PSYCHOLOGICAL ASSESSMENT OF SUICIDAL RISK

PSYCHOLOGICAL ASSESSMENT OF SUICIDAL RISK

Edited by

CHARLES NEURINGER, Ph.D.

Psychology Department
University of Kansas
Lawrence, Kansas

CHARLES   C   THOMAS   ·   PUBLISHER

Springfield   ·   Illinois   ·   U.S.A.

Published and Distributed Throughout the World by

CHARLES C THOMAS • PUBLISHER

Bannerstone House

301-327 East Lawrence Avenue, Springfield, Illinois, U.S.A.

© *1974, by* CHARLES C THOMAS • PUBLISHER

ISBN 0-398-03008-1

Library of Congress Catalog Card Number: 73 14833

Printed in the United States of America

C-1

Library of Congress Cataloging in Publication Data

Neuringer, Charles, 1931-
Psychological assessment of suicidal risk.

1. Suicide—Prevention. 2. Clinical psychology.
I. Title. [DNLM: 1. Psychological tests. 2. Sui-
cide—Prevention and control. HV6545 N494p 1974]
RC574.N48   616.8'5844   73-14833
ISBN 0-398-03008-1

CONTRIBUTORS

CHRISTOPHER BAGLEY, Ph.D.   *University of Surrey, Guilford, Surrey, Great Britain*

JAMES R. CLOPTON, M.A.   *University of Kansas*

SHERMAN EISENTHAL, Ph.D.   *Massachusetts General Hospital, Boston*

NORMAN L. FARBEROW, Ph.D.   *Suicide Prevention Center, Los Angeles*

DOUGLAS J. FREEMAN, M.A.   *Center for Crisis Intervention Research, Gainesville, Florida*

STEVEN GREER, M.D.   *Kings College Hospital, London*

DAN J. LETTIERI, Ph.D.   *National Institute of Mental Health*

MARVIN LEVENSON, Ph.D.   *St. Elizabeth's Hospital, Washington, D. C.*

ROBERT E. LITMAN, M.D.   *Suicide Prevention Center, Los Angeles*

DOUGLAS MacKINNON, M.A.   *University of Southern California*

THEODORE L. McEVOY, Ph.D.   *University of California, Los Angeles*

RICHARD K. McGEE, Ph.D.   *Center for Crisis Intervention Research, Gainesville, Florida*

CHARLES NEURINGER, Ph.D.   *University of Kansas*

JOSEPH THIGPEN, M.A.   *Center for Crisis Intervention Research, Gainesville, Florida*

KARL WILSON, M.A.   *Center for Crisis Intervention Research, Gainesville, Florida*

To Carolyn

PREFACE

THIS VOLUME AROSE out of a pervasive need to examine what has been done in the area of assessing suicidal risk. Having to make some sort of judgment (or prediction) about the future suicidal behavior of an individual is a common experience, not only among clinicians (psychiatrists, psychologists, social workers, physicians, etc.), but also among others who have less exotic dealings with their fellow men (marriage counselors, teachers, hospital clerks, bartenders, druggists, husbands, wives, children, friends, etc.).

The decision that one makes has grave consequences for both the suicidal person and the evaluator. It is a critical episode in the catalog of human encounters, since the consequences of the decision have life-or-death implications.

Much research has been done in trying to develop and evaluate suicidal risk assessment procedures. This book represents an attempt to evaluate such methods and their validity. The contributors are truly "experts" in this area. They have been involved in suicide risk evaluation in particular and in evaluation methodology in general. They share the editor's concern about the status of suicidal risk assessment and have contributed their expertise and knowledge to this volume.

Three general approaches are described and discussed. The first of these involves assessment via lethality scales which are behavioral and demographic in origin. The use of these scales in Suicidology is relatively new and shows great promise of allowing for stable and valid predictions of suicidal behavior. The second approach deals with traditional risk assessment evaluations through the use of psychological tests. The third approach to assessment has developed out of the information gleaned from intensive survey researches of the characteristics of suicidal individuals.

The chapters in this book are original contributions and represent the latest work in the areas of suicidal risk assessment. The only exception to this is the chapter by Bagley and Greer. Their contribution is reprinted from the *British Journal of Psychiatry*. Its importance as a watershed research project made it imperative that it be included in this book and thus be available to American readers. I wish to express appreciation to the authors and to the Royal College of Psychiatrists for their permission to reprint the chapter.

C. N.

INTRODUCTION

THERE IS APPROXIMATELY one "verified" suicide in the continental United States every half hour of every day in the year. The actual suicide rate is probably much higher than indicated in the grim opening statement of this paragraph. Suicide statistics are based on data gathered from reporting sources and do not guarantee the accuracy of the contributors since medical examiners and coroners are known to be hesitant in making suicidal endorsements on death certificates. Thus the "real" suicide rate may be 10 times as high as the apparent rate.

To those who are committed to reducing the suicide rate, its reduction is concrete evidence that lives are being saved. The wellsprings of the need to save lives is influenced by our Western Judeo-Christian Cultural context, which posits that needless loss of life is to be abhorred. Suicide prevention is a "gut level" reaction, upon which one develops sophisticated rationales as an afterthought. The justifications for suicide prevention may be couched in religious terms (e.g., "Only God has a right to choose life and death for us." "The wages of suicide are damnation." They may be explained in socio-economic terms (e.g., "Suicide deprives the community of a productive taxpayer."). The rationales may be sociological (e.g., "Suicide disrupts the fabric of contextual relationships and raises questions about the accepted tenants of society."). The justifications may be humanitarian. They may also be medical and they may be psychological. However, they are all justifications that are evoked to reinforce an emotional abhorrence of solicited death.

Human beings are ordinarily afraid of death and will go to great lengths to avoid the inevitable confrontation. It is emotionally difficult to understand those who seem to rush to embrace it. Suicide is a dramatic event and of great interest to students of human nature. It arouses a certain amount of "existential anxiety" within us because it runs counter to the seemingly axiomatic acceptance of the drive for survival which is the crucial underpinning of our

xi

existence, of our philosophies, and of our psychological theories. Suicide stands as a paradox and is thus a mystery. Why some people choose death, choose not to exist, choose to shut off states of awareness is incomprehensible to our reason, if not our emotions. There are romantic implications to suicide. Perhaps the suicide knows something we do not know or has solved the riddle of life. Such knowledge raises doubts about our reasons for living. This may account for the often mentioned resentments directed toward the suicidal individual. It also accounts for the scientific interest in suicide and the development of suicide prevention procedures. However, in fact, suicide is most often a drab, shabby, and pitiable affair. As part of a concerted suicide prevention effort, techniques to predict self-destructive behavior have been developed. Their main reason for existence is as an aid to intervention. Adequate suicide prevention hinges around being able to predict self-destructive behavior in order to prevent its occurrence. Prediction is forecasting an event. This is what assessment of suicidal risk tries to do. One attempts to make a statement about what will occur in the future *if present conditions remain the same* (i.e., if no new intervening variable enters the forecasting paradigm). Oftentimes conditions do not remain the same, and the task of predicting suicide becomes extremely difficult. One difficulty has been brought about by the suicide forecasters themselves. It concerns their disinclination to allow "present conditions" to persist. A forecast of suicide calls forth an immediate effort at intervention in order to forestall the prediction. We interfere with the orderly process of forecast verification. It is then difficult to accurately predict suicide because events abolish options. It is a source of pride that suicide forecasting has done as well as it has.

If one wants to save lives, the ability to validly predict is paramount. In order to forecast accurately one must have reliable and valid assessment procedures. This is the heart of successful suicide prevention. In this volume is to be found a history of attempts to validly predict self-incurred, premature death. It is a story full of blind alleys, false starts, brilliant ideas, major and minor triumphs, and the dawning of a new way of thinking about suicide.

ACKNOWLEDGMENTS

I WOULD LIKE TO EXPRESS my appreciation to all of the people who helped me in the tedious and mechanical aspects of producing the manuscript. Special thanks go to the Psychology Department secretaries–Jona Dunlap, Marcia Shepard, Sarah Johnson, Linda Speicher, and Gerda Brouhard–for their careful typing of the manuscript and for their forebearance in their dealings with an oftentimes irritable and fretful editor. I would also like to express my appreciation to Payne Thomas of Charles C Thomas, Publisher, for his patience, encouragement, and interest in this volume.

C. N.

CONTENTS

PSYCHOLOGICAL ASSESSMENT OF SUICIDAL RISK

CHAPTER I

PROBLEMS OF ASSESSING SUICIDAL RISK

CHARLES NEURINGER

MANY HUMAN BEINGS are occasionally faced with the task of making some sort of appraisal of another person's suicidal intentions. The frequency of such occasions rises sharply for those individuals in the allied mental health professions. The same is even truer for people who are allied to the mental health profession. Gatekeepers (police, bartenders, druggists, dormitory counselors, etc.) encounter more situations calling for assessments of suicidal risk than does the professional mental health worker who, more often than not, appears on the scene after the self-destructive behavior has occurred. However, for both groups, the occasion that forces some sort of assessment of suicidal risk from the worker is fraught with personal uneasiness and anxiety. Even the professional often feels uncomfortable and unsure about his (or her) own judgments and therefore unsure about whether to initiate action based on his appraisal.

The uncertainty that is felt by the assessor may be due to several conditions. He may not feel confident in his own judgments. He may not have enough knowledge in order to make an adequate judgment. He may feel that he has few or no therapeutic resources to offer the suicidal person. He may hesitate to act because of the consequences of his decision. His own personality may lead him to misread and/or repress critical elements in the construction of the evaluation.

Since suicide is the only "personality" disorder that is lethal, the person who makes the appraisal literally has a life in the palm of his hand. The burden is awesome, and the responsibility is frightening. Avoiding the situation (or disregarding the responsibility) does not help the potentially self-destructive person, and such re-

3

jection may even exacerbate the suicidal trend existing within the individual. The responsibility must be accepted. However, the operative who carries this burden of responsibility has the right to expect all the help possible from psychological science in order to make the most valid assessment of suicidal risk.

The chief problem hindering the development of valid data to be used in making suicidal assessments is due to lack of knowledge about the psychodynamics of "suicide." As will be shown below, even the definition of suicide is open to controversy. It is here being suggested that research may supply badly needed answers to questions about the nature of suicide. Two distinct research efforts are needed. The effort (or direction) first needs to vigorously delve into the very heart of the meaning of suicide. What are its determiners? What are the essential predispositions for suicide? What place do the values of life and death hold in the making of a suicidal decision? These kinds of researches literally call for a program of concerted effort on the part of all those interested in suicide, the value of life, ego processes, etc. In short, research on suicide cannot be separated from the nexus of all personality-environment interactions.

Also critical for the practitioner is research on the assessment of suicidal risk. Psychological science has developed an armamentarium of assessment techniques and procedures for evaluating both their validity and efficiency. Powerful procedures like Factor Analysis, Discriminate Functional Analysis, and Dimensional Analysis exist and are available. Powerful tools such as On-Line Computers, Data Banks, and Random Access Information Retrieval Systems are available. Psychology has produced a number or variety of assessment techniques, reflecting a wide range of strategies. All of these are available. While the solution to the task of understanding the nature of suicide may be far off in the future, the adequate assessment of suicidal risk is a possibility here and now.

Later on in this chapter, the various problems and necessary conditions for valid assessment of suicidal risk will be outlined. But some general problems of assessment of suicidal risk need to be discussed. The assessment of suicidal risk is essentially a problem of prediction. One has to make a statement about what one expects to happen in the future. In addition, the prediction should be valid (i.e., the forecast should be one that is accurate). Shneidman (1957) has outlined the level of validity attached to prediction, postdiction (assessing what has happened in the past), and paridiction (assessing what is happening currently). All of these figure importantly in the assessment of suicide, with the latter two strategies playing supportive roles for prediction. Knowledge about what a person has done in the past and what activities in which he is now engaged are critical for predicting what he will do in the future. What is evidently crucial is that all possible past history data and information about current life style and events be available. One of the great difficulties associated with adequate suicidal assessment is lack of critical information. Not all information is equally important, but there must be a set of potent "facts" which are highly associated with suicidal behavior. Possession of these facts would immeasurably help the worker in making a reasonable assessment. What are these facts? They are, unfortunately, yet unknown. But it is the tasks of research to supply a catalog of the kinds of facts needed for valid appraisal of suicide potential.

Another problem of general prediction involves the question of the specificity or generality of predictive statements. How much specificity should be contained in a predictive statement? Should the prediction be on the order of "S will ingest a lethal dose of barbiturates tomorrow at 3 P.M."? One can get even more explicit than this, by citing "that it will occur in his bathroom" and that "he will be wearing nothing but his underwear, etc., etc." On the other hand, some predictions can be made on a general level. An example of such a prediction might be, "Unless conditions change, X is liable to make some sort of self-destructive move in the near future." The specific prediction is much to be preferred because particular actions can be instituted to short circuit the predicted behavior. However specific predictions are hard to come by and are somewhat dangerous to make, since their probability of being correct is low at the present time because of the level of ignorance of suicidal psychodynamics. When a specific prediction pays off, the results are sensational. Unfortunately, specific predictions, at the present time, do not come as often as one would like. The predictor is "safer" with general forecasts. He will often be correct by reason of his non-specificity. General predictions such as "This man will eventually die," or "Your hair will turn gray as you get older" are unassailable and the "hit" percentage is unusually high. As one moves away from specificity towards generality of prediction, accuracy increases while utility decreases. The aim of science is to be able to make constant *valid* specific predictions. Any adequate assessment of suicidal risk technique should aim at the development of highly probable specific predictions. One might posit that the capacity to deliver such accurate specific and particular predictions is the hallmark of a truly useful assessment technique. No assessment technique is of much use without this capacity. Generalized predictions couched in vague terms are not very useful.

There are several orders of specificity of suicidal behavior prediction. The most inelegant arrangement is in to "commit," "attempt," and "threat." These master categories have been attacked by Shneidman (1963) as being too crude. He has called for a complete rethinking of the nomenclature of suicide. However, most suicidologists persist in using these categories of behavior. There are innumerable subcategories belonging to each of these master categories. The subcategories can be even further subdivided. A useful assessment procedure will provide a nearly exhaustive range of predictive categories. A correlate of knowing what it is that is to be specifically predicted is being able to attach a probability statement to such forecasts. Probability statements are developed from the frequency of past correlations between information and behavior. These data are crucial. It would be of great help to accurately conclude, from the data available to a practitioner that needs to make the assessment that, "Based on all information, he (the practitioner) is 97.32 percent certain that Y will do such and such at a certain time." Being able to make such powerful predictions would go far towards reducing the strain and anxiety stemming from feelings of uncertainty found in individuals forced to make assessments of suicidal risks. What is being argued for here is the adoption of an actuarial approach towards suicide risk assessment. Actuarial predictions are specific and to the point. Global predictions are far too vague.

The actuary makes specific predictions with probability statements attached to each forecast. The possibility of specific and accurate probability statements is in an inverse relationship to the number of factors influencing the range of outcomes (i.e., the more factors influencing the occurrence or nonoccurrence of an event, the greater the difficulty in making a specific prediction). That is why it is critical to get as much information about suicide as is humanly possible. The more one knows about the nature of suicide, the more accurate one can be in making assessments of suicidal risk.

The rest of this chapter is devoted to particular methodological difficulties associated with suicide assessment research. It is one of the author's major beliefs that research should supply the much needed data base for the operative who is confronted with the suicide assessment decision making task. There are a whole host of methodological problems of which the suicide researcher must be aware. The most critical concerns the definition of suicide.

CLASSIFICATIONS OF SUICIDE

The greatest problem in suicide research concerns the adequate definition of the phenomenon. The noun, "suicide," implies a set of varied behavioral actions and experiences. This vagueness of the definition has obscured the nature of the act, thus diminishing its usefulness for developing specific predictions.

It may be of value to survey some of the meanings which the term has taken on. The following list is neither exhaustive nor arranged in any hierarchical order. The categories merely serve to illustrate the wide usage of the rubric.

INTENTIONAL SUICIDE. Here suicide is considered to be an act consciously initiated by an individual, with full awareness of the consequences of the undertaking. There are some special cases of intentional suicide such as (1) "Altruistic Suicide": a term coined by Durkheim (1951) which refers to individuals who give up their lives so that a cause might prosper. (2) "Existential Suicide": propounded by such philosophical writers as Camus (1959) who feels that man comes to the "insight" that life is an absurdity and therefore hollow and empty. There may be no compelling conflicts or affects driving a man to suicide except the profound boredom of existence. (3) "Surcease Suicide": a category exclusively set aside for individuals who, because of intractable pain, decide that they had better kill themselves. Here the individual comes to a "logical" conclusion, and emotions play a minor role. This type of suicide has been described by Shneidman (1960).

PSYCHOTIC SUICIDE. This category covers those suicides that seem to be motivated by psychotic ideation, the intention being not to die. A paranoid schizophrenic patient may die because of an attempt to cut out "bad" parts of himself that reside deep within his body. This type of suicide has been described by Bergler (1946).

AUTOMATIZATION SUICIDE. These individuals, who die because they act in a nonconscious, automatic manner, have been described by Long (1959), although he has doubts about the validity of the lack of motivation involved. This kind of suicide is illustrated by the individual who is extremely tense and ingests a sedative in order to calm himself. The desired effect may not be forthcoming, and a second barbiturate is ingested. If the person still feels tense, he may take more and more barbiturates until he collapses and dies. Under the influence of the sedation, the perceptual fields are said to be narrowed, and the focus of attention is constricted to the act of barbiturate ingestion. Heavy alcoholic intake might produce the same kind of hypnogogic state.

CHRONIC SUICIDE. This category has been propounded by Menninger (1938) and refers to long term self-mutilative and self-defeating mechanisms. Alcoholism, drug addiction, polysurgery, and accident proneness can be given as examples. The intention is to die slowly, inch by inch.

MANIPULATION SUICIDE. Here the individual makes an attempt that does not have an element of lethality. It is in essence a warning, a manipulation, and a plea. This is illustrated by the woman who lightly cuts her wrists so that the wound can be seen easily by her errant spouse. This type of suicide attempt has been described by Farberow and Shneidman (1961).

ACCIDENTAL SUICIDE. It may well occur that a person may die accidently because a suicidal attempt has "backfired." A woman who ingests barbiturates may have the primary aim of manipulation, but her ignorance as to the effects of barbiturates may prove to be fatal. This problem has been discussed by Daston and Sakheim (1960).

NEGLECT SUICIDE. Death may come about through the sheer negligence of an individual. A college professor, with coronary difficulties, may die because he maintains a heavy workload in order to finish some important papers.

PROBABILITY SUICIDE. This category has been developed by Farberow and Shneidman (1961). They discuss individuals who gamble with their lives. Playing Russian Roulette and race track driving are good illustrations of this kind of suicide.

SELF-DESTRUCTIVE SUICIDE. People can be said to be suicidal if they overeat, smoke too many cigarettes, climb mountains, pass on the right when driving on a highway, hunt mountain lions, cross the street against the signal lights, etc. In some way they are taking unnecessary chances with their lives.

SUICIDAL THREATS. A person is said to be suicidal if he threatens to kill himself.

SUICIDAL THINKING. A person is considered to be suicidal if he thinks about killing himself.

TEST SUICIDE. Last, but by no means least, a man is considered to be suicidal if he gives suicidal and/or depressive responses on psychological tests, especially projective personality tests.

A great deal of confusion arises when a researcher ignores the subtle differences between the above mentioned types of behavior and considers suicide to be a single faceted state. Farberow (1950) has shown that there are differences between hospitalized patients who threaten and those who attempt. Rosen (1954) has already pointed out the dangers of lumping suicidal subjects together. Pooling of suicidal subjects can only occur if there is empirical proof that the groups are similar, and since this proof does not seem to be forthcoming, it is mandatory that clear-cut discriminating definitions be made of the kinds of subjects that are going to be used in any research that deal with suicide. The populations used in suicidal research must be clearly and verifiably defined so that subjects can be correctly identified. Only in this way can conclusions, arising from research, be validly tied to the correct parameters. At this time it might be pointed out that adequate classifications is an extremely difficult task for the psychologist interested in suicide research. Stengel and Cook (1958) have likened this process to a pathologist trying to establish the cause of death without having access to the corpse.

SPECIAL METHODS OF INVESTIGATION

On those occasions when the investigator is dealing with deceased individuals, the usual methods that psychologists use are unfeasible since the media for psychological research has always been the living subject either individually or in groups. When suicide is an accomplished fact, the phenomenon is not open to direct inspection and methods involving indirect inference must be developed. Two commonly used modes of investigation will be discussed here. They are (1) the method of residuals and (2) the method of substitute subjects.

Method of Residuals

In this method the residual effects of the deceased are utilized as clues pointing to the state of the individual when alive. Thus suicide notes, diaries, other personal documents, psychological tests administered previous to death, social histories, and the memories of friends and relatives all become grist for the mill. With the dead individual this is probably the best mode of attack available. The work with residuals has produced a great deal of material that is interesting and informative (Farberow and Shneidman, 1955, 1957; Osgood and Walker, 1959; Shneidman and Farberow, 1957, 1959, 1960; Tuckman, Kleiner, and Lavell, 1959), but they have to be treated with a low level of confidence since they are shot through and through with indeterminacies. Working with the residuals is not to be demeaned, but it must be understood that they are neither representative of what the person might be if he were still alive, nor clear reflections of what he was like before his demise. Memory changes in friends and relatives produce distortions that lead the investigator astray. Besides the usual observational perversions existing when one goes back to past events in a person's life, there is in this kind of a method, as Underwood (1957) points out, no way of instituting controls. A control group of nonsuicidal individuals, matched on any and every variable that can be thought of by the investigator as important, cannot hope to cover the areas of uncontrolled variance found within a person's life. Poor control, observational distortion, and unknown validity are the three weaknesses in this method and probably contribute to the mass of contradictory conclusions that are arrived at using this method.

Method of Substitute Subjects

In this method live subjects are considered to be representative of suicidal persons. Arieff, McCulloch, Rotman (1948), Hertz (1948, 1949), Jensen and Petty (1958), Siewers and Davidoff (1943), and Ulett, Martin, and McBride (1950) have used suicidal attempt and depressed patients in making statements about committed suicide. Underlying this method is the assumption that individuals who threaten or attempt suicide are pale carbon copies of those people who commit suicide. This proposition has an attractive but superficial face validity that rests on an assumption of continuity that implies that the difference between the groups is one of quantity or intensity. If this were so, it would certainly be an aid to research, but there is evidence contradicting this view (Farberow, 1950; Rosen, Halles, and Simon, 1954). The method is both logically and empirically unsound and should not be utilized by researchers.

SPECIAL PROBLEMS OF CONTROL

When the investigator focuses on problems that involve suicide attempts, he encounters difficulties similar to those dealt with by psychologists interested in subjects who are emotionally disturbed. However, some unique problems present themselves to the student of suicide. The problems of (1) feedback effects of the attempt, (2) effects of hospitalization, (3) adequate control populations, and (4) validation of predictions will be discussed here.

Feedback Effects of the Attempt

The problem of how to adequately recognize and deal with the feedback effects of the attempt on the attempter has plagued researchers in suicide. Besides the attempt having some cathartic effect that changes the psychological organization of the individual, social and/or therapeutic intervention also acts in such a way as to change the attempter. Many attempters are subjects for investigation after the attempt, and it is a dubious proposition that they reflect the state of the individual before the attempt. Farberow and Shneidman (1959) have tried to resolve this problem by searching hospital records for MMPI's given a month previous to the attempt. Farberow and Devries (1967) have extended the methodology sophistication in this area. There is an obvious danger in using postattempt subjects as representative of presuicidal individuals.

In addition, the direct physical effect of the act itself is a cause of great concern. Bones and tissues are damaged from jumping off a high place. Barbiturates, gunshot wounds to the head, arsenic and lead poisoning, and asphyxia can cause central nervous system damage. Depending upon the amount of brain tissue that is destroyed, temporary or long-standing chronic brain syndromes and psychotic states may ensue. Loss of a limb or disfigurement may lead to the emergence of new unrecognized confounding variables involving body image and self-identity. It is not being suggested that the attempters are a group characterized by brain damage and psychosis but only that extreme caution should be exercised in the selection of subjects. It would seem that a thorough knowledge of the effects of these physical insults to a nonsuicidal person is mandatory in order to set a baseline for the suicidal subjects.

Effects of Hospitalization

Another problem arises when hospitalized suicide attempt patients are utilized as subjects since the hospital treatment for these people is often different than for other patients. Suicidal patients may be placed on maximum security status, watched constantly, followed to the bathroom, can carry nothing in their pockets, may be bombarded with special attention, be on different drug regimes, receive electroshock treatment, made specially impressed by how serious their situation is by the reactions of the hospital staff, be made to feel guilty and/or despised because of their attempt, etc. The research itself may be seen by the patient as a route towards being able to leave the hospital and thus may act in such a way as to insure this or the opposite effect of seeking to remain hospitalized. Using other patients in the same hospital is only a partial control that can be exercised, since intrahospital variation is great. It may be necessary to choose controls from the same ward who have similar treatment programs.

Adequate Control Populations

This problem has already been touched on in the preceding section. Beside the usual problems of finding adequate control groups for research, a control group in suicide research should be as nonsuicidal as possible. Every control group is bound to have some people with "normal" transitory death wishes and fantasies. But even more disturbing is the possibility that subjects may not admit a history of suicidal activities, and because the event can be hidden from scrutiny if there is no documentation, "suicidal" individuals may be used as control subjects. (This is especially true when neuropsychiatric controls are being used.) An attempt to control this possibility can be made by (1) systematic and rigorous screening of the psychiatric-historical background; and for those situations where the desired control group is not neuropsychiatric, (2) screening with psychological tests and/or psychiatric evaluations for manifestations of psychopathology. The presence of psychopathology does not necessarily indicate suicidal trends, but eliminating such individuals increases the probability of having an adequate control group.

Validation of Prediction

When validating predictive scales, the same difficulties manifest themselves in suicide research as in other areas of test construction. However, a validation procedure such as Guilford (1948) used for pilot selection in World War II is not feasible in suicide predictive scale research. Success in flight instruction school was the validating criterion of the pilot selection program. Society (which includes the suicide researcher) does not usually allow sample suicidal groups to "succeed," and so corrective measures (electroshock, ataratic drugs, psychotherapy, etc.) are usually instituted in order to intervene with the suicidal process. This will interfere with the validations of prediction of suicide. It has been argued that the validity of suicidal prediction scales constructed in this manner must of necessity be low (Neuringer, 1962). Newer assessment techniques, especially those dealing with simulation models, should be able to overcome this difficulty. Postmortem investigations of whatever data is available is the method most often used for establishing the validity of predictive scales. Another method involves using criterion variables that are one or more steps removed from suicidal behavior but having a self-destructive flavor (e.g., chronic alcoholism, accident proneness, polysurgery, and self-mutilation). However, this method is based on (1) the unsupported hypotheses of a continuity underlying all suicidal behavior and (2) that other kinds of pathological behavior are suicide equivalents. Utilizing this method as the mode of validation may lead to a situation where the validating criteria are irrelevant to suicidal behavior. Future validation of predictive scales using these kinds of criteria seems to have a limited possibility, but it is profoundly hoped that those investigators interested in validating predictive methods will be able to adopt more powerful models of assessment evaluation.

The author has attempted to alert investigators to some of the methodological problems existent in this very stimulating realm of study. As each investigator attempts to deal with a problem, he will find new methodological questions facing him. But the care taken with the design, selection of subjects, methodology, and controls will help reach towards results that have theoretical, empirical, and therapeutic value.

The various methodological problems described above have particular effects on developing suicidal risk assessment procedures. One has to carefully categorize the type of suicidal behavior to be studied and adequate methods of investigation need to be used. Creative thinking and the vast consortium of sophisticated procedures and instruments will be of great use. Careful attention must be paid to the factors of the influence of feedback. Successful intervention of predicted suicidal behavior destroys the possibility of future validation of that behavior. Careful attention must be paid to that problem. Hospitalization factors must be taken into account; the nature and composition of the control comparison groups are critical.

If all of the methodological problems associated with valid assessment of suicidal risk can be overcome, then the occurrence of false negatives will be severely diminished. The reduction of the number of false negatives (i.e., suicidal people who are erroneous diagnosed as nonsuicidal) is the chief aim of self-destructive risk assessment techniques. It is, in essence, the task of saving lives.

REFERENCES

Arieff, A. J., McCulloch, R., and Rotman, D. B.: Unsuccessful suicide attempts. *Diseases of the Nervous System, 9:*174-179, 1948.

Bergler, E.: Problems of suicide. *Psychiatric Quarterly Supplement, 20:*261-275, 1946.

Camus, A.: *The Myth of Sisyphus*. New York, Vintage, 1959.

Daston, P. G., and Sakheim, G. A.: Prediction of successful suicide from the Rorschach test, using a sign approach. *Journal of Projective Techniques, 24:*355-361, 1960.

Durkheim, E.: *Suicide*. Glencoe, Free Press, 1951.

Farberow, N. L.: Personality patterns of suicidal mental patients. *Genetic Psychological Monographs, 42:*3-79, 1950.

Farberow, N. L., and Devries, A. G.: A multivariate profile analysis of MMPI's of suicidal and nonsuicidal neuropsychiatric hospital patients. *Journal of Projective Techniques and Personality Assessment, 31:*81-84, 1967.

Farberow, N. L., and Shneidman, E. S.: Attempted, threatened, and completed suicide. *Journal of Abnormal and Social Psychology, 50:*230-231, 1955.

Farberow, N. L., and Shneidman, E. S.: Suicide and age. In Shneidman, E. S., and Farberow, N. L. (Eds.): *Clues to Suicide*. New York, Mc-Graw-Hill, 1957.

Farberow, N. L., and Shneidman, E. S.: An analysis of suicidal MMPI data. Paper read at the American Psychological Association convention, Cincinnati, September, 1959.

Farberow, N. L., and Shneidman, E. S.: *The Cry for Help*. New York, Mc-Graw-Hill, 1961.

Guilford, J. P.: Some lessons from aviation psychology. *American Psychologist, 3:*3-11, 1948.

Hertz, Margarite R.: Suicidal configurations in Rorschach records. *Rorschach Research Exchange, 12:*3-58, 1948.

Hertz, Margarite R.: Further study of "suicidal" configurations in Rorschach records. *Rorschach Research Exchange, 13:*44-73, 1949.

Jensen, V. W., and Petty, T. A.: The fantasy of being rescued in suicide. *Psychoanalytic Quarterly, 27:*327-339, 1958.

Long, R. H.: Barbiturates, automatization, and suicide. *Insurance Council Journal*, April, 1959, 299-307.

Menninger, K.: *Man Against Himself*. New York, Harcourt, Brace, 1938.

Neuringer, C.: Methodological problems in suicide research. *Journal of Consulting Psychology, 26:*273-278, 1962.

Osgood, C., and Walker, Evelyn G.: Motivation and language behavior: A content analysis of suicide notes. *Journal of Abnormal and Social Psychology, 59:*58-67, 1959.

Rosen, A.: Detection of suicidal patients: An example of some limitations in the prediction of infrequent events. *Journal of Consulting Psychology, 18:*397-403, 1954.

Rosen, A., Halles, W. H., and Simon, W.: Classification of "suicidal" patients. *Journal of Consulting Psychology, 18:*359-362, 1954.

Shneidman, E. S.: A method of educing the present correlates of perception: An introduction to the method of successive covariation. *Journal of General Psychology, 57:*113-120, 1957.

Shneidman, E. S.: Psycho-logic: A personality approach to patterns of thinking. In Kagen, J., and Lesser, G. (Eds.): *Contemporary Issues in Apperceptive Fantasy*. Springfield, Thomas, 1960.

Shneidman, E. S.: Orientations towards death: A vital aspect of the study of lives. In White, R. K. (Ed.): *The Study of Lives*. New York, Atherton, 1963.

Shneidman, E. S., and Farberow, N. L.: Comparisons between genuine and simulated notes by means of the Mowrer DRQ. *Journal of General Psychology, 66:*251-256, 1957.

Shneidman, E. S., and Farberow, N. L.: A socio-psychological investigation of suicide. In David, H. P., and Brengelmann, J. C. (Eds.): *Perspectives in Personality Research*, New York, Springer, 1960.

Siewers, A. B., and Davidoff, E.: Attempted suicide: A comparative study of psychopathic and general hospital patients. *Psychiatric Quarterly, 17:*520-534, 1943.

Stengel, E., and Cook, Nancy G.: *Attempted Suicide: Its Social Significance and Effects*. New York, Basic Books, 1958.

Tuckman, J., Kleiner, R. J., and Lavell, Martha: Emotional contents of suicide notes. *American Journal of Psychiatry, 116:*59-63, 1959.

Ulett, G. A., Martin, D. W., and McBride, J. R.: The Rorschach findings in a case of suicide. *American Journal of Orthopsychiatry, 20:*817-827, 1950.

Underwood, B. J.: *Psychological Research.* New York, Appleton-Century-Crofts, 1957.

CHAPTER II

ASSESSING INTENTION TO DIE IN SELF-INJURY BEHAVIOR*

DOUGLAS J. FREEMAN, KARL WILSON, JOSEPH
THIGPEN, RICHARD K. McGEE

SUICIDOLOGY HAS BECOME identified as the behavioral science
discipline which addresses itself to the "scientific and humane
study of self-destruction in man." Consistent with this mission,
suicidologists have devoted extensive energy to both conceptual
and statistical analyses of that clinical phenomenon designated
loosely as the "suicide attempt." The literature of suicidology contains many reports of empirical investigations on suicide attempters. Yet there continues to be a pervasive lack of understanding of the behavior, both on the part of clinicians and the researchers. Semantic confusions abound and miscommunication is
the universal medium within which therapists and patients, as well
as investigators, engage one another as they seek to clarify an attempted suicide.

The writing of this chapter was undertaken for the purpose of
discovering and disseminating at least a partial solution to this
critical problem. The means of fulfilling that purpose will involve
a review of the relevant literature on suicide attempts, the formu-
lation of some behavioral concepts related to attempting suicide,
the development and analysis of an instrument for assessing the
patient's intention-to-die, and finally, a discussion of the practical
clinical relevance of increasing our capacity to make distinguish-

* This study was supported by Research Grant MH-16861 from the Center for
Studies of Suicide Prevention at the National Institute of Mental Health to the
Center for Crisis Intervention Research, University of Florida. All of the authors
express gratitude to Rodney Goke for his assistance in the preparation of the
data.

ing diagnostic statements about patients who exhibit life threatening or self-injurious behavior.

PREVIOUS RESEARCH ON SUICIDE AND SUICIDE ATTEMPT

Several writers have described suicide attempters and suicide completers as two separate, but overlapping, populations (Davis, 1967; Dorpat and Ripley, 1967; McGee and Hegert, 1966; Stengel, 1964; and Wilkins, 1967). The attempt population is characterized as younger, as using less lethal means, and as having more women than men, while the population of suicide completers is found to be older, uses more lethal means, and is weighted more toward males than females (Dorpat and Boswell, 1963). Sex differences are one of the most stable findings in the suicide literature.

Shneidman and Farberow (1961) confirm these sex differences in a study of all attempted suicides and completed suicides that came to their attention in Los Angeles County in 1957. Dorpat and Boswell (1963) report that as the seriousness of the suicide method increases, the sex ratio of male:female increases monotonically. They found that 68 percent of the attempters were female. Their findings also indicate that the seriousness of the attempt increases directly with age and that the lethality of the method increases directly with the seriousness of the attempt.

Several writers have made an effort to isolate suicide attempters into more descriptive breakdowns. Callendar (1968) suggests that the suicidal individual passes through specified stages that can serve as a key as to whether his behavior can be considered threat behavior, attempt behavior, or possible completer behavior. Mc-Gee and Hegert (1966) identify four populations which might be said to vary in degree of "suicidality." These groups range from those persons who have (thus far) only talked about suicide, but have done nothing about it; those persons who engage in non-lethal self-injuries or self-poisonings; those persons who are "nearly saved" following self-injury, but subsequently die from that injury after being rescued and exposed to medical or surgical intervention; and that group who die immediately with no possibility for rescue. These four groups differ systematically such that mean age and male-female ratio increase directly with the degree of commitment to dying. The authors conclude that:

> It is evident . . . that suicide is not a dichotomous behavior by which the participants in the act can be meaningfully separated into categories denoting whether or not they actually expire. It is important to note that the populations of people who participate in various types of suicidal behavior are in fact different populations, which are graduated along a continuum. Even within the total group that expires, there are still degrees of "suicidality" based upon method of injury and on demographic variables of age and sex.

It has been frequently pointed out that many persons who engage in a behavior described by the authorities as an attempted suicide actually have little or no intention of dying. For example, Kessel (1966) has described a group of patients who are aware of what is a lethal dosage of a drug, but in their "suicide attempt," actually consume exactly one-half of that dosage. Similarly, Stengel (1964) points out that even lethal dosages of drugs are nonfatal when taken in such a way as to maximize the chances of environmental intervention. If the degree of danger to life is used as the sole yardstick in judging the "seriousness" of an attempt, then many incidents involving the ingestion of lethal drugs would have to be classed as harmless. Stengel is among the first students of suicide attempt to insert the concept of *suicidal intent* as a criterion for evaluating this behavior. However, Stengel uses terms like "strong suicidal intention" or "confused intention" without suggesting any method by which the degree of intention may be reliably determined.

The concept of "seriousness" of an attempt has been confusing and misleading. Stengel (1964) argues against using the extent of physical dysfunction as the criterion, although it is not uncommon clinical practice to define serious (e.g., genuine) attempts as those which would result in death in the absence of life-saving medical intervention. Dorpat and Boswell (1963) were probably the first investigators to attempt to scale the seriousness of attempts. In their investigation they used a five-point rating scale in which a rating of "1" represented a suicide gesture, "3" represented an ambivalent suicide attempt, and "5" indicated a serious suicide attempt. Ratings of "2" and "4" were given to the intermediate categories. However, these authors did not disclose the criteria by which their judges applied these ratings to case history material, nor did they determine and report the reliability of the rating procedure.

Tuckman and his associates (Tuckman and Youngman, 1963, 1968; Tuckman, Youngman, and Kreizman, 1968) have reported a series of investigations into the levels of risk in suicide attempts. They find that multiple attempters have a significantly higher suicide risk than patients making only a single attempt. The criterion used is actual death by suicide within one year following an attempt. Using data collected primarily from police reports and other public documents, these investigators have developed a 14-factor scale against which to evaluate risk in suicide attempt. Applying the scale to over 1,100 cases in Philadelphia, they find scores ranging from zero to ten. However, a cut-off score of four divides the cases into two groups having suicide rates of 0.0 per 1,000 and 35.2 per 1,000.

An inspection of the 14 factors which significantly differentiate high and low risk groups reveals that four of them relate to sizeable differences in suicide rates. As may be expected, two of these are for the demographic variables of age and sex. The other two are living arrangements (alone or with others) and method of injury. Thus, these data provide further confirmation of Stengel's (1964) list of three factors to use in judging seriousness: (1) potential threat to vital body functions, (2) degree of intent to die, and (3) social constellations at the time of the attempt.

It is especially important to note that throughout Tuckman's studies it has been impossible for the investigators to operationalize and measure intention on the part of the patient. Efforts to do so have resulted in too many gaps in the data which necessitated the factor being omitted in the data analysis, or findings which were not in the predicted direction. It is evident that the self-report statement, "I really intended to kill myself," cannot be relied upon as a measure of risk in suicide attempts.

Shneidman (1968) has proposed a taxonomy of orientations or attitudes that one might have toward his own dying. He discusses these under four headings:

1. *Intentioned* (or premeditated). The individual plays a direct role in his own death. Included here are many of the deaths called suicides.

2. *Subintentioned* (or submeditated). The individual plays an indirect, covert, partial, or unconscious role in his demise as when an individual fails to act for his best welfare.

3. *Unintentioned* (or unmeditated). The individual plays no significant role in his own demise, in fact would actively seek to prevent it if he had that option.

4. *Contraintentioned*. The individual plays the role of someone about to act upon his own demise but in actuality has no intention of doing so.

Related to and underlying this classification of intentionality is Shneidman's contention that each human life is characterized by continual, chronic, pervasive attitudes toward cessation, and that these blend together into a style of living which includes the role one plays in his own demise. Surely, if one can infer an orientation toward death from knowing the manner in which one has lived, it is thus equally plausible to infer one's intention to die from the manner in which he performs the act of self-injury.

Weisman (1970) suggests a procedure which offers promise in this direction, but he has only articulated the relevant dimentions and left it for others to develop an application. He proposes a two-dimension rating based upon the risk-rescue factors associated with the method employed for injury and the potential for rescue operations to be successful.

These two factors associated with intent-to-die run consistently through the recent literature on suicide. The method used in the attempt has received the greater amount of attention, but Stengel has noted the importance of the possibility of intervention from others in the attempter's environment. The purpose of this study is to develop a suicide intentionality scale based upon those elements of an attempter's behavior which determine the reversibility of method and probability of intervention. These ratings may serve as the two axes of the two-dimensional rating matrix Weisman proposed.

A CONCEPTUALIZATION OF SUICIDE ATTEMPT BEHAVIOR

The rationale underlying the methodology developed in this paper is relatively simple and direct. It grows directly from the literature just reviewed, the major conclusion of which is that the one single factor necessary for the understanding of a suicide attempt is the intention-to-die on the part of the attempter *immediately prior* to his act of self injury. This degree of intention cannot, as yet, be measured or inferred from presently existing procedures.

Intention-to-die is a construct which, like all others in human behavior, must be inferred from objectively observable and veridical events. The data for the inference cannot meaningfully come from the attempter's demography or personal history, nor should they derive from the subjective assumptions of the police officer or the clinical theories of a therapist. The data for the intentionality inference can be derived only from the *behavior of the person in making the attempt.*

We need make only one simple assumption: persons who make self-inflicted injuries do so within a set of specially contrived circumstances which they have deliberately–perhaps not consciously –created for the purpose of either *providing for, permitting,* or *preventing* their own rescue. Thus, persons who provide for their own rescue have *low intentionality,* those who permit a rescue have *moderate intentionality,* and those who seek to prevent a rescue may be seen as having *high intentionality.* The specially contrived circumstances which are of interest in making this assessment are: (1) the reversibility of the method of self-destruction, and (2) the expected proximity of other people (the probability of intervention by others in the victim's environment). Each of these may be rated on a five-point scale, and these two scales may be combined to yield a matrix of overall intentionality ratings.

The "Reversibility of Method" and the "Probability of Intervention" Scales are reproduced as follows:

Rating of Reversibility of Method

Rating

1 *Complete Reversibility of Method:*

Ingestion of aspirin or other commercial drug items (such as Excedrin®, Bufferin®, and Midol®; antihistamines, or other non-toxic household substances (such as baking powder or mouthwashes).

Also slight cuts not requiring treatment.

2 *Probable and Expected Reversibility of Method:*

Ingestion of 10 or more tranquilizers or nonprescription sleeping pills (such as Sominex®, or pep pills). Ingestion of 10 or more stimulants (such as Serpasil®, reserpine, Raudixin®; Thorazine®, Compazine®, Dartal®, Mellaril®, Permitil®, Trilafon®, Stelazine®, meprobamate; Librium®, valium, Miltown®, and Equanil®).

Also wrist cuts requiring vessel and/or tendon repair.

3 *Questionable Reversibility of Method:*

Ingestion of 10 or more soporific medications, poisons, large amounts or combinations of several drugs, or narcotics (barbiturates: phenobarbital, sodium butisol, Nembutal®, Seconal®, Sodium amytal®, tuinal; non-barbiturate hypnotics: bromides, chloral hydrate, paraldehyde, bromural, Carbrital Kapseal®, halabar; narcotics: morphine, Demerol®, Darvon®).

Deep cuts requiring tendon or vessel repair (except single wrist cuts) and multiple severe cuts.

4 *Improbable and Unexpected Reversibility of Method:*

Attempted drowning, carbon monoxide suffocation, domestic gas suffocation, suffocation.

Deep cuts to the throat.

Jumping from a low place (less than 20 feet).

5 *Remote or No Chance for Reversibility of Method:*

Gunshot in vital area (such as trunk of body or head).

Jumping from a high place (more than 20 feet).

Hanging (feet above ground).

Rating of Probability of Intervention

Rating

1   *Certain Intervention:*

Act committed in the presence of another person.

2   *Probable Intervention:*

Act committed with another person in the immediate vicinity but not visibly present (such as in the same household).

3   *Ambiguous Chance of Intervention:*

Act committed by person alone, with no certainty of immediate assistance; however, a reasonable chance for intervention exists (such as the victim is aware of the impending arrival of others).

Telephone is available and may be used to call a significant other person.

4   *Improbable Intervention:*

Act committed by person alone, with intervention by a passerby possible although not expected (such as a motel room, an office late at night, or home alone with no one expected).

Telephone may be available, but not used by the victim.

5   *Chances of Intervention Remote:*

Act committed by person in a solitary or isolated place without access to telephone (such as a wooded area, cemetery, etc.).

Both scales are 5-point ordinal scales designed to accommodate and represent the circumstances surrounding an individual's suicide attempt. Reversibility of method refers to the ease with which the action can be stopped, or reversed, once the potential victim has set it into motion. The scale ranges from methods with complete reversibility (e.g., aspirin ingestion) through methods with remote or insignificant chances for reversibility (e.g., gunshot wound in a vital area). The intermediate ranges include probable reversibility (e.g., ingestion of tranquilizers or slight wrist cuts), questionable reversibility (e.g., soporific medication and poisons), and improbable reversibility (e.g., carbon monoxide poisoning or drowning). The scale takes into account both the method and the degree to which it is employed.

The degree to which a victim can expect someone to become aware of the event, to recognize it as an attempt, and to intercede determines the probability of intervention. This is largely a function of the proximity or expected proximity of other people in the victim's immediate environment. The scale ranges from ratings of certain intervention (e.g., act committed in the presence of another person) through ratings of remote chance of intervention (e.g., act committed in isolated place without access to tele-

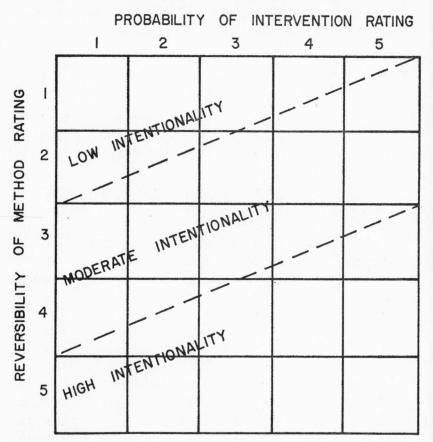

Figure II-1. Intention-to-die matrix based upon a two-dimensional classification of circumstances contrived for a self-injury.

phone). Intermediate ranges include probable intervention (e.g., another person nearby but not visibly present), ambiguous chance of intervention (e.g., victim is aware of impending arrival of others), and improbable intervention (e.g., victim is alone in a setting where intervention by a passerby is possible, but unexpected).

Figure II-1 is a Matrix of Circumstances which derives from combining these two rating scales to form the axes. The intentionality of the patient may be inferred from the resultant of these two factors. Although all irreversible methods indicate high intentionality, methods where reversibility is possible or probable indicate the full range of intentionality to die is partly a function of intervention after the attempt. With methods where death is highly unlikely, the probability of intervention again ceases to be as important. The broken lines in the matrix divide the three degrees of intentionality according to these *a priori* considerations. While originally drawn in this manner, it was expected that they could be shifted appropriately as indicated by actual empirical data.

EMPIRICAL DEVELOPMENT AND USE OF THE ASSESSMENT METHOD

The initial phase of scale development involved carefully writing, editing, and rewriting the rating scale category descriptions until they were finally in the form reproduced above. Criteria which guided writing of these categories were that they include all, or nearly all, of the most frequently occurring events in suicide attempts, and that the full range of possible events be represented in reasonably equal steps. (No claim is made for either rating dimension being more than an ordinal scale in terms of its scaling properties.)

The next procedure was to apply the two scales to a large sample of suicide attempt and death cases. To accomplish this procedure, all attempted suicide and completed suicide cases occurring during the 30-month period ending in July, 1972, in Alachua County, Florida, were analyzed and rated for intentionality. These cases had been reported to the Suicide and Crisis Intervention Center by local law enforcement officers, by the victim, or by other significant individuals involved in the case. In every instance of self-injurious behavior, the Center automatically opened a case file and established contact with the individual. Data gathering activities were routinely followed by the service personnel at the Center.

A total of 277 attempted suicides and 34 completed suicides had been recorded by the Center during this period. Of the attempts, 243 contained sufficient information to be analyzed and rated on the Intent-to-Die Scale. In cases where multiple attempts were recorded, only the first attempt for each individual was assessed in order to reflect the clinical situation of making inferences from the first attempt that comes to an agency's attention. All 34 cases of suicide death were judged on their intent to die. None of these had records of prior attempt included in the group of 243 attempt cases studied.

The results of rating intention-to-die in these 277 cases are summarized in Figure II-2 for self-injury and suicide death cases separately. Each cell contains the total of attempted suicides or completed suicides judged to have occurred under those conditions of method reversibility and intervention probability.

For the sake of clarity, row and column totals and percentages have been omitted, but can be easily computed from the data pre-

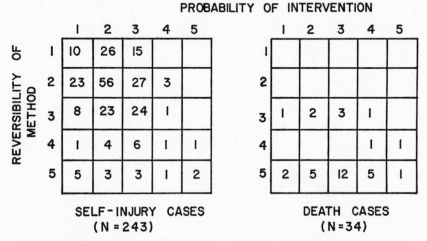

PROBABILITY OF INTERVENTION

REVERSIBILITY OF METHOD — SELF-INJURY CASES (N = 243)

	1	2	3	4	5
1	10	26	15		
2	23	56	27	3	
3	8	23	24	1	
4	1	4	6	1	1
5	5	3	3	1	2

DEATH CASES (N = 34)

	1	2	3	4	5
1					
2					
3	1	2	3	1	
4				1	1
5	2	5	12	5	1

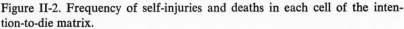

Figure II-2. Frequency of self-injuries and deaths in each cell of the intention-to-die matrix.

sented. For example, 160, or approximately 65 percent, of the self-injuries were judged to involve methods rated "1" or "2" on reversibility, while none of the deaths was judged to have occurred as a consequence of these same acts. Similarly, 25 (or approximately 74%) of the deaths, but only 14 (or approximately 5%) of the attempts were rated "5" on reversibility of method. The data from the two matrices in Figure II-2 can be combined to yield an analysis of the total sample of cases studied. Of all cases rated for intervention, 32.5 percent obtained a level "3" rating, while another 43 percent obtained a level "2" rating. Therefore, it can be ascertained that a large proportion of the individuals in this sample (approximately 75%) attempted suicide alone, but in close proximity or expected proximity to other individuals. Another 18.1 percent made their attempt in the immediate presence of another person. Furthermore, only 6.5 percent of the cases (levels "4" and "5") attempted suicide under conditions which did not allow for reasonable chances for intervention, while over half, 57.8 percent (levels "1" and "2") of the individuals employed a suicide method in which death was highly improbable, if not impossible.

Even more striking are the percentages aligned with levels of intervention chance deployed by the sample of attempters. A highly significant 65.4 percent made their attempt in environmental circumstances that ensured the likelihood of intervention (levels "1" and "2"); 30.9 percent attempted under circumstances characterized by ambivalent intervention opportunities (level "3"); only a meagre 3.7 percent attempted in environments that rendered unlikely intervention opportunities. These results are immediately striking. The largest proportion of individuals in this sample have contrived relatively safe circumstances in which to inflict their self-injuries. In the great majority of these cases one is to conclude that the intention-to-die is relatively low or non-existent.

Reliability of the Rating Procedure

Obviously, the rating of 277 cases was of little practical consequence unless it could be demonstrated that the ratings were made with satisfactory interjudge reliability. Therefore, the procedure

TABLE II-I

RELIABILITY COEFFICIENTS COMPUTED FROM EBEL'S (1951)
METHOD OF INTRACLASS CORRELATION BETWEEN THREE
INDEPENDENT JUDGES

	Reversibility of Method Rating	Probability of Intervention Rating
All cases (N = 59)	.97	.80
Self-injury cases (N = 25)	.89	.71
Suicide death cases (N = 34)	.96	.78

for rating the cases was designed to permit a reliability estimate. Three judges independently rated equal portions of the suicide attempt sample with 10 percent blind overlap. Cases were randomly assigned to each judge such that they unknowingly rated 25 cases in common. Interjudge reliability for these 25 cases was computed by Ebel's (1951) method of intraclass correlation and was found to be r = .89 for the reversibility of method scale and r = .71 for the probability of intervention scale. All three judges each rated each of the 34 suicide cases and yielded a reliability for the reversibility of method scale of r = .96 and r = .78 for the probability of intervention scale. Information concerning how the death was discovered or the expected or actual proximity of others at the time of the attempt often was not present in the cases rated. It was decided to "force" a rating despite this limitation. This strategy might have resulted in the lower agreement for the probability of intervention scale. Complete reliability data for the Intention-to-Die Scale are provided in Table II-I. It is evident that the reliability of this method as applied to this sample is adequate for both clinical and research use, especially since reliability may be further enhanced by more complete reporting and recording of raw data.

Multivariate Prediction of Death

Although many studies have examined the variables that differentiate suicide attempters and suicide completers, few have employed multivariate statistics to relate the variables which may, in fact, interact significantly with each other. Dorpat and Ripley (1967) suggested the need for a multivariate approach in order to gain more practical, clinical value from the data. Therefore, it was decided that a multiple regression design should be employed to reveal the likelihood of incurring death associated with each cell of the Intention-to-Die matrix. For this analysis, the method rating and the probability of intervention rating were used as the predictor variables, and the occurrence of death as a result of that attempt served as the criterion variable. The resulting Probability of Dying matrix is reproduced in Figure II-3. It can be seen that a person who consumes a few aspirin in the immediate presence of another person has an exceedingly low probability of dying. On the other hand, a person who is the agent of a self-inflicted gunshot wound in a vital body area committed in an environmentally remote locale attains the highest intentionality rating, and a probability of resulting death of 70 percent.

It can be readily ascertained from Figure II-3 that the choice

PROBABILITY OF INTERVENTION

	1	2	3	4	5	
1	-.030	.010	.049			LOW INTENTION- ALITY
2	-.052	-.012	.027	.067		MODERATE INTENTION- ALITY
3	.036	.076	.116	.155		
4	.235	.274	.314	.354	.393	HIGH INTENTION- ALITY
5	.543	.582	.622	.662	.701	

REVERSIBILITY OF METHOD

Figure II-3. Probability of dying associated with each cell of the intention-to-die matrix computed by multiple regression analysis.

of method is a much stronger determinant of the probability of dying than is the likelihood of intervention at the time of the attempt. As the method rating increases from level "1" to level "5," there is an across-the-board increase of .59 chance of incurring death, while on the other hand, as the intervention rating increases from level "1" to level "5," there is an increase of only .16 chance of dying as a result of the attempt. Choice of method, therefore, contributes approximately four times the amount of variance to the prediction of death probability than does the probability of intervention. Nevertheless, an increase of 16 percent in the chance of incurring death is substantial and must not be overlooked, especially when a victim may contrive to provide or permit a rescue which actually fails to materialize. In such a case, a "successful" suicide may be an accidental "failure" of an attempt to continue living.

It might seem strange that a case located in the 5,5 cell only has a 70 percent chance of resulting in death. The following is a capsule description of a case from our sample that fell in the 5,5 cell and survived a most serious and highly intentioned act.

F. C., a 47-year-old black female, had been having frequent and severe conflicts with her family and was generally weighted down with numerous worries. She was in a very agitated and depressed mood when she drove her car off a seldom-travelled highway into an adjoining wooded area. It was there that she shot herself in the abdomen with a German-made, .22 calibre Rohm pistol. A young boy, playing in the woods nearby, heard the shot. After finding F. C. slumped over the front seat of her car, he called the local law enforcement agency which, in turn, put in motion the rescue operations that eventuated in F. C.'s surviving this most highly intentioned self-injury.

Predicting Intentionality Indices

Once the methodology for assessing intention-to-die had been developed, an attempt was made to predict the intentionality index (or probability of dying as a result of the self-injury event) of various sub-groups within the total sample of 277 cases. It was recognized that the limitations of this relatively small sample size made such an analysis somewhat tenuous since various subgroups were under-represented. Nevertheless, this pilot study was carried out with the notion that the method could be applied to larger samples at a later time. At this point, however, it is relevant to report some of the more salient trends in the data.

A multiple regression analysis was utilized in an effort to ascertain how adequately the various demographic data could predict a particular sub-population's mean intentionality index. This was carried out with the notion that if it could be demonstrated that demographic characteristics make a significant contribution to the determination of intentionality level, this would be of enormous clinical value.

It was found that the mean probability of dying for the entire population of self-injurers and the death group was .123 with a standard deviation of .215. The mean probability of dying, or mean intentionality rating, for males is a bimodal curve, peaked at the oldest age levels with an average .43 intentionality after increasing steadily from the lowest average intentionality of .12 for the 35-40 year old age range. The other smaller peak was in the 20-25 year old age range with average intentionality of .29. This was an increase from .18 for the below 20 age group and declined to .19 for the 26-30 age group. Two effects seemed to create this early peak in intention-to-die. The first was the higher intentionality of students who injured themselves. Students in this sample had up to twice the intentionality index depending on the age range. Another factor contributing to the peak in the 21-25 age range for males was the increased frequency of black attempters. Although only 14 black males were in the entire sample (including two students), seven were in this age range and averaged .46 in intentionality. This could be artifactual as the three black non-student males in the 26-30 range averaged .02 in intentionality, but it might indicate a trend toward younger black males making more serious and more frequent self-injuries than in the past.

Sixty-six percent of the total sample was female and 54 percent of the female attempters were less than 25, while 95 percent were below 45 years old. For the 88 percent of female attempters who were below 40, a low intentionality curvilinear mean was found for the different age levels. The below 20 age group averaged .03

in intentionality which increased to .07 for the 25-30 age group and then decreased to .03 intentionality average for the 36-40 age group. Black females were consistently slightly lower in intentionality, whereas black males were consistently slightly higher in intentionality. White female students could have accounted for some of the peaking in intentionality. They demonstrated a much sharper curve, peaking in the 20-25 age range at a mean intentionality of .13. While only 12 percent of female attempters were over 40, the average intentionality increased to a large peak in the 46-50 age group and declined in frequency and seriousness into old age. With the fewer cases in this range of the sample, it was hard to make any generalizations.

Some generalizations that can be made from the data are that the sex of the attempter is a very significant factor in predicting the circumstances surrounding a self-injury. While a great many attempts can be expected from young females, the great majority will be of low intentionality. Age, to a lesser extent, is also a factor with increasing age generally associated with higher intent ratings. However, this does not seem to be uniform across the age span, with college age students having increased intentionality for their age group and lower intentionality being more common in the late thirties. Although few attempts have been recorded in older groups, relatively higher intentionality is evident in the middle-aged, especially for women, and in the oldest group. Student status is also found to increase intentionality.

Although race was not found to significantly increase the explanatory powers of the regression equation, this could be a function of the inadequate sample of black attempters, especially males. Although the frequencies were low, a disturbing proportion demonstrated moderate and high intentionality in attempts, especially among young black men. Perhaps this represents a new phenomenon with which suicide centers should be prepared to cope in the future.

Although some demographic data explain some of the self-injury behavior in the sample studied, much is left unaccounted for by only knowing the age, sex, and student status of the individual. Only 20 percent of the variance was explained by these variables. It is important to know that an older male has more likelihood of making a highly intentioned attempt. But enough exceptions exist at nearly every demographic combination to caution against generalizing to a single individual. The only group in this sample that demonstrate uniformly low intentionality in their self-injuries are adolescent females.

Caution must also be taken in generalizing from the sample population to other localities. As a college town, Gainesville, Florida, is over-represented by the young middle and upper-middle classes. The county also has a substantial lower class population, both white and black. Class is a pervasive variable that has not been adequately recorded in these cases and whose effects are therefore unknown in this sample. However, there may be an important source of data which could be used to further analyze and refine the intention-to-die measurement. Murphy, Clendinin, Darvish, and Robins (1971) have developed and reported a data gathering instrument whereby law enforcement officers in the St. Louis area investigate and report the circumstances of accidental and intentional self-inflicted injuries. From the thousands of such reports which must be on file, each of which contains data sufficient to reliably rate both the probability of intervention and reversibility of method scales, it should be possible to extend this pilot study to a broad population including many subgroups of adequate size. Perhaps other areas offer the possibility of replicating and cross-validating these initial findings.

Clinical and Theoretical Implications

There are some interesting implications which follow from the ability to precisely measure the intention-to-die construct and thereby designate the degree of that intention in any individual case of self-injury. Furthermore, there are potential uses of this methodology in attempting to predict the suicide risk, defined as probability of death due to self-injury, in population subgroups. These two areas deserve discussion in greater detail.

Clinical Implications

Anyone who has spent much of his professional clinical practice in a hospital or other agency setting to which patients present for psychological treatment following acute suicidal episodes is thoroughly aware of the attitudes which characterize the perception of a patient who has "attempted suicide." There is smug and not-too-subtle degradation expressed almost universally by the clinical staff. The patient is automatically placed in a lose-lose situation as soon as anyone reports, however honestly, that he has attempted to kill himself. The first reaction is to wonder why, if he tried to kill himself, is he still alive and seeking treatment? There are several answers to that question.

First, a low threshold answer is that he didn't *really* try to kill himself, but only wanted to make it look like he was trying to kill himself in order to gain sympathy or other concessions from those who could not be otherwise manipulated. Therefore, the clinician is immediately on guard lest his peers see him as capable of being manipulated by this patient, who now has a known history of being manipulative. Treatment responses are developed from a set which includes an expectation of, and a readiness to counter, the patient's further attempt to "put something over" on the environment. It is hard for a patient to overcome this set of attitudes.

Another equally pejorative situation for the patient occurs if one concludes that he really did try to kill himself, but was so stupid or incompetent that he could not carry out his plan. It is even worse when the method of injury involves a highly reversible process which is not even life-threatening at worst. To conclude that a person intended to die when he ingested a few tablets of a non-prescription drug brands him as a very stupid or inept individual. Naturally, this attitude plays right into the patient's own sense of worthlessness and potential for failure at everything he does. Behaving as if the event was a genuine attempt to die, which failed due to the patient's lack of knowledge or courage, signals an agreement on the part of the would-be helper with all of the disparaging feelings the patient holds toward himself already.

A third possible answer as to why the person is still alive when it is reported that he tried to kill himself is that the person making the report is simply in error; that it wasn't a suicide attempt at all. Again, as in the first answer above, the responsibility for the error is shifted back onto the patient. Thus, the report is usually rendered in a tone of voice and in a manner which says, in effect, "I don't believe it, and you would be well advised not to believe it either."

Shneidman (1968) has cautioned against the development of pejorative attitudes on the part of clinical treatment personnel. He says that, "It is all too easy to say that an individual only attempted suicide or to dismiss the case as beneath the need for human compassion, if one assesses the act as contraintentional." Ansel and McGee (1971) use the semantic differential technique to measure positive attitudes toward suicide attempters, and find that with only one exception, the attitudes of groups of helpers become more positive in relation to the degree of intention-to-die which they perceive in the case history description of the event. The greater the perceived intentionality of the patient, the more positive is the expressed attitude toward the patient. The data from this study offer unequivocal confirmation to many published observations that clinical helpers often assume a pejorative attitude toward suicidal behaviors (Ayd, 1961; Farberow and Shneidman, 1958; Glaser, 1965; Jacobziner, 1965; Mintz, 1961; Motto, 1965; Shneidman, 1968; Sifneos, 1966; Sudnow, 1967; Tabachnick, 1961; Umscheid, 1967; Wolford, 1965). It is essential that clinical personnel reorient their conceptualizations concerning the meaning and interpretation of acts of self-injury.

There may be several paths to take in achieving such a reorientation, but the one proposed here is a radical semantic departure from current clinical jargon. It is that the term "suicide attempt" be stricken from the vocabulary of practitioners altogether. Rather than continue to label a sequence of behavior as something which it in fact *is not,* it is reasonable to re-label it according to what it, in fact, *is.* This study has shown that the vast majority of events heretofore called "suicide attempts" are in fact not that at all, but rather are, behaviorally speaking, events of *self-injury* or *self-poisoning.* The *attempt* is, in nearly all cases, not that of dying, but of living. In some cases, the intent to continue living is less obvious, i.e., more ambivalent. In only a very few does the behavior suggest that the intent is very probably to die; in nearly all of those cases the act is successful and death follows. In those few high intentioned cases where death does not follow, the event can legitimately be called an attempt at suicide which has failed. However, this occurs in our data in only 22 out of 277 cases (8%). It is reasonable to attach the concept "attempt to kill himself" only to those patients who, by the method proposed herein, can be said to have high intention of dying, and to thereby avoid the semantic trap which results from indiscriminately applying it to that great majority of self-injury patients for whom it is not only not true, but grossly misleading.

Once this attitude is adopted, it becomes possible to ascertain what it is that the patient is really trying to do by his act. In many cases, it is probably to establish a communication with a significant individual in the interpersonal environment (Shagoury, 1971). If so, clinical treatment can be based upon learning why other more conventional forms of communication are not attempted or why they may have failed. Such an approach is only meaningful if the concept "to die" is totally removed from the semantic meaning of the term *suicide attempt*. This is most easily accomplished by refusing to use the term and substituting an accurate one in its place.

Theoretical Implications

The problems in classifying and describing self-injurious behavior appropriately and in grouping individuals who engage in such suicidal behaviors are exceedingly complex. Neuringer (1962), in an important paper outlining the methodological problems in suicide research, concludes that attaining an adequate definition of the phenomenon is probably the most critical issue we have to face. It is with this in mind that the authors propose a theoretical system for the assessment of suicidal risk which underscores the importance of the individual's intention to die in assessing his suicidal risk.

Lethality is a concept in suicidology which has never been precisely defined, operationally or otherwise. It is generally taken to mean "the probability that a person will take some potentially self-destructive action." Thus, in rating lethality, telephone workers have typically been evaluating a caller's present state in order to place a bet or predict the chances that a self-injury might follow.

Lethality is, then, a statement of a future event, whereas intentionality as developed in this chapter, is a statement concerning an event (a self-injury) which has already taken place.

The assessment of a person's lethality has generally been taken as the only index of his suicidal risk; his intention-to-die has rarely been taken into consideration. Based upon these considerations, it is the contention of the present authors that the following series of assumptions and concepts would lead to a more complete understanding of suicidal behavior:

1. The population of persons who die by suicide is a subpopulation of all persons who inflict self-injuries.

2. Death by suicide is a probability event that differentiates persons according to both their intention to die as well as their assessed lethality.

3. Intentionality is the probability that death will occur as a consequence of the circumstances in which a self-injury event occurs.

4. Expected intentionality is that mean, or base line level, of intentionality which characterizes the self-injuries of a definable, homogeneous subgroup, and would, therefore, be expected given a self-injury by any member of that subgroup.

5. Lethality is the probability that a self-injury event will occur in any form.

With this theoretical system, it is possible to approach a mathematical assessment of suicidal risk, such that:

Suicide Risk =

(Lethality $\times$ Expected Intentionality) + Chance Factors

Furthermore, it may be shown that the lethality of the population or subpopulation can be assessed and inferred by applying the formula:

$$\text{Lethality}_j = \frac{\text{frequency of self-injurious behavior}}{\text{population size} \times \text{time}}$$

Also, the expected intentionality associated with self-injurious behavior in a subpopulation can be inferred from the proportion of these events that result in death:

$$\text{Expected intentionality} = \frac{\text{frequency of suicide death}}{\text{frequency of self-injurious behavior}}$$

Therefore, in any population or subpopulation, suicide risk can be inferred from past events by applying the formula:

$$\text{Suicide risk} = \frac{\text{frequency of suicide death for the subpopulation}}{\text{population size} \times \text{time}}$$

If the probability that the self-injury event will occur in any form (assessed lethality) is 1 in 5, and the probability that death will occur as a result of that event's occurrence (expected intentionality, based upon empirical data obtained from previous self-injury events engaged in by members of that particular subgroup) is 1 in 2, then the risk of suicidal death is assessed at .10 plus the error term. While intention-to-die is ascertained after the event, lethality is anticipated before the event on the basis of perturbation (Shneidman, 1971) and possibly from available population base-rate data.

As stated above, this theoretical system construes all three of its major elements (suicide death, lethality, and intention-to-die) as probability events. As a result, important implications become apparent. For example, certain subgroups within the total population of potential self-injurers engage in self-injury more often than do other subgroups (their lethality is higher). White, adolescent females immediately come to mind as a subgroup within the self-injury population that engage in a relatively large number of self-injury events. However, this same group is concurrently characterized as having a very low mean intentionality index. The circumstances surrounding their self-injuries very often lead one to infer very low intention-to-die. On the other hand, elderly while males, as a group, might be characterized as having a lower assessed lethality (they engage in relatively fewer self-injury behaviors), yet their expected intentionality index is exceedingly high.

Therefore, it is conceivable that the adolescent females and the elderly males could have equal or near-equal assessed suicide risks, *as groups,* when this formula is utilized. Nevertheless, it is readily apparent that *when* an elderly male does engage in a self-injury behavior, his intention-to-die is likely to be very high, whereas the adolescent female's self-injury attempt, which occurs much more often, is likely to be much less intentioned. This particular bit of information about two potential events, both characteristically called "suicide attempts," and both of near-equal risk, could be very valuable to the clinicians, suicide prevention center personnel, police officers, and any others who face the task of trying to predict the behavior of a suicidal individual.

This study has been designed to be a first step in being able to better predict the suicidal risk of an individual given certain circumstantial information. This step involves designing a scale which could be applied to self-injury patients in order to ascertain their intention-to-die. Intentionality is then related to probability of dying by means of multivariate regression analysis. A further extension involving more sophisticated studies might include the assessment of suicidal risk of an individual from a formula that could account for the base rates of self-injury events in particular subpopulations.

REFERENCES

Ansel, Edward L., and McGee, R. K.: A study of attitudes toward suicide attempters. *Bulletin of Suicidology, 8:*22-28, 1971.

Ayd, F. J., Jr.: Suicide, a hazard in depression. *Journal of Neuropsychiatry, 2:*52-54, 1961.

Callendar, W. D.: A socio-psychological study of suicide-related behavior in a student population. *Dissertation Abstracts, 28A:*3765, 1968.

Davis, F. B.: The relationship between suicide and attempted suicide. *Psychiatric Quarterly, 41:*752-765, 1967.

Dorpat, Theodore L., and Boswell, John W.: An evaluation of suicidal intent in suicide attempts. *Comprehensive Psychiatry, 4:*117-125, 1963.

Dorpat, T. L., and Ripley, Herbert S.: The relationship between attempted and completed suicide. *Comprehensive Psychiatry, 8:*74-79, 1967.

Ebel, R. L.: Estimation of the reliability of raters. *Psychometricka, 16:*407-424, 1951.

Farberow, Norman L., and Shneidman, Edwin S.: Suicide and the police officer. *Police, 54,* July-August, 1958.

Glaser, K.: Attempted suicide in children and adolescents; psychodynamic observations. *American Journal of Psychotherapy, 12:*220-227, 1965.

Jacobziner, H.: Attempted suicides in adolescents by poisoning. *American Journal of Psychotherapy, 12:*247-252, 1965.

Kessel, N.: The respectability of self-poisoning and the fashion of survival. *Journal of Psychosomatic Research, 10:*29-36, 1966.

McGee, R. K., and Hegert, Thomas: A detailed analysis of suicide in Orange County, Florida, 1963-1965. Department of Clinical Psychology, Gainesville, Florida, 1966 (mimeo).

Mintz, R. S.: Psychotherapy of the suicidal patient. *American Journal of Psychotherapy, 15:*348-367, 1961.

Motto, J. A.: Suicide attempts: A longitudinal view. *Archives of General Psychiatry, 13:*516-520, 1965.

Murphy, George E., Clendenin, William W., Darvish, Harriet S., and Robins, Eli: The role of the police in suicide prevention. *Life-Threatening Behavior, 1:*96-105, 1971.

Neuringer, Charles: Methodological problems in suicide research. *Journal of Consulting Psychology, 26:*273-278, 1962.

Shagoury, Joan B.: A study of marital communications and attitudes toward suicide in suicidal and non-suicidal individuals. University of Florida, Gainesville, Florida, 1971, doctoral dissertation.

Shneidman, E. S.: Orientations toward death: A vital aspect of the study of lives. In Resnik, H. L. P. (Ed.): *Suicidal Behaviors.* Boston, Little, Brown, 1968, 19-48.

Shneidman, E. S.: Perturbation and lethality as precursors of suicide in a gifted group. *Life-Threatening Behavior, 1:*23-45, 1971.

Shneidman, E. S., and Farberow, N. L.: Statistical comparisons between attempted and committed suicides. In Farberow, N. L., and Shneidman, E. S. (Eds.): *The Cry for Help.* New York, McGraw-Hill, 1961, 19-47.

Sifneos, P. E.: Manipulative suicide. *Psychiatric Quarterly, 40:*525-537, 1966.

Stengel, Erwin: *Suicide and Attempted Suicide.* Baltimore, Penguin, 1964.

Sudnow, D.: Dead on arrival. *Trans-Action, 5:*36-43, 1967.

Tabachnick, N.: Countertransference crisis in suicide attempts. *Archives of General Psychiatry, 4:*527-538, 1961.

Tuckman, Jacob, and Youngman, William F.: Suicide risk among persons attempting suicide. *Public Health Reports,* U.S. Dept. of Health, Education, and Welfare, *78:*585-587.

Tuckman, J., and Youngman, W. F.: Assessment of suicide risk in attempted suicides. In Resnik, H. L. P. (Ed.): *Suicidal Behaviors.* Boston, Little, Brown, 1968, 190-197.

Tuckman, J., Youngman, W. F., and Kreizman, Garry: Multiple suicide attempts. *Community Mental Health Journal, 4:*164-170, 1968.

Umscheid, Theophane: Caring for is caring about. *American Journal of Nursing, 67:*1230-1232, 1967.

Weisman, Avery D.: Suicide, death, and life-threatening behavior. Presented at meeting of Task Force on "Suicide Prevention in the Seventies," Phoenix, Arizona, January 30-February 1, 1970.

Wilkins, J.: Suicidal behavior. *American Sociological Review, 32:*286-298, 1967.

Wolford, Helen G.: A psychiatric nurse in a suicide outreach program. *Psychiatric Quarterly 39:*8-14, 1965.

CHAPTER III

RESEARCH ISSUES IN DEVELOPING PREDICTION SCALES

Dan J. Lettieri

WITH THE PROLIFERATION of suicide prevention centers in the United States (several hundred to date), the task of rapidly and effectively assessing an individual caller's suicide potential has come to the fore as the *sine qua non* research problem. Much of the pioneering work in the area of evaluation and assessment of suicide potential has stemmed from the Los Angeles Suicide Prevention Center. The prediction instrument to be described here is in large measure a product of (1) the availability of extensive, clinically-rich case file records maintained on callers over the years at the Los Angeles Center* and (2) the advent and accessibility of sophisticated, computerized statistical prediction methodologies.

The word prediction may be generally understood as the estimation of one phenomenon from a knowledge of others to which it is related *empirically*. In this context, a prediction instrument is one which uses certain information (e.g., item scores) applying to a person at one point in time in order to estimate the probability of his becoming or remaining suicidal at some later point in time.

TIME-BOUND AND TIME-LIMITED PREDICTION

In a very real sense, the concept of prediction must be understood in terms of "time-bound" and "time-limited" prediction. Measures taken at time 1 are used to predict some phenomenon

---

* The author wishes to thank the staff of the Los Angeles Suicide Prevention Center for their cooperation and offers special acknowledgment to Drs. T. Brown, R. Litman, C. Wold, and N. Farberow without whose assistance these scales could not have come to fruition.

at time 2, where time 1 occurs temporally prior to time 2. In this regard, such prediction may theoretically be viewed as progressive rather than regressive, and there is some discussion of the appropriateness of using regression methodologies for progressive prediction (Grygier, 1966). The researcher must be cognizant that prediction instruments are both time-bound and time-limited. Such tools are time-bound in the sense that the time at which the initial measurements are made (viz., time 1) reflect and capture a particular psycho-social state of the individual, and great care must be given to the choice of time at which such measures are initially taken. For example, if one were interested in predicting the driving patterns of an individual, then it would be appropriate to take the initial measures when the individual was driving as opposed to when he was sleeping. Similarly if one wished to predict some future suicidal behavior, it would seem wise to have base line measures taken when the person was engaging in some suicidal behavior. But prediction instruments are also time-limited, or ideally should be, to maximize their efficiency. The time-limit refers to that interval between the initial, or base-line, time 1 measures and the predicted outcome at time 2.

The time interval between times 1 and 2 can conceivably range from moments to eons; further it is recognized that the smaller the interval, the potentially greater will be the power and accuracy of the predictive tool. The essential issue rests with the degree of control over the amount of unforeseen, uncontrollable variation which may affect and interact and hence mollify the value of the base line measures. Certainly an instrument which predicts that some behavior will or will not occur within the next three minutes can conceivably achieve greater efficiency and power than a tool which attempts to predict the occurrence of some phenomenon within the distant future. The concept of *ceteris parabus* is applicable here. In most instances, practical requirements force us into a choice of time limits. In the current study, the predictive instrument was limited to make predictions for a period up to two years from the initial base line measures. This decision was not arbitrary; rather it was discovered that if a person would indeed commit suicide, he would do so within a period up to two years from his last contact with a suicide prevention center (Wilkens, 1970).

SELECTIVE PREDICTION AND HOMOGENEITY

Two recently developed methodologies, association analysis technique (Williams and Lambert, 1959) and predictive attribute analysis (Macnaughton-Smith, 1963), stress that relationships between predictive cues or items and the criterion variable may vary greatly in a sample that is relatively heterogeneous; moreover it is recognized that the power and efficiency of a prediction instrument increases with decreases in the heterogeneity of the groups of persons about which predictions are to be made. An instrument is maximally efficient if it correctly predicts or classifies all persons into the appropriate categories under study. The state of the art of psychological prediction, however, is far from achieving the maximally efficient instrument. It would seem that there are at least two important ways the researcher may adjust his predictive device to increase its homogeneity or decrease its heterogeneity. The first is to carefully take measures of individuals at time 1 when they are all in some similar psychological state–in this case, at a time when they are calling a suicide prevention center because of current, personal suicidal feelings, thoughts, and threats. In short, they are all in a suicidal crisis situation. A second way is to statistically control various kinds of subgroupings of suicidal callers on certain basic and relevant parameters such as age or sex. Thus, of the pool of callers, various subgroupings could be distilled such that within each of the subgroups homogeneity would be increased–in essence a type of gross within-group matching procedure.

THE CRITERION PREDICTION VARIABLE

As has been noted, prediction instruments are best made for defined classes of persons, for example: suicide threateners vs. attempters vs. completers, males vs. females, young vs. old, poor vs. rich, white vs. black, single vs. married. The more delimited, and hence homogeneous, the group under study, the more likely the increased efficiency of the instrument. This notion applies, in a broader sense, to the criterion variable as well. An instrument which aims at predicting future suicidal behavior of general sorts will most probably be less efficient and accurate than one which has a more focused, highly specific criterion of suicidal behavior. The ultimate problem for suicidologists is the prevention of suicidal death. The instrument developed here focuses specifically on the prediction of future suicidal death as opposed to the more global concept of future suicidality which may include such behaviors as threats, attempts, gestures, and ideations.

Methodological Characteristics of Prediction Instruments

Length and Scope of Predictive Instruments

It has often been assumed that clinical judgment will become more accurate when more relevant information is available. The research findings, however, do not support this, and in fact most studies of clinical prediction have not shown a positive relationship between a judge's predictive accuracy and the amount of information available to him (Goldberg, 1968). There is thus little support to believe that vast amounts of information or very long predictive instruments, will, in the long run, be any more efficient predictors than concise and germane predictive tools. In fact, if one finds that two measurements vary closely together, one of them is unnecessary; it can contribute nothing to the information provided by the other. What is worse, if one puts measurements which are highly correlated (redundant) together into a predictive scheme, one really uses one measurement twice, thus potentially giving it an importance which is twice what it should be. It is precisely for these reasons that a *stepwise* discriminant function analysis (Dixon, 1968) is among the best predictive methodologies currently available (Ward, 1968). The selection and combination of predictive items may be done by a variety of methods ranging from the simple adding up of points for "good" and "bad" factors to more complex methods (e.g., stepwise discriminant function analysis) which take account of not only the association of each factor with the criterion but also the relationships between the factors themselves. The essential feature of D.F.A. (discriminant function analysis) is that it affords a means of selecting from a large number of items those which have the most predictive value and of combining these with the aim of making the combination a more powerful predictor than any of the individual items alone. The stepwise discriminant function, an elegant version of multiple regression analysis, systematically and in stepwise fashion seeks only the most pertinent, discriminating items for inclusion in the final scale and discards the redundant items.

In summary, the phrase which best describes the research strategy here employed is "time-bound, time-limited selective prediction of suicidal death." Selective and time-limited because the prediction estimates apply differentially to different, select groups of persons within delimited time periods; and suicidal death because the phenomenon to be predicted is suicidal death, as contrasted to other suicidal phenomena such as future attempts, threats, ideations, etc.

Uses of Prediction Instruments

A prediction instrument can distinguish between different kinds of risks (e.g., suicidal attempt vs. suicidal death), and it can separate low risks from the high risks. Such a tool may take several forms: a table showing risk groups or a score or equation which gives individual probabilities of risk.

A prediction tool may also be used to estimate the risks of various kinds of suicidal phenomena which are genuinely in the future; for example one may try to identify children with a high probability of becoming suicidal when older so as to give them preventive treatment now. But such tools can also be used for persons whose suicide potential is already known, in order to estimate the expected risk on the basis of information applicable at an earlier stage, e.g., when to release a recurrently hospitalized suicide attempter for suicide attempts. This latter type of prediction may well be used in research on the effectiveness of treatment. If persons given various treatments (whose outcomes may already be known) are classified according to the risks that would have been expected before the onset of treatment, a baseline is formed against which the outcomes of the treatments can be judged. The development of such a tool, properly called a base expectancy instrument, is in no way as facile as it may appear.

METHOD

Goals of the Study

The overriding goal of the study was to develop a set of scales capable of making predictions as to the likelihood of a suicidal caller's future death by suicide. In short, one wanted to predict death by suicide. It was not the intent to develop indices to predict the likelihood that a particular individual would engage in future non-fatal suicidal behaviors. A subsidiary and practical goal was to develop such scales appropriate for use at a crisis phone clinic at the very time that a person was calling the clinic for some suicidal problem. Thus the scales would have to be simple enough to be used by the phone worker while on the phone with the suicidal person and both empirical and efficient enough to allow for a relatively accurate and standardized assessment of the suicidal risk involved.

Subjects

It is eminently clear that suicide prevention centers often act as screening devices to detect potentially suicidal persons; moreover, the callers to such agencies present a higher suicide risk group than found in the general population. While it has been argued that many seriously suicidal persons do not contact such centers, evidence indicates that at least 1½ percent of the callers do go on to take their own lives by suicide. The actual figure is probably much higher. However, the vast difficulty in follow-up of such callers necessarily makes the estimate highly conservative. Over the years the Los Angeles Suicide Prevention Center has kept detailed records of its callers and has extensive documentation on at least 52 callers that have gone on to suicide; although the actually known number of suicides from this population is several-fold larger.

From the files of the Los Angeles Suicide Prevention Center, a random selection was made of 530 callers who were known to be alive at the time of the study. This group was then to be compared to the sample of 52 callers who were known to be dead (see Table III-I). Neuringer (1962) cautioned that researchers may incorrectly and prematurely put suicidal committers (dead) into the comparison (alive) group. A preliminary pilot study by the author indicated that the bulk (over 90%) of callers who later suicided, did so within two years from their last suicidal call to the SPC. Similar findings are reported by Wilkens (1970) in Chicago. Persons chosen for the alive comparison group were screened to be certain that they were still alive and had remained alive at least two years from their last suicidal call. No known suicidal deaths were included in the alive comparison group.

A further screening was necessary to be certain that the case records contained information on the currently suicidal (social, demographic/epidemiologic, personal and psychological) state of the subject. It was critically important that the information to be used for measures of the dependent variables reflected the "current" suicidal state of the subject at the time he called the agency and not simply retrospective perceptions by the clinical worker. This screening reduced the 530 alive cases to 465. The 65 cases which were dropped from the study design consisted of persons who were not currently suicidal at the time they were seen at the SPC. Often these were hospital released suicide attempters who came for ongoing treatment, referral, etc., but were not suicidal at that time. In summary, the two groups of subjects were thus defined by (1) having called the SPC and voiced a current suicidal problem; (2) information was available on their characteristics when they were actively and currently suicidal; and (3) the alive

TABLE III-I

Sample Size

G R O U P S	Currently suicidal who remain alive "ALIVE GROUP"	N=465
	Currently suicidal who go on to commit suicide "DEAD GROUP"	N=52

group was known to be alive for a minimum of at least two years from their last suicidal call or episode.

Inventory of Variables

INDEPENDENT VARIABLE. In prediction studies the independent variable is usually the criterion variable, viz., the phenomenon to be predicted. In this instance it was whether or not the person died by suicide.

DEPENDENT VARIABLES. An extensive review of the literature was made with the aim of including in the final item pool all those items which had shown any merit as potentially predictive variable. Many items were included in each of the following broad classes: demographic/epidemiologic; symptomology; stress factors; life style characteristics; current suicidal plans, past suicidal behavior; available resources, both interpersonal and economic; history of emotional disturbance; employment and life-role features, etc. An initial list of 100 items was developed by the staff of the LA SPC; after repeated reliability checks, only 75 items which attained better than 85 percent reliability (i.e., percent agreement among 12 raters on a random sample of 10 cases) were included in the final item pool for analysis. Twelve clinical associates for the SPC rated the cases on all items. Ratings were made blind as to whether the case was dead or alive; furthermore, ratings were systematically made on the basis of only that information which was relevant to the subject's most current suicidal call as presented in the case folders. The author wanted to capture the emotional and psychological state of the caller at the height of his suicidal crisis.

Analysis

The method of choice was a stepwise discriminant function analysis (Dixon, 1968) performed on the 52 dead cases vs. the 465 alive cases. As might be anticipated, the variables of age and sex produced high weightings; it was consequently decided to divide the total samples into age X sex groupings to increase homogeneity within each of the sub-groupings such that four groups each were formed for both the dead and the alive samples. The four basic groupings were: (1) older males (40 years old and

TABLE III-II

Analysis	SUBGROUPS COMPARED		
1.	OLDER MALES (ALIVE) N=59	VS.	OLDER MALES (DEAD) N=17
2.	YOUNGER MALES (ALIVE) N=115	VS.	YOUNGER MALES (DEAD) N=13
3.	OLDER FEMALES (ALIVE) N=80	VS.	OLDER FEMALES (DEAD) N=11
4.	YOUNGER FEMALES (ALIVE) N=211	VS.	YOUNGER FEMALES (DEAD) N=11
TOTAL N:	N = 465 (ALIVE)		N = 52 (DEAD)

*Note that a preliminary function analysis was performed on all dead vs. all alive cases (N-52 vs. N-465). On the basis of this preliminary analysis it was decided to perform the four above described age X sex analyses. A comparison of the efficiency of the four separate scales vs. the preliminary scale indicated that the four way approach was more efficient predictively.

over), (2) younger males (under 40 years), (3) older females (40 years old and over), and (4) younger females (under 40 years). Four separate stepwise discriminant function analyses were performed as shown in Table III-II. The stepwise procedure afforded the advantages of statistically choosing only those items which were powerful discriminators or predictors and eliminating redundant items, as well as devising long and short forms of the predictive scales. Only those items which attained an F ratio sig-

TABLE III-III

THE EIGHT VARIATIONS OF THE PREDICTION SCALES

Sex X Age Group	*Form of Scale*	*Number of Items in the Scale*
Older Males	Long	13
Older Males	Short	7
Younger Males	Long	9
Younger Males	Short	5
Older Females	Long	10
Older Females	Short	4
Younger Females	Long	8
Younger Females	Short	3

nificance level .10 were included in the long form of the scales, while an F ratio p level at least .05 was mandatory for an item to remain in the short form of each scale. Table III-III depicts the eight scale variations, that is, the four basic scales each with a long and short version. Neuringer and Kolstoe (1966) have argued for the merit of .10 significance levels.

Applications

The primary purpose for a long and short form of each of the age X sex scales is one of practicality. It was known that due to some caller's reluctance to give information, not all the items on the longer form of a scale would be answerable by the phone worker. It was felt that in such instances the short form of a scale would be applicable. It must be recognized that the various scales here developed have certain restraints which must be observed. First, the scales are for use by phone workers at the time a suicidal person calls such an agency and openly voices a current suicidal problem. The scales are not applicable to persons who deny their suicidality. Second, the scales are time-bound and time-limited. They are time-bound to that instant in time when a caller is currently suicidal and expressing a suicidal problem. They are time-limited to a two year prediction period, that is, a prediction made now applies to the period up to the next two years. This restricted time-limit was one of the design features built into the study, and its rationale has been discussed above. Third, the original study population had age ranges between 18 and 65. The scales should consequently be used only on persons within this age range.

Evaluation of Efficiency of Predictive Scales

The ultimate test of the efficiency of any prediction instrument rests with its viability and robustness on new populations. There are several other ways to assess the efficiency of a prediction scale, namely how well it predicts the criterion when a total population is used as a base, rather than a sample. In the case of predicting infrequent events, such as suicidal death, this becomes a very challenging test for any predictive tool. Based on Los Angeles Suicide Prevention Center yearly data, tabulations were calculated as to the breakdown of age X sex subgroups (see Table III-IV). Fur-

TABLE III-IV

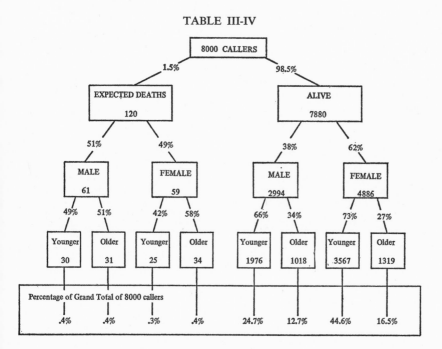

TABLE III-V

Scale	Format	#Items	Labeled Dead a	Alive b	Expected Dead (g)	a/e	a/g	b/f	b/g	c/e	c/h	d/f	d/h	e/i	f/i	g/i	h/i
			c	d	Alive (h)												
			(e)	(f)	(i)												
Older Males	Long	13	29 / 71 / 100	2 / 947 / 949	31 / 1018 / 1049	29	94	0.2	6	71	7	99.8	93	10	90	3	97
Older Males	Short	7	29 / 173 / 202	2 / 845 / 847	31 / 1018 / 1049	14	94	0.2	6	86	17	99.8	83	19	81	3	97
Younger Males	Long	9	23 / 316 / 339	7 / 1660 / 1667	30 / 1976 / 2006	7	77	0.4	23	93	16	99.6	84	17	83	1.5	98.5
Younger Males	Short	5	21 / 257 / 278	9 / 1719 / 1728	30 / 1976 / 2006	8	70	0.5	30	92	13	99.5	87	14	86	1.5	98.5
Older Females	Long	10	28 / 158 / 186	6 / 1161 / 1167	34 / 1319 / 1353	15	82	0.5	18	85	12	99.5	88	14	86	2.5	97.5

Scale	Format	# Items	Labeled Dead (a) / c / (e)	Alive (b) / d / (f)	Expected Dead (g) Alive (h) (i)	a/e	a/g	b/f	b/g	c/e	c/h	d/f	d/h	e/i	f/i	g/i	h/i
Older Females	Short	4	25 / 290 / 315	9 / 1029 / 1038	34 / 1319 / 1353	8	74	0.9	26	92	22	99.1	78	23	77	2.5	97.5
Younger Females	Long	8	18 / 357 / 375	7 / 3210 / 3217	25 / 3567 / 3592	5	72	0.2	28	95	10	99.8	90	10	90	0.7	99.3
Younger Females	Short	3	18 / 535 / 553	7 / 3032 / 3039	25 / 3567 / 3592	3	72	0.2	28	97	15	99.8	85	15	85	0.7	99.3
All 4 AGE X SEX SCALES	Long	(40)	98 / 902 / 1000	22 / 6978 / 7000	120 / 7880 / 8000	10	82	0.3	18	90	11	99.7	89	12.5	87.5	1.5	98.5
All 4 AGE X SEX SCALES	Short	(19)	93 / 1255 / 1348	27 / 6625 / 6652	120 / 7880 / 8000	7	77.5	0.4	22.5	93	16	99.6	84	17	83	1.5	98.5
Preliminary Scale	Long	(11)	95 / 1734 / 1829	25 / 6146 / 6171	120 / 7880 / 8000	5	79	0.4	21	95	22	99.6	78	23	77	1.5	98.5

1. Each of the four "age X sex" scales (older males, younger males, older females and younger females) will be examined in terms of nine dimensions. Each of these is alphabetically keyed to figure at bottom of page:

a=number of persons labeled by scale as dead, and actually expected as dead in next two years. These can also be viewed as TRUE POSITIVES.

b=number of persons labeled by scale as alive, but actually expected as dead in next two years. These can also be viewed as FALSE NEGATIVES.

c=number of persons labeled by scale as dead, but actually expected alive in next two years. These can also be viewed as FALSE POSITIVES.

d=number of persons labeled by scale as alive, and actually expected as alive in next two years. These can also be viewed as TRUE NEGATIVES.

e=total number of persons which the scale labels as dead.

f=total number of persons which the scale labels as alive.

g=total number of persons actually expected dead in next two years.

h=total number of persons actually expected alive in next two years.

i=grand total of persons in a particular age X sex grouping who will call a suicide prevention center in one year's time.

2. The scales are designed to predict death by suicide within the two years following the last suicidal call. The scales are *not* designed to predict future attempts which are not fatal, nor are the scales set to predict suicidal risk within the very immediate future (that is, within the next couple of days) from the suicidal call.

3. The following format will be used to present the predictive efficiency of each of the scales:

LABELED BY SCALE AS   ACTUALLY EXPECTED
                                                          (Statistically)

DEAD   ALIVE

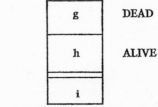

a	b		g	DEAD
c	d		h	ALIVE
e	f	TOTALS	i	

4. As a further aid, the following ratios (expressed in %) will be presented: a/e; a/g; b/f; b/g; c/e; c/h; d/f; d/h; e/i; f/i; g/i; and h/i.

ther, the efficiency of each of the derived scales was then tested on the yearly population data, so as to give a more representative picture of the actually expected number of predictive hits and misses. A detailed analysis of the efficiency of each of the scales is presented in Table III-V.

The Scales: Questions and Answer Sheets

The final products of the study were four basic suicidal death prediction scales, each with a long and short version. The questions are presented in the beginning of Table III-VI, and the answer sheets along with a summary of instructions for use of the scales can be found in Table III-VII. The instructions for the usage of the scale can be found in Table III-VIII. In practice, the

TABLE III-VI

SCALE FOR OLDER MALES

Item	Content of Item

1. *Divorce Status*
   If the patient is clearly and legally divorced, score "Yes."
   If the final divorce papers are not in, or the patient is only separated, score as "No."
   Patient is currently divorced:
   0   No
   1   Yes
2. *Depression-Somatic Aspects*
   This aspect of depression refers only to somatic (physical) expressions such as loss of weight, appetite, sleep, excessive fatigue. Other kinds of depression such as affective (mood) depression or social depression (wanting to be alone, etc.) are *not* to be scored on this question.
   Recently the patient has experienced *somatic* problems such as disturbed appetite, sleep disorders, or excessive fatigue:
   0   None or slight
   1   Moderate to severe
3. *Irritation—Rage—Violence*
   Obsessional thoughts, while irritating, are *not* a part of this item.
   Nor is frustration.
   Recently the patient has:
   0   Not felt irritated or angry more easily or more often than usual
   1   Felt irritated or angry more easily or more often than usual
   2   Been enraged and/or violent (throwing furniture, striking others, etc.) one or more times
4. *Accept Help Now*
   "Refused help now" means the patient refused to do any of the things the worker suggested, stopped coming after one interview, or rejected help from

Item	*Content of Item*

friends and relatives. If he agreed, even reluctantly, score as "accepted help now."
The patient has:
0   Accepted help now (i.e., the assistance of relatives, friends, or professionals) or is disposed to doing so
1   Refused help now

5. *Type of Actual Loss—Divorce*
The patient has had a recent (last 6 months) divorce:
0   No
1   Yes

6. *Repetition of Attempts*
(Score all attempts the patient may have made, including recent ones).
0   None
1   One attempt
2   Two or more attempts

7. *Role Failure*
The patient has had a failure in the performance of a major role, work for man. Seen in downward vertical mobility, bankruptcy, or unemployment for men.
0   No
1   Yes

8. *Dual Suicidality*
Both partners (man and wife, homosexual pair, parent-child) may be suicidal.
0   No
1   Yes

9. *Family Available*
Do not consider as "family" more removed blood relatives like uncles and aunts, cousins, etc. unless they are mentioned specifically by the caller. Available does *not* pertain to whether they are *willing* to help, only to whether they are in the area and *could* help.
The patient has:
0   Many (3 or more) family members (spouse, siblings, children, parents) who are available (i.e., in the vicinity or who could reasonably come to the area or patient go to them)
1   Few (1 or 2) family members who are available
2   No family members who are available

10. *Repeatedly Discarded*
A "pattern" consists of at least 3 such occurrences unless the first two are sufficiently alike to indicate that a pattern is forming.
The patient has a pattern of divorce or repeatedly being discarded by a lover or spouse.
0   No
1   Yes

11. *Thinking*
Marked confusion and disorganization means that what the patient said did not make any sense; his thoughts were not connected. Suspicious means that he feels people are against him. Hallucinations refer to hearing voices or seeing things which others do not see. Delusional means he believes he has special powers, feels others are plotting against him, etc.
Recently the patient's thinking:
0   Has not been markedly confused, disorganized, and/or suspicious

Item	*Content of Item*

1   Has been markedly confused, disorganized, and/or suspicious
2   Recently the patient has been hallucinating and/or delusional

12. *Anxiety Panic*
   "Extremely anxious and/or panicky" means that the patient is close to losing control of himself, no longer able to stand his feelings.
   Recently the patient has:
   0   Not been more nervous, anxious or agitated than usual or just mildly more nervous, anxious or agitated
   1   Been extremely anxious, panicky and/or thinking of running away (or even may have done so)

13. *Dependent-Independent*
   Persons who cannot survive without others taking active care of their physical and emotional needs are "highly dependent." Persons who prefer to function without help from others or reject support from others are "highly independent." Some people manipulate others for money—these manipulators only appear to be dependent (financially) but in fact are often psychologically quite independent and use other people rather than depend on them. Such manipulators are often best scored an "independent." The dimension of dependence-independence as used here is more psychological than financial.
   Patient is:
   0   Highly dependent, or neither highly dependent or highly independent
   1   Highly independent

SCALE FOR YOUNGER MALES

1. *Marital Status*
   This refers to his present marital status. If patient is separated, divorced, widowed, or never married he is not currently married, hence score "No." Separated means spouse walked out and has been gone overnight or longer. Common-law marriages are to be considered married, i.e., scored "Yes." Homosexual "marriages" are to be scored "No."
   Patient is currently married:
   0   No
   1   Yes

2. *Caucasian*
   If patient is not white score as "No." Non-white includes: Blacks; Orientals; Indians; Spanish, Mexican nationals, etc.
   0   No
   1   Yes
   Patient is caucasian:
   0   No
   1   Yes

3. *Thinking*
   Marked confusion and disorganization means that what the patient said did not make any sense, his thoughts were not connected. Suspicious means that he feels people are against him. Hallucinations refers to hearing voices or seeing things which others do not hear or see. Delusions means that he believes he has special powers, feels others are plotting against him, etc.
   Recently the patient's thinking:
   0   Has not been *markedly* confused, disorganized, and/or suspicious
   1   Has been markedly confused, disorganized, and/or suspicious
   2   Recently the patient has been hallucinating and/or delusional

Item	*Content of Item*

4. *Omnipresent Suicidal Feelings*
   If suicidal thoughts are something the patient has recently had on occasion, score "No"; but if thinking of suicide has become a preoccupation, something which he dwells on frequently, score "Yes."
   Recently the patient has been thinking of suicide nearly all the time:
   0   No
   1   Yes
5. *Homicide Component*
   Score "Yes" if the patient is thinking of killing someone other than (or in addition to) himself.
   Recently the patient has been thinking of killing someone else:
   0   No
   1   Yes
6. *Dual Suicidality*
   Both partners (man and wife, homosexual pair, parent-child)
   May be suicidal:
   0   No
   1   Yes
7. *Type of Actual Loss—Divorce*
   The patient has had a recent (last 6 months) divorce:
   0   No
   1   Yes
8. *Criminal Behavior*
   This means that the patient has been arrested and charged with a crime such as drunk or disorderly conduct, drug abuse, sexual offense, or any other crime; i.e., the patient is known to the police. Anyone who has spent a night in jail has had a problem with the law. Traffic violations are not to be included as criminal behavior.
   The patient has had a problem with criminal behavior (may or may not be a current problem):
   0   No
   1   Yes
9. *Culture Trap*
   This refers to a person who evaluates himself wholly or nearly so on performing his traditionally defined sex role (score "Yes" if he does this).
   The patient accepts overstrenuously the traditional culturally defined sex roles and goals, i.e., work or job performance.
   0   No
   1   Yes

SCALE FOR OLDER FEMALES

1. *Single Status*
   This means that the patient has never been married. Common-law marriages are to be considered as married. Homosexual "marriages" are to be considered as "single," i.e., score as "Yes."
   Patient is single, i.e., never married. (Score as 0 if patient is married, separated, divorced, or widowed.)
   0   No
   1   Yes
2. *Socioeconomic Status*
   An annual income under $5,000 is "low"; "middle" is $5,000 to $15,000; and "high" is over $15,000. "Low" is for patients who are in the marginal

Item	*Content of Item*

group, without means, often destitute or on welfare. If the person is a skilled craftsman or regularly employed on an adequate job, score "middle." Score as "high" those persons who have considerable property, an important job, considerable savings, investments, or income.

0   Low (up to $5,000)
1   Middle ($5,000-$15,000)
2   High (above $15,000)

3. *Time*

If the plan is sufficiently developed so that the time of the suicide act might be estimated, score "Yes."

The patient is considering suicide sufficiently to estimate whether the probable time of her act would be in the next 24 hours, within the next month, or more than a month away:

0   No
1   Yes

4. *Family Available*

Do not consider as "family" more removed blood relatives like uncles, aunts, cousins, etc. unless they are mentioned specifically by the patient. Available does *not* pertain to whether they are willing to help, only to whether they are in the area and could help.

The patient has:

0   Many (3 or more) family members (spouse, siblings, children, parents) who are available (i.e., in the vicinity or who could reasonably come to the area or patient could go to them)
1   Few (1 or 2) family members who are available
2   No family members who are available

5. *Drinking Currently*

Recently the patient has been drunk one or more times or has been drinking excessively.

0   No
1   Yes

6. *Prior In-Patient Psychiatric Treatment*

This means that the patient has been in a psychiatric hospital one night or more.

0   None
1   One in-patient experience
2   More than one

7. *Alcoholism*

"Moderate" means that the patient has had some problem with alcohol, distinguished from "severe" in that it did not cause a major disruption or alteration in her life.

The patient has had a long history of difficulty with alcohol (not necessarily a current problem).

0   No
1   Moderate
2   Severe (i.e., patient has lost a job or a marriage because of this or has been a down and out alcoholic)

8. *Living Arrangement*

Family members include spouse, common-law husband, or blood relatives such as siblings, uncles, aunts, or cousins. In-laws are *not* considered part of the family.

Item	*Content of Item*

The patient is living with persons other than members of her family. (Score as 0 if she is living alone or with some other member of her family.)
0   No
1   Yes

9. *Lethality of Prior Suicidal Behavior*
The patient has:
0   Never previously (before this) thought of or engaged in any suicidal behavior(s)
1   Previously thought of suicide and/or vaguely considered suicidal behavior(s)
2   Previously deliberated on or planned specific suicidal behavior(s) but has never engaged in them
3   Engaged in suicidal behaviors but this behavior had little likelihood of being fatal
4   Engaged in suicidal behavior and this could have been fatal

10. *Repeatedly Discarded*
At least 3 such occurrences constitute a pattern unless the first two are sufficiently alike to indicate a pattern forming.
The patient has a pattern of divorce or repeatedly being discarded by a lover or spouse:
0   No
1   Yes

SCALE FOR YOUNGER FEMALES

1. *Friends in Vicinity*
This means someone in a close personal relationship, available to help. This does not mean impersonal neighbors, landlords, or apartment managers who may be of help in an emergency but are not in a personal relationship with the patient.
The patient has:
0   One or more good friends in the vicinity
1   No good friends in the vicinity

2. *Dependent-Independent*
Persons who cannot survive without others taking active care of their physical or emotional needs are highly dependent. Persons who prefer to function without help from others or reject help from others are "highly independent." For further explanation see Older Male Scale Item 13.
The patient is:
0   Highly dependent, or neither highly dependent nor highly independent
1   Highly independent

3. *Warm Interdependent Relationships*
Most people have numerous close, long time friends and relatives from whom they derive and give support. Score "limited ability" if the patient has only been able to form long-lasting mutually supportive relationships with a few persons in her life. Score "inability" if she has not been able to maintain any such relationships.
The patient has shown lifelong:
0   Good or moderate ability to maintain warm, mutually interdependent relationships
1   Limited ability to maintain warm, mutually interdependent relationships
2   Inability to maintain warm, mutually interdependent relationships

Item	*Content of Item*

4. *Occupation*

If patient has more than one occupation, score the highest number:
1.   Housewife
2.   Student
3.   Blue collar (manual laborer, waitress, carpenter, mechanic, police-woman, etc.)
4.   Clerk, secretary, office worker
5.   Executive or owns business
6.   Professional

5. *Irritation—Rage—Violence*

Obsessional thoughts, while irritating, are *not* a part of this item. Nor is frustration.

Recently the patient has:
0   Not felt irritated or angry more easily or more often than usual
1   Felt irritated or angry more easily or more often than usual
2   Been enraged and/or violent (throwing furniture, striking others, etc.) one or more times

6. *Homicide Component*

Score "Yes" if the patient is thinking (mentions) of killing someone other than (or in addition to) herself.

Recently the patient has been thinking of killing someone else:
0   No
1   Yes

7. *Lethality of Prior Suicidal Behavior*

The patient has:
0   Never previously (i.e., before current episode) thought of or engaged in any suicidal behavior
1   Previously thought of suicide and/or vaguely considered suicidal be-havior(s)
2   Has previously deliberated on or planned specific suicidal behavior(s) but has never engaged in them
3   Engaged in suicidal behavior(s) but this behavior had little likelihood of being fatal
4   Engaged in suicidal behavior and this could have been fatal

8. *Criminal Behavior*

This means that the patient has been arrested and charged with a crime such as drunk and disorderly conduct, drug abuse, sexual offense, or any other crime, i.e., the patient is known to the police. Anyone who spent a night in jail has had a problem with the law. Traffic violations are *not* to be considered as a "problem with the law."

The patient has had a problem with criminal behavior (may or may not be a current problem):
0   No
1   Yes

TABLE III-VII

SUICIDAL DEATH PREDICTION SCALES

There are four suicide risk scales for use with phone work. The four scales pertain to the following four age X sex subgroupings: (1) older males, (2) younger males, (3) older females, (4) younger females.

Steps for Using the Scales
1. Determine the sex of the caller.
2. Determine the age of the caller; if the exact age is not known then try to find out whether the caller is under 40 years old, or 40 years and older.
3. Once you have the sex and general age of the caller, select the appropriate risk scale. The "Older scales" refer to persons 40 years old and older; while the "Younger scales" refer to persons not yet 40 years old.
4. Once you have the correct risk scale try to get all the information asked for by the scales. In some instances it may not be easy to get all the answers to the questions asked by the particular scale, in that case you can use short forms of the scale in the following ways:

Scale	Form	Number of Questions You Must Answer
Older Males	Long	Answer all 13 items.
Older Males	Short	Answer the *first 7* items.
Younger Males	Long	Answer all 9 items.
Younger Males	Short	Answer the *first 5* items.
Older Females	Long	Answer all 10 items.
Older Females	Short	Answer the *first 4* items.
Younger Females	Long	Answer all 8 items.
Younger Females	Short	Answer the *first 3* items.

5. You must answer the questions exactly as worded. It is always best to use the long forms of the scales. These scales give more accurate predictions of the suicidal risk. If you absolutely cannot get all the answers needed to fill out the long form of the scale, then resign yourself to using the short form which is not as accurate. In general, the short form will have a tendency to include many more people as high risk, when in fact they should not be so considered; furthermore, the short form has a slight tendency to call some truly high risk people as not such high risks.
6. If you have time or the need, it is a good idea to assess risk first by using the long form of the appropriate scale, and then do it again using the short form.
7. The suicidal risk scales are so arranged that persons receiving scores of 7 or higher are to be considered high risk, and will likely be dead by suicide within 1 to 2 years from the time of the call (i.e., the suicidal episode). A person who gets a score of 7 or higher should be followed up carefully.
8. Using the weightings listed on the scale sheets
   a. First answer the questions required by the scale question sheet.
   b. Once you have got the answers (expressed in terms of 0, 1, 2, etc.) look at the weightings associated with those scores. Add up the weightings and see which range the total sum falls into. That is the final prediction of risk.
9. Here is a simplified example of how to get the weightings and the suicide risk score. Let us use the Younger Female Scale (Short Form with 3 items only). As an example let us assume that a young female calls in and you learn that she has no good friends in the vicinity (Item #1 gets scored as 1); also you determine that she is highly independent (Item #2 gets

scored as 1); and finally that she has a limited ability to maintain warm interdependent relationships (Item #3 gets scored as 1). Given these three pieces of information, if you look up the weights associated with these responses on the weighting sheet, you should get the following weights which are to be added up:

Col. 1 Item	Col. 2 Score	Col. 3 Weight	Col. 4 (Chosen Weights Which Are Added Together)
1 1		1.5	1.5
2 1		5.4	5.4
3 1		1.1	1.1
		Add Col. 4 =	8.0

Now look at the ranges at the bottom of the sheet and you'll see that a score of 8.0 fits into the range 7.2 to 9.1. This means that the final risk rating is HIGH. This also means that the scale predicts this person will probably be dead by suicide in 1 to 2 years.

10. *A final note:* These scales apply to persons who phone an agency and clearly voice some suicidal ideation, threat, or behavior. Do not use the scales for persons who *say* they are *not* suicidal.

Always try to use the long form of the scales. These are more accurate. You must always get answers to all the required questions. Occasionally, it is OK to take a guess at one answer if you don't get it answered directly by the caller.

TABLE III-VIII

SCALE FOR OLDER MALES   (40 and over)

LONG FORM OF SCALE USING ALL 13 ITEMS

Col. 1		Col. 2	Col. 3	Col. 4
Item #	Title of Item	Score	Weights	Assigned Weights
1	Divorce Status	0 1	8.0 10.9	
2	Depression - Somatic Aspects	0 1	8.0 11.1	
3	Irritation - Rage - Violence	0 1 2	8.0 5.2 2.3	
4	Accept Help Now	0 1	8.0 10.6	
5	Type of Actual Loss - Divorce	0 1	8.0 14.8	
6	Repetition of Attempts	0 1 2	8.0 10.7 13.4	
7	Role Failure	0 1	8.0 2.6	
8	Dual Suicidality	0 1	8.0 0.6	
9	Family Available	0 1 2	8.0 10.5 13.0	
10	Repeatedly Discarded	0 1	8.0 3.5	
11	Thinking	0 1 2	8.0 6.3 4.7	
12	Anxiety - Panic	0 1	8.0 11.3	
13	Dependent - Independent	0 1	8.0 5.1	
		ADD TOTAL OF COL. 4:		

Be sure to circle the appropriate scores in Column 2, fill in the appropriate weights in Column 4, add up the total of Column 4, and circle the final suicidal risk rating at the bottom of the page.

SUICIDAL RISK RATING IS FOUND BY EXAMINING-
WHICH RANGE ABOVE TOTAL FITS:

RANGES	74.8 80.2	80.3 85.7	85.8 91.3	91.4 96.9	97.0 102.5	102.6 108.1	108.2 116.5	116.6 124.8	124.9 133.1
RISK RATING	1	2	3	4	5	6	7	8	9
		LOW			MODERATE			HIGH	
PREDICTION			ALIVE				DEAD		

SCALE FOR OLDER MALES   (40 and over)

SHORT FORM OF SCALE USING FIRST 7 ITEMS

Col. 1 Item #	Title of Item	Col. 2 Score	Col. 3 Weights	Col. 4 · Assigned Weights
1	Divorce Status	0 1	4.0 5.9	
2	Depression – Somatic Aspects	0 1	4.0 6.1	
3	Irritation – Rage – Violence	0 1 2	4.0 2.6 1.3	
4	Accept Help Now	0 1	4.0 7.0	
5	Type of Actual Loss – Divorce	0 1	4.0 8.3	
6	Repetition of Attempts	0 1 2	4.0 5.2 6.4	
7	Role Failure	0 1	4.0 0.6	
			ADD TOTAL OF COL. 4:	

SUICIDAL RISK RATING IS FOUND BY EXAMINING
WITHIN WHICH RANGE THE TOTAL OF COL. 4 FITS:

RANGES	21.9 23.1	23.2 24.4	24.5 25.7	25.8 27.0	27.1 28.4	28.5 29.8	29.9 33.8	33.9 37.8	37.9 41.7
RISK RATING	1	2	3	4	5	6	7	8	9
		LOW			MODERATE			HIGH	
PREDICTION			ALIVE					DEAD	

Be sure to circle the appropriate scores in Column 2, fill in the appropriate weights in Column 4, add up the total of Column 4, and circle the final suicidal risk rating at the bottom of the page.

SCALE FOR YOUNGER MALES   (Under 40)

LONG FORM OF SCALE USING ALL 9 ITEMS

Col. 1		Col. 2	Col. 3	Col. 4
Item #	Type of Item	Score	Weights	Assigned Weights
1	Marital Status	0 1	5.0 9.4	
2	Caucasian	0 1	5.0 0.8	
3	Thinking	0 1 2	5.0 7.2 9.4	
4	Omnipresent Suicidal Feelings	0 1	5.0 6.9	
5	Homicide Component	0 1	5.0 1.9	
6	Dual Suicidality	0 1	5.0 1.5	
7	Type of Actual Loss — Divorce	0 1	5.0 2.7	
8	Criminal Behavior	0 1	5.0 6.8	
9	Culture Trap	0 1	5.0 6.5	
		ADD TOTAL OF COL. 4:		

Be sure to circle the appropriate scores in Column 2, fill in the appropriate weights in Column 4, add up the total of Column 4, and circle the final suicidal risk rating at the bottom of the page.

SUICIDAL RISK RATING IS FOUND BY EXAMINING
WITHIN WHICH RANGE THE TOTAL OF COL. 4 FITS:

RANGES	31.1 34.1	34.2 36.4	36.5 38.7	38.8 41.0	41.1 43.4	43.5 45.8	45.9 50.2	50.3 54.6	54.7 59.0
RISK RATING	1	2	3	4	5	6	7	8	9
		LOW		MODERATE			HIGH		
PREDICTION		ALIVE					DEAD		

SCALE FOR YOUNGER MALES   (Under 40)

SHORT FORM OF SCALE USING FIRST 5 ITEMS

Col. 1		Col. 2	Col. 3	Col. 4
Item #	Title of Item	Score	Weights	Assigned Weights
1	Marital Status	0 1	4.0 7.3	
2	Caucasian	0 1	4.0 0.4	
3	Thinking	0 1 2	4.0 5.5 7.0	
4	Omnipresent Suicidal Feelings	0 1	4.0 5.4	
5	Homicide Component	0 1	4.0 1.6	
		ADD TOTAL OF COL. 4:		

SUICIDAL RISK RATING IS FOUND BY EXAMINING
WITHIN WHICH RANGE THE TOTAL OF COL. 4 FITS:

RANGES	14.0 14.8	14.9 15.7	15.8 16.7	16.8 17.7	17.8 18.7	18.8 19.7	19.8 22.4	22.5 25.1	25.2 27.7
RISK RATING	1	2	3	4	5	6	7	8	9
		LOW			MODERATE			HIGH	
PREDICTION			ALIVE					DEAD	

Be sure to circle the appropriate scores in Column 2, fill in the appropriate weights in Column 4, add up the total of Column 4, and circle the final suicidal risk rating at the bottom of the page.

SCALE FOR OLDER FEMALES   (40 years and over)

LONG FORM OF SCALE USING ALL 10 ITEMS

Col. 1 Item #	Title of Item	Col. 2 Score	Col. 3 Weights	Col. 4 Assigned Weights
1	Single Status	0 1	5.0 6.2	
2	Socioeconomic Status	0 1 2	5.0 6.2 7.4	
3	Time	0 1	5.0 6.0	
4	Family Available	0 1 2	5.0 6.7 8.5	
5	Drinking Currently	0 1	5.0 0.0	
6	Prior In-Patient Psychiatric Treatment	0 1 2	5.0 3.4 1.7	
7	Alcoholism	0 1 2	5.0 9.8 14.6	
8	Living Arrangement	0 1	5.0 7.5	
9	Lethality of Prior Suicidal Behavior	0 1 2 3 4	5.0 5.5 5.9 6.4 6.9	
10	Repeatedly Discarded	0 1	5.0 2.9	
		ADD TOTAL OF COL. 4:		

Be sure to circle the appropriate scores in Column 2, fill in the appropriate weights in Column 4, add up the total of Column 4, and circle the final suicidal risk rating at the bottom of the page.

SUICIDAL RISK RATING IS FOUND BY EXAMIINING WITHIN WHICH RANGE THE TOTAL OF COL. 4 FITS:

RANGES	39.6 42.0	42.1 44.5	44.6 47.0	47.1 49.5	49.6 52.0	52.1 54.6	54.7 60.4	60.5 66.2	66.3 72.1
RISK RATING	1	2	3	4	5	6	7	8	9
		LOW			MODERATE			HIGH	
PREDICTION			ALIVE					DEAD	

·SCALE FOR OLDER FEMALES   (40 years and older)

SHORT FORM OF SCALE USING FIRST 4 ITEMS

Col. 1		Col. 2	Col. 3	Col. 4
Item #	Title of Item	Score	Weights	Assigned Weights
1	Single Status	0 1	0.0 3.5	
2	Socioeconomic Status	0 1 2	0.0 1.2 2.3	
3	Time	0 1	0.0 2.1	
4	Family Available	0 1 2	0.0 1.0 2.1¨	
			ADD TOTAL OF COL. 4:	

SUICIDAL RISK RATING IS FOUND BY EXAMINING
WITHIN WHICH RANGE THE TOTAL OF COL. 4 FITS:

RANGES	0.0 0.3	0.4 0.8	0.9 1.3	1.4 1.8	1.9 2.3	2.4 2.8	2.9 5.2	5.3 7.6	7.7 10.0
RISK RATING	1	2	3	4	5	6	7	8	9
		LOW			MODERATE			HIGH	
PREDICTION			ALIVE					DEAD	

Be sure to circle the appropriate scores in Column 2, fill in the appropriate weights in Column 4, add up the total of Column 4, and circle the final suicidal risk rating at the bottom of the page.

SCALE FOR YOUNGER FEMALES (Under 40)

LONG FORM OF SCALE USING ALL 8 ITEMS

Col. 1		Col. 2	Col. 3	Col. 4
Item #	Title of Item	Score	Weights	Assigned Weights
1	Friends in Vicinity	0 1	3.0 4.5	
2	Dependent — Independent	0 1	3.0 8.7	
3	Warm Interdependent Relationships	0 1 2	3.0 4.2 5.3	
4	Occupation	1 2 3 4 5 6	3.4 3.8 4.2 4.6 5.0 5.4	
5	Irritation — Rage Violence	0 1 2	3.0 1.9 0.7	
6	Homicide Component	0 1	3.0 5.5	
7	Lethality of Prior Suicidal Behavior	0 1 2 3 4	3.0 3.5 4.0 4.5 5.0	
8	Criminal Behavior	0 1	3.0 0.7	
		ADD TOTAL OF COL. 4:		

Be sure to circle the appropriate scores in Column 2, fill in the appropriate weights in Column 4, add up the total of Column 4, and circle the final suicidal risk rating at the bottom of the page.

SUICIDAL RISK RATING IS FOUND BY EXAMINING
WITHIN WHICH RANGE THE TOTAL OF COL. 4 FITS:

RANGES	19.8 21.4	21.5 23.1	23.2 24.8	24.9 26.5	26.6 28.2	28.3 29.9	30.0 33.4	33.5 36.9	37.0 40.4
RISK RATING	1	2	3	4	5	6	7	8	9
		LOW		MODERATE			HIGH		
PREDICTION		ALIVE					DEAD		

SCALE FOR YOUNGER FEMALES   (Under 40)

SHORT FORM OF SCALE USING FIRST 3 ITEMS

Col. 1		Col. 2	Col. 3	Col. 4
Item #	Title of Item	Score	Weights	Assigned Weights
1	Friends in Vicinity	0 1	0.0 1.5	
2	Dependent — Independent	0 1	0.0 5.4	
3	Warm Interdependent Relationships	0 1 2	0.0 1.1 2.2	
			ADD TOTAL OF COL. 4:	

SUICIDAL RISK RATING IS FOUND BY EXAMINING
WITHIN WHICH RANGE THE TOTAL OF COL. 4 FITS:

RANGES	0.0 0.4	0.5 0.9	1.0 1.4	1.5 1.9	2.0 2.4	2.5 2.9	3.0 5.0	5.1 7.1	7.2 9.1
RISK RATING	1	2	3	4	5	6	7	8	9
		LOW		MODERATE			HIGH		
PREDICTION		ALIVE					DEAD		

Be sure to circle the appropriate scores in Column 2, fill in the appropriate weights in Column 4, add up the total of Column 4, and circle the final suicidal risk rating at the bottom of the page.

phone worker attempts to readily identify the age and sex of the caller, so as to know which question sheet is appropriate. Every attempt is made to answer all of the questions for that scale which is age and sex appropriate to that particular caller. If *all* the necessary information is obtained, the worker can then use the long form answer sheet to tally up the caller's predictive index. If the call is terminated abruptly or information is not obtainable, hopefully the worker has gathered enough information to make as assessment based on the short form answer sheet. In actual operation the various question and answer sheets can be color-coded to facilitate the worker's task of finding and turning to the appropriate scales. For instance the question and answer sheets for males and females can be printed on various shades of blue and pink paper, respectively.

REFERENCES

Dixon, J.: *BMD: Biomedical Computer Package Handbook.* University of California at Los Angeles, 1968.

Goldberg, L. R.: Simple models or simple processes? Some research on clinical judgments. *American Psychologist, 23:*483-496, 1968.

Grygier, T.: The effect of social action: Current prediction methods and two new models. *British Journal of Criminology, 6:*269-293, 1966.

Macnaughton-Smith, P.: The classification of individuals by the possession of attributes associated with a criterion. *Biometrics, 19:*364-366, 1963.

Neuringer, C.: Methodological problems in suicide research. *Journal of Consulting Psychology, 26:*273-278, 1962.

Neuringer, C., and Kolstoe, R. H.: Suicide research and non-rejection of the null hypothesis. *Perceptual and Motor Skills, 22:*115-118, 1966.

Ward, P. G.: The comparative efficiency of differing techniques of prediction scaling. *Australian and New Zealand Journal of Criminology, 1:* 109-112, 1968.

Wilkens, J.: A follow-up of those who called a suicide prevention center. *American Journal of Psychiatry, 127:*155-161, 1970.

Williams, W. T., and Lambert, J. M.: Multivariate methods in plant ecology. *Journal of Ecology, 47:*83-101, 1959.

CHAPTER IV

RORSCHACH INKBLOT TEST ASSESSMENT OF SUICIDAL RISK

CHARLES NEURINGER

THE RORSCHACH TEST is the most commonly used method for estimating suicidal risk. Its popularity is slowly being supplanted by more sophisticated psychometric instruments such as the MMPI and the various lethality scales. However, the test still exerts a seductive influence on psychologists who are not acquainted with the risk assessing alternatives that arise from the new discipline of suicidology. However, the Rorschach is still a potent tool for assessing suicidal risk if it is used correctly. Reviews of the capacity of the Rorschach to adequately predict suicidal ideation and behavior have not been overly sanguine (Brown and Sheran, 1970; Goldfried, Stricker, and Weiner, 1971; Lester, 1970; Neuringer, 1963). However, the reviews do not call the Rorschach test itself into question, but raise doubts about its appropriate usage and interpretation.

Analysis of the use of the Rorschach for predicting and identifying suicidal behavior indicate that inconsistent results can be traced to the inconsistent utilization of the test. Whatever usefulness the Rorschach has for the understanding of suicide has been obscured by confusing and varying definitions of suicidal behavior and ideation and inconsistent and often ludicrous measures of suicide. People evaluated before committing suicide have been grouped together with those who have been measured before a suicide attempt. Researchers have inspected Rorschach protocols of individuals who have been administered the test one to five years previously and have not found a relationship between the protocols and consequent suicidal behavior. Ignoring the time lag, they have concluded that the Rorschach is an inappropriate instrument for predicting suicidal behavior.

74

The vague classification of suicide, as used by researchers, has already been discussed by Neuringer (1962). He points out that the rubric has been used in over fourteen different ways in suicide research. Even observable and verifiable attempts may have profoundly different motivational bases. The person who takes a small dosage of barbiturates in order to threaten, warn, or manipulate another person, and the individual who has shot himself through the head but has been saved by medical science, are usually both classified "as suicide attempters." It is then not surprising that their Rorschach protocols differ.

Studies of suicide with the Rorschach may be roughly classified into four groups. They are investigations of (1) determinants and ratios, (2) single signs, (3) multiple signs, and (4) content. In this presentation the varying investigations will be described and discussed from a methodological standpoint and possible new approaches to remedying certain problems will be suggested. This review is restricted to empirical comparative studies. There are some excellent theoretical case studies, and descriptive papers available (Bachrach, 1951; Beck, 1945, 1960; Boreham, 1968; Cutter, 1968; Daston, 1967; Holzberg, Cahen, and Wilk, 1951; Lindner, 1950; Piotrowski, 1950; Rabin, 1946; Teicher, 1947; Ulett, Martin, and McBride, 1950; White and Schreiber, 1952; Varvel, 1941) which are strongly recommended to the reader.

DETERMINANTS AND RATIOS

The research paradigm for the study of determinants and ratios involves a comparative assessment of the Rorschach protocols of a suicidal group and a nonsuicidal group. The earliest study of this kind was conducted by Berk (1949). He presented the results of a comparison conducted between the records of 25 male suicidal attempt schizophrenics and 30 nonsuicidal male schizophrenics. The suicidal patients produced significantly more FC and At responses than did the controls. Out of the vast number of comparisons made, these two significant differences may well have been due to chance. If, however, they appear again in a replication study, some confidence could be placed in these findings. Fisher (1951), also utilizing male suicidal attempt schizophrenics and nonsuicidal schizophrenic patients, reported that his suicidal subjects gave *fewer* FC responses and longer IRT's than the controls. Berk has not reported any significant difference between IRT's in his study. However, it should be noted that different methods of statistical analysis were used by these investigators.

Broida (1954) also utilized schizophrenic patients but differed from the studies already cited in that the suicidal patients were chosen on the basis of ward psychiatric judgments and not solely on the basis of overt suicidal behavior. These patients' protocols were compared with those of severely depressed but not suicidal controls (based on the ward psychiatrist's judgment). The suicidal patients only produced significantly fewer A responses than the controls.

Costello (1958) utilized the records of suicide attempt males and females of mixed diagnostic origin, and a control group matched on sex, age, IQ, and diagnosis. He reported that the suicidal patients produced fewer R, M, and C responses than the suicidal subjects. Hertz (1949), also utilizing a mixed "clinical" group of suicidal and control protocols, found that C responses were more prevalent among the suicidal than control Rorschachs. This runs counter to Costello's findings.

Pratt (1951) compared the Rorschach protocols of suicidal and homicidal subjects. In her suicidal group were found the protocols of 43 attempters of varying seriousness and eight successful suicides. These were compared with the Rorschachs of 48 homicidal and with a group of normal records. The suicidal vs. normal analysis yielded information that the suicidal subjects produced fewer R, M, FC, V, and P responses and more CF, Y, and S responses than the normals. When the suicidal and homicidal protocols were compared, it was found that the suicidal subjects gave significantly more P and M responses. Seriously suicidal subjects had more R, CF, Y, and S responses in their protocols than non-seriously suicidal persons. Crasilneck (1954) also compared the records of serious and non-serious suicide attempters. He reported that the protocols of the more serious cases yielded more F+, FC, and fewer CF responses than the less serious cases. The Pratt and Crasilneck findings are inconsistent. But it must be noted that Crasilneck utilized suicide attempt Rorschachs from one hospital, while Pratt collected her protocols from a wide variety of sources.

If one scrutinizes those studies utilizing psychiatric patients, one finds that several determinants (more A, At, fewer R, M, m, C, and IRT) appear, but only once. The FC responses appear twice but in opposite directions. If all the determinant studies are considered at once, there appears to be contradictions concerning P, M, C, and CF. Only the presence of more S and fewer R responses among the suicidal groups were not contradicted, but these results were found only in Pratt's study. This should not be surprising to the reader since the studies described here were different in design. There were a variety of different research methodologies reported (suicidal schizophrenic vs. non-suicidal schizophrenics; mixed diagnostic group comparisons; suicide defined by the commission of an attempt; suicide defined by a ward psychiatrist's judgment; serious vs. non-serious; some studies utilizing matched subjects, others not, etc.). One can see why the results seem contradictory. Their seeming contrariness is due to the variety of research designs. In essence the studies are not at all comparable. It makes no sense to conclude that the fault for these "inconsistencies" lies with the Rorschach test.

Some of the studies discussed above have reported data on ratio comparisons. It would be expected that the findings concerning the ratios would not be very fruitful since the results of determinant comparisons have not been very fruitful. Crasilneck (1954) reported that greater $FY + YF + Y$ ratio scores were found among the more serious suicidal protocols as compared with the less serious suicidal records. This he christened a "deep depression" sign. A ratio in which he compared "deep depression to reactive depression" ($F+\% + TRT + SMWt/TR + M\% + A\%$) also yielded significant differences. He found that the serious individuals showed more deep depression than their less lethal cohorts. The more serious subjects also showed greater positive scores on his "histrionic" ratio $[FC - (CF + C)$ wt] than the controls. This same ratio was characterized as a "stability" ratio by Hertz (1949), and she reported similar results for her subjects. She also developed a "sensitivity" ratio $[FCh = (ChF + Ch)]$ on which her suicidal subjects scored significantly higher in the positive direction than her controls.

SINGLE SIGNS

Some investigators have been interested in a single characteristic (that may involve a determinant) which they feel to be intimately related to suicide.

Sakheim (1955), in his empirical investigation (to be more fully described later) of the then known Rorschach hypotheses about suicide, found verification for Beck's (1954) hypothesis of shading shock (indicating oppressive anxiety) in card IV and for Piotrowski's (1950) hypothesis on utilization of "M through animals" (e.g., two ants writing a book) which is hypothesized to be indicative of pessimism and disillusionment with people. Hertz (1949) also reported that her suicidal subjects showed more shading as well as color shock than her controls (through the FCh − (ChF + Ch) and FC − (CF + C) ratios). Fisher's (1951) study of Hertz's ratios did not corroborate her findings. However, evidence for color and shading shock was claimed by Pratt (1951) who reported that her suicidal subjects rejected more of the cards that she felt reflected color shock (II, VIII, IX and X) and shading shock (IV, V, VI, and VII) than the controls. The evidence for color and shading shock is difficult to evaluate since its operational definition varies among the investigators.

Sapolsky (1963), basing his research on an interpretation of the "psychoanalytic" hypothesis that suicide represents a wish to return to the womb and desire to be reborn, felt that subjects with suicidal tendencies would be attracted to and utilize the lower center (D6 in Beck's system) on card VII. This location he feels to be the "vaginal area" in the "mother card." He gathered together 28 protocols of neuropsychiatric patients who responded to D6 and then utilized the protocols of 28 other neuropsychiatric patients (matched for age, sex, number of responses, percentage of D responses and diagnoses) who had not responded to D6. The psychiatric histories of these 56 patients were examined for suicidal ideation or behavior. The criterion for suicidality was at least one mention of suicide. Sapolsky reported that there were significantly more "suicidal" histories among the responders than among the non-responders to D6. However, any conclusions to be drawn from it should be tentative, since Sapolsky had not presented data indicating that a significant number of suicidal subjects utilized D6, but only that among utilizers of this blot area were to be found a large number of suicidal subjects.

Two attempts were made to replicate Sapolsky's findings (Cooper, Bernstein, and Hart, 1965; Drake and Rusnak, 1966). Both studies failed to confirm the relationship between the D6 area on Card VII and suicidal behavior. Sapolsky (1967) took issue with the results of the latter study, indicating that the criteria for suicidal behavior were too harsh and that the data had not been correctly analyzed. Sapolsky reconstructed a contingency table from Drake and Rusnak's data and found it to demonstrate a statistically significant relationship between response to the D6 area and suicidality. Cutter, Jorgenson, and Farberow (1968) correlated the seriousness of suicidal attempt intent with the use of the D6 area and reported that no relationship existed between the extent of suicidal intent and response to that area of Card VII. Neither did they find any relationships between amount of previous suicidal behavior and the Sapolsky variable.

Applebaum and Holzman (1962) reported success with a single sign composed of shading within a colored area. They felt that any response that combines color and shading regardless of whether form is primary or not is related to suicidal behavior. They examined the protocols of committed and attempted suicides, neuropsychiatric controls, police officers, women with thyroid conditions, psychiatric residents, and college girls for evidence of the presence of at least one color-shading response. After a comparison of the incidence of color-shading responses among these records, they reported that the frequency among the suicidal subjects was significantly greater than among the controls. However, Neuringer, McEvoy, and Schlesinger (1965) could not corroborate their findings for female commit and attempt suicidal, neuropsychiatric, criminal offender, and normal subject records. These two studies are not strictly comparable since different subject populations were used by the investigators.

Applebaum and Colson (1968) reexamined the relationship between the color-shading response and suicidal behavior utilizing psychiatric patients. Utilizing a criteria of bare mention of color-shading in any way (even to deny the presence of the determinant), they found a significant relationship between the color-shading response and suicidality. Cutter, Jorgenson, and Farberow (1968) were unable to confirm the relationship between color-shading responses and suicidal lethality. Cutter et al. investigated the correlation between levels of lethality of suicidal intent (ranging from no attempt to very dangerous suicidal behavior) with color-shading responses and reported an r biserial correlation coefficient of .03 to exist between the two variables. Neither was there a relationship between amount of previous suicidal behavior and the appearance of the color-shading response.

Aside from studies dealing with the D6 area on card VII, for which the results are highly inconclusive, the other studies have concentrated on color and shading either as a shock effect or as a combinatory response. It is difficult to draw any conclusions about color and shading from these investigations because of the various ways it has been formally and operationally defined as well as the presence of non-comparable experimental designs. The use of color and shading variable to predict suicide should be handled with great suspicion.

MULTIPLE SIGNS

The developers of multiple sign approaches feel that their methodology is bound to be more useful than the determinant and single sign approaches. They argue that the psychodynamics of suicide are so complicated that no single determinant or sign could adequately reflect the many facets of the suicidal phenomenon. They feel that if the researcher could even grasp some of its characteristic expressions, then he stands a better chance of identifying and understanding it in the future. Typically, it is the presence of a certain number of signs that defines whether a protocol is suicidal or not. The actual signs themselves play a subservient role to the overall number of the signs present and the signs may differ from protocol to protocol or may change temporarily in the same individual. Thus cutoff scores, in terms of numbers of signs, are crucial for making inferences about suicide. This approach represents an attempt to circumvent the failure of previous research to uncover reliable determinants or single signs.

Two multiple sign approaches have been developed. Hertz's (1948, 1949) method is based on signs (which she calls configurations) derived primarily from clinical experience. Martin (1951) chose to use a more empirical approach towards developing his set of signs.

On the basis of extensive clinical experience with suicidal individuals, Hertz (1948) hypothesized that self-destructive tendencies ought to be reflected in 14 different ways. These signs were given the following titles: (1) Neurotic Structure, (2) Deep Anxiety, (3) Depressed States, (4) Constriction, (5) Active Conflict, (6) Obsessive-Compulsive Personality Components, (7) Hysterical Features, (8) Ideational Symptomatology, (9) Agitation Phenomena, (10) Resignation, (11) Sudden and Emotional Outbursts, (12) Withdrawal from the World, (13) Paranoid Tendencies, and (14) Chaotic Sexuality.

The definitional criteria for each of the signs is somewhat complicated and often difficult to comprehend. Below is her definition of "Neurotic Structure."

> Reduced R; Low Human M; human M < animal M; shading disturbance; color disturbance; failure and rejection trends; high F%; high A + At%; low FC; reactions to color inhibited, evaded or unstable; m; free floating anxiety; dysphoric use of achromatic color; occasional F− not due to intellectual limitations; high (Dr + Do + S − s) % contents reflecting special longings, desires, wishes, inner conflict, over-valent materials; Ad + Hd A + H; behavior manifestations pointing to insecurity, lack of confidence, tension, strain, inhibition, self-criticism, doubts, evasiveness, and repression (p. 5).

The examiner is asked to examine the protocol and utilize the above-cited criteria and make a judgment as to the presence or absence of the sign. Unfortunately, Hertz neither gives further definitional elaboration for her signs or indicates how many of these elements need to be present before the sign can be judged to have appeared in the record.

Hertz reviewed the case history materials of 113 neurotics, 116 psychotics, and 96 normal individuals that had been referred to her in order to determine whether they contained any indications of suicidal ideation, threat, attempt, or commission. Based on this evaluation, she then divided the subject's Rorschach protocols into suicidal and non-suicidal groups and examined them for the presence of the signs. It is unfortunate that Hertz did both of these analyses herself since this procedure raises the possibility of contamination. She reported that the suicidal psychiatric, non-suicidal psychiatric, and normal protocols yielded respectively 7.8, 4.8, and 2.8 mean number of signs. She also reported that six or more signs correctly identified 92 percent of the suicidal subjects. This cutoff yielded 35 percent and 3 percent false positives respectively for the non-suicidal "clinical" and normal groups. Further intergroup analyses forced Hertz to reduce the number of signs from 14 to 10. However, the cutoff remained at six signs.

Hertz (1949) then conducted a validation study in which she analyzed 178 consecutive non-selected protocols without prior knowledge of the case history data. Utilizing a cutoff score of 5, she characterized the records as either being suicidal or not. When the case history material was examined, it was found that she had correctly identified 170 of the 178 protocols.

The results of the validating study are impressive. Unfortunately, because of the ambiguous way they are stated, Hertz has not adequately communicated her definitional criteria and this has led to difficulty in duplicating her results. Only one study attempting to utilize her method met with partial success.

Sakheim (1955), using 40 suicide attempt psychiatric and non-suicidal psychiatric controls matched on age, sex, education, and IQ, and making a good attempt to utilize only serious suicidal cases, applied his interpretation of Hertz's signs to their Rorschach protocols and found that only "Deep Anxiety," "Depressed States," "Withdrawal from the World," and "Resignation Trends" differentiated between the two groups. He also reported that a cutoff of 5 or more signs identified a significant number of suicidal individuals.

On the debit side, Fisher (1951) applied what he felt were the Hertz criteria to the protocols of 20 schizophrenic suicide attempters and controls without success. Berk (1949) also reported negative results in terms of the individual signs and cutoff scores.

Further investigation with Hertz's signs has not been done. This has been only partially due to the ponderousness of her signs and amount of work involved in analyzing the protocols. The primary reason for lack of interest in Hertz's scheme has been due to the appearance of another multiple sign approach which requires less effort on the part of the examiner and which defines its signs clearly and concisely.

Martin's (1951) multiple sign approach utilized a strictly empirical methodology without any initial hypotheses as to which characteristics of suicidal thinking, feeling, or perception led to what kind of Rorschach responses. Martin examined the Rorschach records of 36 male suicide attempt and 36 non-suicidal patients matched on diagnosis, age, educational level, IQ, occupation, and number of Rorschach responses.

After comparing the protocols of the two groups for the presence of numerous kinds of signs, he finally found a residue of 16 signs which differentiated the suicidal from the nonsuicidal subjects at the .10 level of significance.

These signs were: (1) No. $D < 6$ or > 20; (2) $D\% < 60$ or > 79; (3) No. $CF > 0$ to < 3; (4) Total C responses > 1; (5) Sum $C > 1.0$ to < 3.5; (6) C and/or CF responses appear first on Card VIII-X: yes; (7) C and/or CF responses appear with zero $(FY + YF + Y)$: yes; (8) No. $(FV + VF) < 1$; (9) No. $FY + YF + Y < 1$; (10) Total shading responses < 1; (11) Difference between M: Sum $C < 1.5$; (12) No. $(H + Hd) > 6$; (13) No. Categories < 6 or > 13; (14) percent VIII-X/R > 29; (15) No. $P < 3$ or > 6; and (16) P failure with $F + \% > 60$: Yes.

Martin then validated his 16 signs on two new groups matched to his original groups. In this study only signs 3, 5, 6, 7, and 8 differed at the .05 level of significance. He retained his original list and also added a 17th sign (T/IR 27 seconds). There is some question about the wisdom of retaining all his signs since some of them did not continue to differentiate at the .10 level of significance. One sign differentiated at the .90 level (appeared in 13 of the suicidal and 11 of the control records). Martin seems to have felt that the cutoff percentage of correct identifications vindicated this procedure (a cutoff of 7 or more signs, he reports, correctly identified 69% of the suicidal patients). Martin speculated that since a great number of his signs involved color and/or shading, they indicated that the suicidal person was very affectively reactive, but with poor control.

Daston and Sakheim (1960) added a matched committed suicide group to Martin's validating groups and compared them for signs. They found no significant difference in the number of signs between the protocols of their commit suicide group and Martin's attempt suicide group. The Daston and Sakheim committed suicide group was, as expected, significantly differentiated in terms of number of signs from Martin's control group. These results limit the Martin Checklist's ability to distinguish between those people who commit suicide and those who attempt it. Daston and Sakheim reported that signs 3, 5, 7, 8, 11, and 17 differentiated between Martin's suicide attempt and control groups at the .05 level of significance. This may surprise the reader since, with the same data, Martin reported that only signs 3, 5, 6, 7, and 8 differentiated. However, Daston and Sakheim used a different statistical method than the one used by Martin. They further reported that signs 7, 11, and 17 successfully differentiated the suicide committers from the controls and that sign 16 successfully differentiated the attempt suicide from the commit suicide group. They also reported that the 7 or more sign cutoff correctly identified 62 percent of the suicide commit records. They concluded that their study corroborated and further validated Martin's findings.

Weiner (1961) extended the range of applicability of the Martin Signs beyond schizophrenics. He applied the checklist to all the adult patients who had been at a psychiatric service in a general hospital for over six months. Different age, sex, diagnostic, and patient statuses were represented. His subject population was composed of 28 males and 43 females. Forty-two of these were hospitalized and 29 were outpatients. Twenty-four of these subjects had made suicide attempts. He concluded that the number of signs were not related to age, sex, number of responses, or to in-or-out patient status, but was related to suicidal status and to severity of the diagnosis. He concluded that the Martin Checklist was useful in general for identifying suicidal persons but one should be cautious about cases where the diagnosis was severe. However, only two signs (5 and 13) differentiated the suicide attempt and control groups. Neuringer, McEvoy, and Schlesinger (1965) were not able to reproduce Weiner's positive results in terms of sex differences.

Successful demonstration of the utilization of the Martin Signs with single cases has been made by Boreham (1967) and Daston (1967). Cutter, Jorgenson, and Farberow (1968) found that the Martin Signs could be successfully related to level of suicidal lethality of intent (i.e., as the dangerousness of suicidal behavior rose, there is a corresponding rise in the number of Martin Signs appearing in the protocols).

The Martin multiple sign approach seems to have yielded some interesting and reliable results. There are some inconsistencies, but they can be traced to different subject populations. Certainly more extensive use with the approach is indicated. Hertz's method might have yielded important contributions if it had had more definitional clarity. However, it needs to be pointed out that the multiple sign approach as utilized by Hertz and Martin has some severe limitations. These studies are all "after-the-fact" with protocols of patients who have already committed or attempted suicide, and a long range predictive study is badly needed here.

The multiple sign methodology tends towards only an identification of suicidal persons procedure. This is not to demean the diagnostic task, for it is very important and certainly can help to save lives, but there is little contribution made to the understanding of and teasing out of the psychodynamic variables in suicide. However, neither are the studies of single signs or determinants superior to multiple sign investigations as far as this capacity is concerned.

CONTENT

Studies relating content of responses to suicidality are rare. This is somewhat surprising since content, although it is somewhat subjective and prone to individual differences in interpretation, may at times communicate affective states very directly. However, investigators (Osgood and Walker, 1959; Spiegel and Neuringer, 1963) working with suicide note contents found that it was extremely difficult to find examples of explicit statements reflecting suicidal intention or ideation. None of the Rorschach studies of content to be described here report any direct expression of suicidal ideation (e.g., "a man killing himself"). For some reason this direct expression through content seems to be inhibited, and thus suicidal thoughts and intentions remain hidden from the examiner. This is unfortunate since such contents, if they existed, could probably offer the most immediate identifications of suicidal ideas and planning.

Pratt (1951) reported that, when compared to homicidal subjects, suicidal individuals produced more mutilation, abstraction, ice, weapon and fighting responses, and fewer blood responses. Fisher and Hines (1951) compared the content productions of a group of hospital job applicants, non-suicidal schizophrenics, and suicide attempt schizophrenics in terms of explicit and implicit hostility. Explicit hostility was defined by a response which reflected overt hostility (e.g., "somebody fighting someone") while implicit hostility was characterized by responses which were thought to be more subtle and covert (e.g., "knife," "guns,"). Fisher and Hines reported no significant differences between the three groups as far as the production of explicit or implicit hostility responses were concerned.

Broida (1954) attempted to vindicate Lindner's (1950) hypothesis concerning the suicidal implications of certain kinds of contents associated with card IV. Lindner felt that this card could reflect suicidal trends if they existed. Suicidal ideation is betrayed, he felt, by such depressive and deteriorating responses as "a decaying tooth," "rotting tree trunk," or "pall of black smoke." Broida administered cards I, II, III, and IV to his subjects and also tried to elicit these kinds of responses in the testing of the limits situation if they were not given spontaneously during the performance. He found that 15 percent of the suicidal subjects gave Lindner type responses while none were reported for the controls. No significant difference in occurrence of these responses were found in the testing of the limits situation. On the other hand, Cutter, Jorgenson, and Farberow (1968) report a significant correlation between "deteriorating content" on Card IV, which they describe as a Lindner sign, and lethality of suicidal intention. They also found this sign to appear more often in Rorschachs that were administered a very short time before a suicidal death as compared to protocols administered long before the self-destructive behavior.

Lester (1967) investigated the relationship between attempted suicide and body image. His concern was to study the effect of levels of body-image integrity and inward direction of aggression. He reported no relationship between body image contents and suicidal behavior.

Perhaps the most comprehensive study of Rorschach contents in suicidal persons was conducted by Costello (1958). He intensively examined the protocols of suicidal attempt and control subjects matched for age, sex, IQ, and diagnoses. Costello isolated all content responses that occurred at least 25 percent of the time. If any such responses occurred twice as often in one group as compared to the other group, they were considered to be typical for that group. The following typical responses for the suicidal group were reported: Card I: Map responses; Card II: Whole two humans in passive posture; Card V: Winged whole in flight; Card VI: Object response to top detail; Card VII: Map response; Card IX: Man's head response to bottom pink detail; Card X: Whole plant response.

Studies of content are always fascinating because of their direct communication. However, the content communication of the above-cited studies is difficult to interpret. Moreover, extreme caution should be exercised here since none of these studies have been validated. Attempts to validate Lindner's specific content hypothesis about depression and deterioration lead to equivocal results. Fisher and Hines' study was concerned directly with hostility and found no evidence for an abundance of the variable in suicidal individuals. Neither was hostility found among Costello's protocols to any great degree, although Pratt found these kinds of responses to be extremely common. However, it should be remembered that Pratt compared her subjects with homicidal subjects, a comparison which may have highlighted certain classes of responses by contrast.

DISCUSSION

A wide variety of studies has been presented to the reader. However, an integration of their results is not a difficult task since few trends were apparent among them. Martin's Checklist results come closest to consistently identifying suicidal persons across varying conditions. There certainly does not appear to have been found any particular determinant, sign, set of signs, or content which appears to be associated with suicide under all or even most conditions, i.e., there is no pathognomic sign on the Rorschach for suicide which is so strong that it transcends all the various states of suicidality or the differing conditions under which the test data was elicited. This is not to say that the data derived from the researchers described here is not valid. They are valid operationally (i.e., when tied down to the particular conditions under which they were gathered). Repetition of these studies would certainly strengthen any conclusions that can be drawn from them. It is because of the absence of a single transcendent clue to suicide on the Rorschach that careful notation of the research design and methodology becomes imperative.

Some general remarks may be made about the difficulties confronting the suicide researcher which tend to reduce the effectiveness and fruitfulness of his efforts. Except for one instance, the studies described here have been "paper researches." Protocols of suicide individuals are found and then analyzed instead of finding suicidal persons and administering the Rorschach to them. As Underwood (1957) has pointed out, a great deal of precision is lost in this kind of methodology because one cannot control many important variables. Unfortunately, the suicide researcher is often forced into this kind of design because the number of available "live" suicidal subjects is severely limited at any given time (Rosen, 1954). Another problem, not unrelated to the above, involves a peculiar statistical artifact in suicide research which may mediate against the appearance of significant results. Neuringer and Kolstoe (1966) reviewed all the known empirical studies of suicide and found that all but one utilized the .05 level of significance. They also pointed out that in suicide research the sample sizes tend to be small, the treatment conditions variable, and the controls poor. These conditions mediate against tests of significance approaching the .05 level of confidence. They suggest that these conditions be corrected whenever possible in order not to reject a good hypothesis when in fact it is true. It may be that the

Rorschach investigators in the area of suicide have been penalized because they are dealing with a phenomenon whose frequency of occurrence is extremely low. It should also be pointed out that Lester (1970) rejects this view and feels that greater precision is needed because of the presence of methodological difficulties.

There are also some general methodological criticisms that can be leveled against the various suicide researchers. Without mentioning specific studies, it could be pointed out that confusion as to the conclusions that can be drawn from the data often stems from an omnibus definition of suicidal subjects in which all kinds of subjects (threateners, ideators, committers, attempters, depressed patients, etc.) are lumped together to compose the pool of suicidal protocols. As has been mentioned before, even suicide attempters may be vastly different in terms of motive and psychodynamics. The violation of temporality also has mitigated against the possible emergence of valid and useful data. Rorschachs administered before the suicidal behavior may not be tapping the same areas as those given after the event. And yet, "before" and "after" protocols have been lumped together. In addition, the time span between Rorschach and suicidal event has often been ignored. Farberow and Shneidman (1959) have shown that this is a very important factor in terms of the responses that suicidal individuals give to the MMPI.

It is the author's intention to demonstrate that much of the so-called contradictions concerning the results of suicide research lay not with the Rorschach, but with the designs and methodologies. Although the methodological difficulties and criticisms already mentioned, either as general statements or as related to the studies reviewed here, have contributed heavily to this equivocality, the greatest share of this is due to the erroneous comparison of noncomparable studies. One cannot conclude that this or that study does not agree or confirm another study when the designs are vastly different. The results of a study utilizing suicide attempt schizophrenic protocols compared to schizophrenic control records (either matched or unmatched) are bound to be different from a study utilizing mixed psychiatric populations with "suicidality" defined by a ward psychiatrist or a mention as a case history.

Sakheim (1955) has suggested that the paucity of protocols could be circumvented by pooling all of the available data at one central depository. The author would like to further suggest that these protocols be annotated with the subject's history, his suicidal behavior, and the conditions under which the protocol was elicited. Even more important than this is the careful documentation of suicidal intent. The usual categorization of ideation, threat, attempt, and commit are somewhat artificial and too encompassing. The problem of intent has been worked on by Farberow (1962) and McEvoy (1963). However, the most extensive thinking in this area has been done by Shneidman (1963). He attempts to relate suicidal intent to general orientations towards life and death. It may be that the application of his new taxonomies to suicidal Rorschach data may open up new vistas.

If the Rorschach is of any value it should detect suicidal trends, since vast changes in affect and cognition are presumably involved. And it has yielded some interesting data. Unfortunately, few generalizations can be made because of the variability of conditions under which the data is gathered. Although the suicide rate is small, its impact is great. And since greater coordinated effort towards identification, prediction, and understanding of suicidal ideation and behavior is a worthy task, there is no reason why the Rorschach test with its many excellent qualities should not be one of the leading weapons in the armamentarium if it is utilized in a judicious manner.

The methodological problems mentioned in the previous paragraphs are critical for researchers and for those trying to establish "universal" Rorschach indicators of future suicidal behavior. But research findings of this kind are not of much help to the clinician who is faced with the difficult task of inspecting a protocol and coming to some sort of conclusion about whether or not his patient or client is going to kill himself in the very near future. The clinician's conclusion can lead to various consequences. If he decides that the level of suicidal seriousness is low, he will suggest or initiate certain strategies. If his conclusions are in the opposite direction, other contingencies will come to mind. There is a rule-of-thumb suggestion that should be followed. That suggestion is that "when in doubt, estimate a high level of suicidal danger."

When dealing with suicidal individuals it is better to find oneself surrounded by false-positives than by false-negatives. The consequences of being diagnosed as suicidal (when the actual suicidal danger is low) can be most irritating. The patient may find himself in a maximum security ward, watched constantly, not allowed to wear a belt, or have shoelaces, etc. But the wages of being diagnosed as a false-positive may be death.

It is here suggested that the clinician rely most heavily on content. If suicidal content appears on the Rorschach, it should be taken very seriously since its manifestation could be an indication that self-destructive behavior is close to the surface, and that the suicidal person may be using the test protocol as a medium of communication to the examiner about his intentions and feelings. The clinician should not make an inference about suicidal intention from the Rorschach alone. Case history material and data from other tests will help maximize the accuracy of decision making. The clinician should strive to have all the data possible available to him. The presence of previous suicidal attempts and threats should compound the danger associated with the presence of suicidal Rorschach content.

Unfortunately, social history data are often not available. Even more regrettable is the absence of suicidal content on the Rorschach. Various processes may obscure and hinder the clear manifestation of suicidal thoughts in Rorschach contents. When this occurs, the next best clue to suicidal intent seems to be the Martin Checklist signs. Although the Martin signs are not "perfect," they seem to be the most potent indicators of suicidal manifestations that have been found for Rorschach data. It would not be foolhardy to suggest that the Martin signs be routinely calculated for every Rorschach protocol. A great number of lives could be saved in this manner.

REFERENCES

Applebaum, S. A., and Holzman, P. S.: The color-shading response and suicide. *Journal of Projective Techniques, 26:*155-161, 1962.
Applebaum, S. A., and Colson, D. B.: A reexamination of the Color-Shading Rorschach Test response and suicide attempts. *Journal of Projective Techniques and Personality Assessment, 32:*160-164, 1968.
Bachrach, A. J.: Some factors in the prediction of suicide. *Neuropsychiatry, 1:*21-27, 1951.

Beck, S. J.: *The Rorschach Experiment.* New York, Grune & Stratton, 1960.

Berk, N.: A personality study of suicidal schizophrenics. Unpublished doctoral dissertation, New York University, 1949.

Boreham, J.: The prediction of suicide. *Rorschach Newsletter, 12:*5-7, 1967.

Broida, D. C.: An investigation of certain psychodiagnostic indications of suicidal tendencies and depression in mental hospital patients. *Psychiatric Quarterly, 28:*453-464, 1954.

Brown, T. R., and Sheran, T. J.: Suicide prediction: A review. *Life Threatening Behavior, 2:*67-98, 1972.

Cooper, G. W., Bernstein, L., and Hart, C.: Predicting suicidal ideation from the Rorschach: An attempt to cross validate. *Journal of Projective Techniques and Personality Assessment, 29:*168-170, 1965.

Costello, C. G.: The Rorschach records of suicidal patients. An application of a comparative matching technique. *Journal of Projective Techniques, 22:*272-275, 1958.

Crasilneck, H. B.: An analysis of differences between suicidal and pseudosuicidal patients through the use of projective techniques. Unpublished doctoral dissertation, University of Houston, 1954.

Cutter, F.: Role complements and changes in Consensus Rorschachs. *Journal of Projective Techniques and Personality Assessment, 32:*338-347, 1968.

Cutter, F., Jorgenson, M., and Farberow, N. L.: Replicability of Rorschach signs with known degrees of suicidal intent. *Journal of Projective Techniques and Personality Assessment, 32:*428-434, 1968.

Daston, P. G., and Sakheim, G. A.: Prediction of successful suicide from the Rorschach test, using a sign approach. *Journal of Projective Techniques, 24:*355-361, 1960.

Daston, P. G.: Applicability of a Rorschach sign approach to a British suicide. *Rorschach Newsletter, 12:*19-20, 1967.

Drake, A. K., and Rusnak, A. W.: An indicator of suicidal ideation on the Rorschach: A replication. *Journal of Projective Techniques and Personality Assessment, 30:*543-544, 1966.

Farberow, N. L.: Suicide: The gamble with death. Paper read at the Los Angeles County Psychological Association convention, May, 1962.

Farberow, N. L., and Shneidman, E. S.: An analysis of suicidal MMPI data. Paper read at the American Psychological Association convention, Cincinnati, September, 1959.

Fisher, S., and Hinds, E.: The organization of hostility controls in various personality structures. *Genetic Psychological Monographs, 44:*3-68, 1951.

Goldfried, M. R., Stricker, G., and Weiner, I. B.: *Rorschach Handbook of Clinical and Research Applications.* Englewood Cliffs, Prentice-Hall, 1971.

Hertz, M. R.: Suicidal configurations in Rorschach records. *Rorschach Research Exchange & Projective Techniques, 12:*3-58, 1948.

Hertz, M. R.: Further study of "suicidal" configurations in Rorschach records. *Rorschach Research Exchange & Journal of Projective Techniques, 13:*44-73, 1949.

Holzberg, J. D., Cahen, E. R., and Wilk, E. K.: Suicide: A psychological study of self-destruction. *Journal of Projective Techniques, 15:*339-354, 1951.

Lester, D.: Attempted suicide and body image. *Journal of Psychology, 66:* 287-290, 1967.

Lester, D.: Attempts to predict suicidal risk using psychological tests. *Psychological Bulletin, 74:*1-17, 1970.

Lindner, R. M.: The content analysis of the Rorschach protocol. In Abt, L. E., and Bellak, L. (Eds.): *Projective Psychology.* New York, Knopf, 1950.

Martin, H. A.: A Rorschach study of suicide. Unpublished doctoral dissertation, University of Kentucky, 1951.

McEvoy, T. L.: An investigation of aggressive fantasy in suicide. Unpublished doctoral dissertation, University of California at Los Angeles, 1963.

Neuringer, C.: Methodological problems in suicide research. *Journal of Consulting Psychology, 26:*273-278, 1962.

Neuringer, C.: The Rorschach Test as a research device for the identification, prediction and understanding of suicidal ideation and behavior. *Journal of Projective Techniques and Personality Assessment, 29:*71-82, 1965.

Neuringer, C., and Kolstoe, R. H.: Suicide research and non-rejection of the null hypothesis. *Perceptual and Motor Skills, 22:*115-118, 1966.

Neuringer, C., McEvoy, T. L., and Schlesinger, R. J.: The identification of suicidal behavior in females by the use of the Rorschach. *Journal of Medical Psychology, 72:*127-133, 1965.

Osgood, C., and Walker, E. G.: Motivation and language behavior: A content analysis of suicide notes. *Journal of Abnormal and Social Psychology, 59:*58-67, 1959.

Piotrowski, A.: *A Rorschach Compendium.* Utica, State Hospital Press, 1950.

Pratt, C.: A validation study of intropunitive and extrapunitive signs on the Rorschach test, based upon records given by suicidal and homicidal subjects. Unpublished doctoral dissertation, Purdue University, 1951.

Rabin, A. L.: Homicide and attempted suicide: A Rorschach study. *American Journal of Orthopsychiatry, 16:*516-524, 1946.

Rosen, A.: Detection of suicidal patients: An examination of some limitations in the prediction of infrequent events. *Journal of Consulting Psychology, 18:*397-403, 1954.

Sakheim, G. A.: Suicidal responses on the Rorschach test: A validating study. *Journal of Nervous and Mental Disorders, 122:*332-344, 1955.

Sapolsky, A.: An indicator of suicidal ideation on the Rorschach test. *Journal of Projective Techniques, 27:*332-335, 1963.

Sapolsky, A.: Comment on Drake and Rusnak. *Journal of Projective Techniques and Personality Assessment, 31:*95, 1967.

Shneidman, E. S.: Orientations toward death. In White, W. W. (Ed.): *The Study of Lives.* New York, Atherton, 1963.

Teicher, J. D.: A study of attempted suicide. *Journal of Nervous and Mental Disorders, 105:*283-298, 1947.

Ulett, G. A., Martin, D. W., and McBride, J. R.: The Rorschach findings in a case of suicide. *American Journal of Orthopsychiatry, 20:*817-827, 1950.

Underwood, B. J.: *Psychological Research.* New York, Appleton-Century-Crofts, 1957.

Varvel, W. A.: The Rorschach test in psychotic and neurotic depressions. *Bulletin of the Menninger Clinic, 5:*5-12, 1941.

Weiner, I. B.: Cross-validation of a Rorschach checklist associated with suicidal tendencies. *Journal of Consulting Psychology, 25:*312-315, 1961.

White, M. A., and Schreiber, H.: Diagnosing "suicidal risks" on the Rorschach. *Psychiatric Quarterly Supplement, 26:*161-189, 1952.

CHAPTER V

SUICIDAL RISK VIA THE THEMATIC APPERCEPTION TEST

THEODORE L. McEVOY

FOR THE CLINICIAN, a review of the literature on the Thematic Apperception Test as a diagnostic instrument in the assessment of suicidal risk is disappointing. It is disappointing both because the literature is sparse and not systematic, and even more so because it is generally negative. The needs of a clinician are different from those of a researcher or a theoretician, and those differences should be kept in mind in examining both the evidence and the issues. In working with a patient who is potentially suicidal, the clinician needs a sign, some reliable index, that will aid differentially in making judgments. Is there a high probability that a particular patient will make a serious, perhaps lethal, suicidal attempt (providing that no intervention is made)? Is there reason to believe that a patient is seriously disposed to run dangerous risks or inflict bodily harm on himself? It would appear that these kinds of questions, dealing with a specific person at a specific time, are not clarified by recourse to projective testing via the Thematic Apperception Test. Thus far no clearly reliable signs or indices have emerged, nor does it appear probable that they will. For the busy clinician this chapter may have no further interest, at least not in practical terms.

The researcher and the theoretician may be intrigued, as least with the issues and methodological problems, if not the research findings. Before engaging these, however, some review of general findings is in order.

It is suitable to anticipate, in brief, some of the more obvious problems. One of the first of these has to do with the relationship between suicidal behavior and aggression. It has been widely held

95

that suicidal activities are expressions of aggression, usually expressions of self-directed aggression. Accordingly, most studies of suicidal persons via the TAT have focused upon themes and measurements of aggression. A few studies have been less oriented to an aggression hypothesis and have simply searched for any empirically emerging indices which would differentiate suicidal from non-suicidal persons. Attendant upon the thesis that suicidal behavior and self-directed aggression are dynamically related is the equally important question of whether the TAT is a valid test for measuring this hypothetical relationship.

A question of quite a different order is whether suicidal activities or suicidal persons are homogeneous or reasonably congruent in some critical way. With respect to suicidal acts, the heart of this question is whether persons who kill themselves are really like persons who commit sublethal suicidal acts, including no-risk acts such as suicidal threats. In the main, clinicians, theoreticians, and even researchers have been more interested in suicidal acts and persons who die in their act than those who don't; on the other hand most of the available data have been marshalled about persons who make nonlethal attempts of varying seriousness or who only talk about or threaten suicide. Unfortunately, the research literature often is not explicit about what specific behaviors are being called suicidal. This tendency to blur real differences under broad categories is most unfortunate, inasmuch as there is growing and compelling evidence to conclude that suicidal phenomena and suicidal persons are variable and not homogeneous.

There is a unique theoretical and methodological problem related to the seriousness of a suicidal act. For the psychologist, the theoretical question of suicidal behavior is a question of intention rather than outcome. Theories and definitions of suicide uniformly stress the state of mind, the motivation, the expectation—in short, the intention of the suicidal person. But events are ofter perverse, and real consequences are not necessarily consistent with intention. In the extreme there are tragic cases of miscalculation or purely accidental death in the person who neither expects nor wants to do it. Likewise there are miraculous or freak cases of survival in the face of incredible odds. In between there are less dramatic but numerous instances in which a real discrepancy exists between the expected and real outcome. The clinician, like the coroner, must be practical, and in the final analysis must take into account the possibility of accidental outcome. The researcher has his own problems as regards this discrepancy and should adjust his methods accordingly.

To summarize, there are then four general considerations which should be kept in mind as one reads the literature on the Thematic Apperception Test relating to suicidal risk and suicidal behavior. Each of these warrants more careful consideration after a review of the general findings and a discussion will follow. The four considerations are:

(1) Is suicidal behavior a form of self-directed aggression?

(2) Is the Thematic Apperception Test a valid instrument for the assessment of some psychological condition, e.g., aggression and/or suicidal predisposition?

(3) Are suicidal phenomena (and suicidal persons) homogeneous; stated differently, are the dynamics of sublethal suicidal acts, including suicidal threats, the same as the dynamics of lethal suicidal acts?

(4) Do the intentions of persons engaging in suicidal behavior correspond with the real outcomes of suicidal activities?

A REVIEW OF THE LITERATURE

A careful review of the literature yields discouraging little on this subject. Reports on single cases must be regarded cautiously and have been excluded from consideration here, though they may be of interest to the person who is a serious student of the Thematic Apperception Test or the clinician dealing daily with suicidal patients. The small number of studies are not easily comparable because of marked differences among them in methodology as well as subjects. Because they are few in number, each may be briefly considered.

Broida (1954) undertook an investigation in which twenty "suicidal" patients were compared with twenty "nonsuicidal" patients. The twenty suicidal persons were described as being mostly psychotic and included ten persons who had made *bona fide* suicidal attempts and ten persons who had made known suicide threats or had been engaging in suicidal ruminations. It was not reported how the *bona fide* cases were defined, hence the seriousness of the attempt cannot be assessed. Moreover, no comparisons were made between those persons who made *bona fide* suicidal attempts and those persons who either threatened or ruminated about suicide. This investigation employed only one card of the TAT, card 3BM, often referred to as the "suicidal" card. Comparative thematic analysis of the responses failed to reveal any significant differences between the two groups ("suicidal" and "nonsuicidal") with respect to the production of depressive, suicidal, or any other type of theme. Broida noted that the "suicidal" group produced a greater frequency of happier endings than the nonsuicidal patients. It would be hazardous to interpret this finding.

Shneidman and Farberow (1958) undertook an investigation of the TAT heroes of suicidal and nonsuicidal subjects. Their "suicidal" groups included: 16 neurotic females who had attempted suicides, 16 neurotic males who had attempted suicide, 8 schizophrenic males who had made suicidal attempts, and 5 neurotic males who had committed suicide. The authors did not attempt to assess the seriousness of intention or expectation; rather the suicidal subjects were grouped according to lethal or nonlethal outcome. The study focused only upon the characteristics of fantasy heroes; other thematic analyses were not undertaken. A Q-sort technique was employed to determine the characteristics of the fantasy hero for each subject. It proved possible to separate subjects according to sex using this method, but the judges could not differentiate the suicidal from the nonsuicidal persons. Shneidman and Farberow proposed that the differences which might appear on individual cards between the subjects might have been obscured by pooling all the cards in assessing a single hero for each subject. This possibility remains undemonstrated at this time.

Another study, employing several projective techniques including seven cards from the Thematic Apperception Test, was undertaken by Fisher and Hinds (1951). Of three groups studied, one was labeled as "suicidal," i.e., persons with known histories of suicidal attempts. The "suicidal" group included twenty subjects (all diagnosed as schizophrenic) and they were compared with a nonsuicidal group, schizophrenic group and a so-called normal group (i.e., nonsuicidal, nonpsychotic). The authors were primarily interested in ways of managing aggression; the hypothesis regarding the suicidal group was that these persons should reveal a disposition to introject aggressive impulses in significantly greater degree than the other two groups. The "suicidal" group was made up of 17 men and 3 women with an average age of 29 years 3 months and average IQ of 105, from lower middle-class backgrounds and hospitalized in a state mental hospital. Each had made an overt suicidal attempt within a three month period prior to the study. In terms of sex, age, intellectual level, and class background, they were not markedly different from the other two groups. (It should be recalled that the study employed the Rorschach and other projective techniques as well as the TAT.)

The results revealed that there were no demonstrable differences among the groups in the sheer amount of hostility projected. However, the schizophrenic suicidal group was distinguished from the other two groups in that they did display a disposition toward turning hostility on themselves; they dissipated themselves in self attack and so seemed unable to assert themselves realistically in meeting ordinary frustration and obstacles. As one might have expected, the results were mixed and complex. The two psychotic groups overlapped with each other in many ways in their management of hostility. Specifically, there was no difference between the two groups on masochistic scores developed on the TAT responses. However, in carefully reviewing the data, the authors found that there was, for the suicidal group, a negative correlation between a measure of self blame derived from the Rosenzweig Picture Frustration Test and the scores for overt aggression based on the Thematic Apperception Test. The hypothesis, tentatively advanced, was that an increase in normal assertiveness was accompanied by a decrease in self-blaming hostility; conversely, self-attack dissipated hostility and incapacitated the person to respond suitably in other situations. Ideally this hypothesis would be tested in a replicated study. The mixed implications are of interest theoretically but of limited value clinically.

Levenson and Neuringer (1972) in a straightforward study using the TAT alone, investigated the hypothesis that suicidal adolescents perceived their environment as being more oppressive than do other (i.e., nonsuicidal adolescents). Selected TAT cards were used in comparing three groups: (1) "suicidal," (2) psychiatric, nonsuicidal, and (3) nonpsychiatric, nonsuicidal. The responses were analyzed for number of environmental presses. The findings were not significant statistically.[1]

A recent study employing the Thematic Apperception Test was undertaken by Lester (1970). The TAT responses of several persons, who subsequently committed suicide, were examined. The subjects were divided into two groups depending on suicidal methods—some employed active methods and some employed passive methods. No differences were found between the two groups in terms of their fantasied aggression in the TAT responses.

McEvoy (1963) undertook a study of fantasied aggression which had three objectives: (1) the development of a reliable method for assessing the seriousness of intention or expectation of the suicidal person with respect to a lethal outcome; (2) an exploration of the value of the TAT as a useful instrument for further research in suicide; and (3) to test hypotheses specifically related to the intensity and direction of fantasied aggression as projected by suicidal persons toward the hero figure.

Three categories of suicidal persons were identified. Using Farberow's (1950) terminology, these were labeled as a "to be" group (those whose expectations toward death was to survive), a "to be or not to be group" (gamblers with death whose intentions and expectations were equivocal), and a "not to be" group (those whose expectations were to die).

One hundred and thirty suicidal persons were examined. Some of these had died in their suicidal attempt and others had not, but, in the consensus of three experienced clinical psychologists, all of them had made *bona fide* suicidal attempts. Using two nine point

---

1. In another similar study using the Picture Frustration Test, the authors also had negative findings. They concluded that the "intropunitive" hypothesis of suicidal behavior needed reexamination. See Levenson, M., and Neuringer, C.: Intropunitiveness in suicidal adolescents. *Journal of Projective Techniques and Personality Assessment, 34:*409-411, 1970.

assessment techniques graded for lethality, one for method and the other for intent, suicidal case histories of each of the 130 victims were independently rated by three judges. The 130 subjects were also classified as psychotic or psychiatric nonpsychotic. Six groups were possible, but only three emerged with sufficient numbers as to be useful. Two were "not to be" groups, one psychotic (N = 28); the other, psychiatric but not psychotic (N = 17). The other group was made up of psychiatric nonpsychotic persons labeled "to be" (N = 16). It was not possible to constitute the other three hypothetically possible groups because there were, apparently, too few instances of these groups in the available sample of 130.[2] Particularly in the case of gamblers with death, the "to be or not to be" groupings, there was less agreement among judges, perhaps because it is necessary to have more detailed information in these cases than in other cases in order to make reliable judgments.

In addition there were two nonsuicidal groups, one psychotic (N = 25) and one psychiatric nonpsychotic (N = 25). For each of the subjects in all five groups, protocols for three TAT cards were available, namely 3BM, 6BM, and 13MF. These were rated by Stone's TAT Aggressive Content Scale (1953; 1956) and were also subjected to a "theme" or content analysis.

With regard to the use of the TAT as an instrument for assessing suicidal disposition or risk, the general findings may be stated briefly: The Thematic Apperception Test failed to reveal significant differences in aggressive fantasies or themes between these suicidal groups regardless of diagnostic categories or between suicidal and nonsuicidal persons. (Indeed, a pooling of all 130 suicidal cases combining the 69 which were not classified and the 61 which were, and comparing them with the pooled nonsuicidal group of 50 subjects failed to reveal any significant differences in aggressive themata.)

Other aspects of this study will be discussed later in this chapter. However, with regard to the primary findings it must be concluded that despite the methodological difficulties, here the evidence is discouraging, but consistent with the other studies. At

2. Accordingly, 69 of the 130 cases were not used in the principal data analyses.

present, the TAT has not demonstrated usefulness in the study or assessment of suicidal risk.

Summary and Critique

The literature on the Thematic Apperception Test in the assessment of suicidal behavior is sparse and not easily compared for purposes of generalizations. Perhaps the only general conclusion is that the test has not proved to be useful for this purpose. Nor does it likely appear to do so in the near future until after several methodological problems are successfully resolved. Some critical ones are reflected in all of these studies; we will note three.

(1) *Timing:* In almost all instances there is a marked time lapse between a suicidal action and the gathering of the TAT response. Let us examine first cases involving suicidal death. Ordinarily the suicides have not been predicted and such data as exist are by happenstance. The researcher can study only a few persons (it is not known whether these are random and typical); he can only use those chance data that exist in clinical records (often obtained under unknown conditions). Since such data are scarce he must be conserving; inevitably this means that he will use TAT records which have been gathered weeks, months, or sometimes years prior to the suicidal death. It is possible to justify such time lapses only if one assumes that the critical variables are enduring; that is that there are permanent character differences between suicidal and nonsuicidal persons. Such an assumption is hazardous; indeed clinical experience would suggest that suicidal disposition is more commonly acute than chronic. Research conditions could hardly be less favorable.

By contrast, sublethal suicidal activities pose less of a problem. It is possible to test persons within hours of a suicidal attempt, though one can never be sure of how long a time delay is critical. In practice, however, much longer time delays have been accepted. Often weeks or even months may lapse after a suicidal activity and before psychological examination. So far, no study has dealt effectively with this problem. The longer the time lapse, the more essential that the critical qualities are characterological and enduring rather than situational and acute or recurring. An equally serious problem is related to the sequence of events. Usually, in instances of sublethal suicidal activity, the psychological examination comes *after* the suicidal action. One is left with the disturbing question of what, if any, effects the suicidal action itself has on the suicidal person, especially in altering the critical features that existed prior to the suicidal action. For example, does suicidal activity discharge tension or aggression? Does it resolve conflicts? Both the clinician and theortician are concerned with the presuicidal state, and it is not known whether or not it bears close resemblance to the postsuicidal state.

Of course, it may be possible to use presuicidal data as in cases of lethal outcomes, but one would only encounter the formidable problems of time lapse, happenstance data, and nonrandom subjects. One final note. In studies where both lethal and nonlethal suicidal groups were compared, the suicides were tested before the suicidal event, the attempters were in almost all instances, tested after the event. Such differences in the critical sequence make strict comparisons impossible; pooling all of the subjects into a "suicidal" group may further confound the situation.

(2) *Sampling:* Partly because of the dependence upon chance data and partly because suicidal behavior is commonly treated as psychopathological, studies are complicated by the problem of psychiatric and nonpsychiatric subjects. It is not appropriate, in this context, to examine the question of whether suicidal behavior is itself evidence of psychopathology. Suffice it to say that persons who have not been labeled for any other reason psychoneurotic or psychotic do sometimes make suicidal attempts, frequently lethal. In the main, these studies have utilized subjects who have had long psychiatric histories. It is not clear what effects this may have produced on the data. Nor is it known how representative of all suicidal persons these subjects have been. Better sampling procedures are clearly desirable; they are uncommonly difficult to employ in these kinds of studies because of the practical problems.

(3) *Grouping of suicidal activities:* Suicidal activities are remarkably variable. There are overt and covert threats, obscure ruminations, nonlethal attempts that range from symbolic gestures (such as ingesting a few aspirin) to permanently maiming actions (such as breaking one's back in a jump from a moderate height), and lethal attempts, sometimes resulting in death accidentally and

sometimes clearly by design. In the main these activities and the persons engaging in them are thrown together in a single "suicidal" group or separated into gross categories, most commonly, suicidal threats, suicidal attempts, and suicidal deaths. The many differences which may exist between persons who engage in one variation as compared with those in another variation are obscured. Implicit in this practice is the assumption that there are common critical features in suicidal behavior, that the vast variety of acts have common meaning, and that "suicidal persons" are dynamically the same. While lethal suicidal behavior has always been and still is of greatest concern and interest clinically and theoretically, the greatest research data exist about persons who never die in a suicidal act–indeed they do not expect nor intend to do so. It is possible that persons who engage in suicidal ruminations, make threats, or engage in relatively benign "suicidal" acts are not suitable subjects for testing hypotheses about persons who kill themselves. This problem is discussed more fully below.

Until these methodological problems are resolved, progress in rigorous research appears to be difficult. The disappointing results in the use of the Thematic Apperception Test in the assessment of suicidal potential is partly secondary to these problems. They are, equally, a result of the sparse and incomplete work which has been done but which does not lend itself to systematic comparison. Finally, one might venture the conclusion that at present the evidence available from the Thematic Apperception Test casts doubt on the general hypothesis that suicidal behavior is a form of self-directed aggression, or that suicidal persons are more intrapunitive than nonsuicidal persons. This is a negative finding of uncertain validity. No positive common hypothesis can be deduced from these limited data.

TAT AND THE STUDY OF AGGRESSION

One of the more pervasive theories about suicide is that it is a manifestation of self-directed aggression. Consequently, some of the studies using the TAT in the assessment of suicidal disposition or tendency have focused upon intropunative or various facets of the expression of aggression. In order to test these hypotheses about the dynamics of suicidal behavior, it must be demonstrated that the TAT is a valid instrument for the measurement of aggressive disposition and overt aggression.

The relevant research literature has grown in recent years but is still plagued by inconsistency, inconclusiveness, and complexity. It is beyond the scope of this paper to systematically review and evaluate this literature. However, since the question about the validity of the TAT is so central here, some general overview is required. The most critical question is this: "Is there a direct positive relationship between fantasied aggression in the responses to the TAT and independent evidence of aggressive behavior?," or a somewhat similar question, "Can TAT responses, scored for aggressive indices, discriminate between persons who manifest marked overt aggression and persons who manifest little overt aggression?" Studies spanning two decades leave these questions unanswered. There are studies (James and Mosher, 1967; Mussen and Naylor, 1954; Stone, 1953; Weismann, 1964; Kagan, 1956)[3] which show a positive and direct relationship between fantasied and overt aggression and which are discriminating: there are also studies that fail to demonstrate any differences between groups which differ in overt aggression in terms of their fantasied aggression on the TAT (Coleman, 1967; McNeil, 1962; Scodel and Lipetz, 1957). It is true that the studies are not easily compared because of important differences in experimental design, but so much inconsistency leaves serious question about assumptions concerning the validity of the TAT to effectively demonstrate a direct relationship between fantasied and overt aggression.

This growing research has challenged the projective hypothesis in important ways. Specifically, with regard to the Thematic Apperception Test, there is growing, but disputed, evidence that the formal structure of the card itself acts as an important, sometimes the most important, influence in determining the content of the responses. Whereas Coleman (1967), Epstein (1966), and Murstein (1965), among others, assert that this is the case, the results of James and Mosher (1967) are inconsistent. There are "high-pull" cards with respect to aggressive themes, and it is difficult to

---

3. In the Kagan study the TAT cards were not used, but very similar test cards were developed and administered in a similar fashion.

determine what effect these stimulus cues have upon responses. Under some circumstances they clearly do have marked effects.

Many TAT cards have only a "medium" or "low pull" with respect to aggressive themata. Perhaps more neutral cards would be better suited to studying aggressive disposition, since aggressive stories would seem to be clearly "projections" and not produced by the stimulus cues themselves. Alas, here the evidence is again contradictory. Whereas Saltz and Epstein (1963) and Murstein (1965) have concluded that "low pull" cards discriminate better than "high pull" cards, James and Mosher (1967) found "high pull" cards to discriminate significantly, but found "low pull" cards non-discriminating.

These confusions have not been diminished by the speculation about the inhibiting effects of threatening stimuli. According to some research, "high pull" cards should produce aggressive themata irrespective of whether persons are overtly aggressive or not because of the stimulus cues. In some instances it is argued that they do not produce some themata in inhibited or non-aggressive persons because these persons respond to anxiety or other inhibitions and respond neutrally. Both Megargee (1967) and Saltz and Epstein (1963) offer partial evidence for this interpretation.

It is unfair to review these studies so hastily and incompletely. However a careful reading of the literature does raise serious questions about the validity of the Thematic Apperception Test in assessing hypotheses about aggression. The confusion of these diverse findings is clarified in part by a study undertaken by Megargee and Cook (1967). Their hypothesis is that results vary with different measures of fantasied aggression and also with different measures of overt aggression. This discovery is not surprising, but is rather discouraging. Among other things, it signifies that aggression is not well understood and is poorly defined. There are a multitude of behaviors that may be loosely categorized as aggressive that may not be, in fact, closely related. Moreover, the measures of fantasy are also not well understood and not easily comparable. These authors recommend, with judicious caution, that future studies would do well to incorporate multiple measurements, or else stick with one of the better researched scales.

For the researcher, there are obviously many variables to be sorted out and complex relationships clarified. For the clinician who might wish to use the TAT in the prediction of overt aggression or, more particularly, suicidal behavior in the individual case, these results are quite discouraging.

SUICIDE AND AGGRESSION

Suicidal behavior has been associated both theoretically and clinically with depression and self-directed aggression or intropunitiveness. Particularly, aggression has played prominently in theories, and so it is reasonable that some of the research in suicidal phenomena, including some of the studies cited here should have focused upon aggressive variables or cues. It is clearly beyond the scope of this paper to unravel the complex relationships, if any, between aggression and suicidal activities. It is, however, appropriate to point out that some of the studies reviewed here have rested on the logic that (1) suicidal persons handle or express aggression in a way which differentiates them from nonsuicidal persons, and (2) these differences are reflected in fantasy and are projected in their responses to the Thematic Apperception Test (or said differently, the Thematic Apperception Test is a valid and effective instrument for assessing the magnitude and the form for expressing potential aggression).

We wish only here to draw attention to a few pertinent considerations. A reading of the literature on aggressive behavior is as bewildering as a reading of the literature in suicide. Modern ethology has drawn our attention to aggression as an intraspecific phenomenon probably manifest in humans in two very different contexts. In one instance, it is a reaction to invasion or encroachment upon one's territory or living space; in the other instance it is a response aroused by intragroup competition and the establishment or status (Diamond, 1967; Lawick-Goodal, 1971; Lorenz, 1966). In either instance it is not described as a drive or a force bursting to find expression, but rather a predetermined response or disposition activated by certain conditions. There is a question as to whether either is ever expressed intropunitively. A different theory from psychology is the frustration-aggression hypothesis which posits that frustration leads to aggressive reactions, including intropunitive ones (Dollard et al., 1939; Rosenzwerg, 1944).

This hypothesis seems to be suitable for testing the disposition of suicidal persons to be more inclined to self-blame or self-punishment. In a study designed to test this hypothesis, Levenson and Neuringer (1970) find negative results and conclude that the "intropunitive" hypothesis of suicidal behavior needs reexamination.

The association of suicidal acts and self-directed hostility or violence probably stems, in the Western mentality, from the writings of St. Augustine who first condemned suicide on the grounds that it was a violation of the Mosaic commandment "Thou shalt not kill." Suicidal behavior has, subsequently, been equated with murder, both morally and, more recently, psychodynamically (St. John-Stevas, 1961).

There are several reasons for questioning the theory that suicidal behavior is a form of self-directed aggression or hostility, two of which we will note. In many instances, especially in suicidal threats or gestures, it is abundantly clear that the behavior is punitive or manipulative *toward others* rather than toward oneself. And suicidal fantasies are often of the punishing variety "You'll be sorry when I'm gone," in which the inventor of the fantasy enjoys immensely the guilt and sorrow of those he seeks to punish (Jensen and Petty, 1958). Secondly, it should be noted that many suicidal persons do not appear to be aggressive or violent. Their behavior toward themselves bears little resemblance to aggression which is manifest towards others. Ethologists have described vividly the differences between intraspecific aggression with all of its emotional excitement and the killing or maiming of predation (Lorenz, 1966). One is struck by the marked variability of affect among suicidal phenomena (consider the deliberate and poised manner of Socrates and contrast it with the histrionics of some suicidal gestures or the desperation and despair of other victims). Are we to conclude that each of these is fundamentally an expression of self-directed aggression? Then too one must minimize the importance of impulse, anxiety, coping behavior, or other prominent features of the suicidal drama including the complex social meaning of many of the suicidal dramas.

Perhaps we have fixed upon death or self-destruction as the key to understanding suicide because we have very much wanted one unifying key to a myriad of phenomena. If there is not one such common denominator, then one cannot expect to find a reliable index; the mixed results of these studies may be partly related to that difficulty.

HETEROGENEITY OF SUICIDAL BEHAVIOR AND LETHALITY OF INTENTION

That suicidal phenomena are markedly heterogeneous is apparent to everyone. Indeed, there are distinctions routinely made and reflected in ordinary language usage: suicidal threat, suicidal attempt, and suicidal death. These distinctions are clearly too gross, and the informed observer can quickly specify many ways in which these categories are inadequate or even inaccurate. Suicidal threats are sometimes direct and sometimes veiled; they are sometimes threateningly manipulative and other times one of many manifestations of despair and depression. Suicidal attempts are serious or not; they differ with respect to mode (e.g., ingestion, cutting, shooting) and with respect to social context. And suicidal deaths are also variable. Sometimes they are clearly accidental, sometimes they are consciously contrived. They too differ with respect to mode and social context–alone and secretive or sometimes in a public context with help nearby. These are only a few of the more obvious signs that reveal the heterogeneity and, perhaps, noncomparability of suicidal phenomena.

For our purposes, however, the most critical issue is whether persons who make lethal suicidal attempts are like persons who undertake less than lethal actions. This is critical here since most studies of suicidal behavior employing the TAT do rely upon data about persons who have engaged in sublethal activities whereas most interest is in understanding and identifying persons who may precipitate their own death.

In a study of 287 cases of attempted suicide, Reimer (1967) reports reliable differences between categories of persons who engage in such activities. There are persons who make suicidal gestures, usually ingesting small amounts of analgesic or sedative medications. They usually are persons who might be described as hysterical and narcissistic and appear to be motivated to manipulate others or win attention. These persons are in marked contrast with intellectually determined, or premeditated, attempters who engage in careful planning, often careful to avoid attention. Typically they choose a method of high lethal probability such as hanging or shooting, and typically they are persons who exert considerable rational control over their emotions and actions. The impulsive suicidal person is yet another and more difficult to describe narrowly.

Stengel and Cook have undertaken one of the most extensive (1958) studies of attempted suicides. They report that in only a minority of cases was there real danger to life or evidence that the victim had intended to die. Furthermore, only a small percentage of the attempted suicides went on to kill themselves in the future.[4] Of course they report the usual differences in suicidal methods and sex ratios in comparing attempted suicides with committed suicides. What is of greater interest is their general finding that *an examination of the social character of suicidal activities reveals that much of what happens in suicidal attempts is life preserving rather than life destroying.*

Although it has been repeatedly emphasized that intention is a critical aspect of suicidal behavior, and it is eminently apparent that expected and effected outcomes are often not the same, rarely is any effort made to assess intention as a variable. In one study utilizing the TAT in suicidal assessment, this problem was addressed directly. The development of means for judging the intention of the suicidal person, with respect to bodily harm or death, was undertaken by McEvoy (1963). One of the compelling clues in assessing the intention of a suicidal person is to evaluate the suicidal method. In many instances this single clue is so compelling as to overshadow any other data, hence it proves practical to devise two assessment schemes; one an assessment of the "lethality of method" and the other the assessment of "lethality of intention."[5]

The two scales or schemes are reproduced in the following two tables:

---

4. The authors report that 14 percent were known to have gone on in the near future to kill themselves.

5. A common observation made by workers investigating suicidal attempts is that often a method, objectively of low death potentiality, is believed by the victim to be of high death potentially or vice versa. This is especially true with respect to drugs and poisons.

TABLE V-I
LETHALITY OF INTENT

1. No intention and/or expectation of dying. Act is a momentary impulse (e.g., to control others, expiate guilt, etc.).
2. No intention and/or expectation of dying. Act is a planned attempt (e.g., to control others, expiate guilt, etc.).
3. a. Ruminations of dying and fantasies of rescue precede act, but no serious intention of dying (or)
   b. act is impulsive under the influence of alcohol. No real intention of dying, though the risk of injury is present.
4. a. Death is recognized as a possible outcome, but victim is willing to risk it in an act that is a strong cry for help (or)
   b. death is recognized as a possible outcome. Ruminations precede act; alcohol is ingested for "courage."
5. Intention is ambiguous due to wholly inadequate information. Death may be accidental, or excessive amount of alcohol may cloud issue.
6. Death is recognized as a "real" and somewhat probable outcome. Act is impulsive. If alcohol is taken, it was before the impulse may have facilitated it.
7. Act is planned with suicidal ideation preceding. Although strongly ambivalent, there are strong intentions of dying. Victim makes a "calculated" gamble with death, since some behavior is directed toward survival. If alcohol is taken, it is done deliberately to "boost" courage.
8. Strong intention and expectation of dying. Act is planned, survival depends on "chance," not "calculated" intervention.
9. Intention and/or expectation is to die. Victim consciously takes steps to prevent chance survival. Only the most fortuitous circumstances preclude death.

Note: In rating lethality of intention, it is desired that a subjective evaluation be made of the victim's intentions (e.g., not to die, to gamble with death, to die)*, independently insofar as it is possible, of the real method employed. Although the data are, in most cases, inadequate and/or incomplete, an attempt should be made to rate the case if it seems at all possible. A level of confidence in the rating may be made at the conclusion.

* In some cases the victim believes that the method (dosage, agent, etc.) will lead to death or serious consequences when, in fact, this is objectively improbable. In rating intention, care must be taken to evaluate victim's expectations whether or not these are realistic.

TABLE V-II
LETHALITY OF METHOD

1. Death is an impossible result of the "suicidal" behavior (or act).
2. Death is very highly improbable. If it occurs it would be a result of a secondary complication, an accident, or highly unusual circumstances.
3. Death is improbable as an outcome of the act; if so, it is probably due to unforeseen secondary effects.
4. Death is improbable, so long as first aid is administered by victim or other agent. Victim makes a communication.
5. Death is a 50-50 probability directly or indirectly. Or, in the opinion of the average person, the chosen method has an equivocal outcome.
6. Death is a probable outcome unless there is "immediate" and "vigorous" first aid or medical attention by victim or other agent. Victim may make a communication.
7. Death would ordinarily be considered the outcome to the suicidal act, unless saved by another agent in a "calculated" risk.
8. Death is a highly probable outcome. "Chance" intervention and/or unforeseen accidental circumstances save victim.
9. Death is averted only by the most fortuitous circumstances and vigorous intervention by an outside agent.

Note: In rating the lethality of the method, one should confine evaluation to the objective facts as they are reported in the history. In many, if not most, cases the information may be inadequate or perhaps unreliable.

It should be pointed out that these procedures are not, in any formal sense, scales. Furthermore, the available data were not very uniform, so that interjudge reliability could not be adequately evaluated. Despite these limitations it has proved possible to identify two groups differing markedly in their motivation in which there was a high degree of agreement by independent judges using these rating methods. Clear-cut cases are identifiable, but at a loss of many cases too equivocal or incomplete to produce agreement.

For each potential subject in the study, a case history was prepared including all the available information relating to the suicidal act. These cases were then assessed independently by three expert judges using both assessment techniques. It was decided to identify the groups using only the "lethality of intention" ratings since this is psychologically more meaningful. Cases in which all three judges rated the intention of the victim 7, 8, or 9 were included in groups identified as those whose expectations were "not to be." Ratings of 9 had been assigned to the victim who had taken steps to insure a lethal outcome, 8 was assigned to persons who acted in a planned manner, and expecting to die, took no counter steps to make the outcome equivocal. Ideally, only cases uniformly rated 8 and 9 would have been utilized. It was, however, not possible to obtain a sufficient sample in this manner, and so cases in which ratings of 7 were made were also considered. The description of the rating 7 indicates that the victim does make a calculated gamble with death, indicating some real equivocation in his behavior, but there is a clear-cut evidence that death is a very probable consequence. In only one of the included cases, however, did more than one rater rate a subject 7 and the lowest average rating accepted as the cut off point for this group was 7.67.

Using the same procedure, those cases which uniformly received ratings of 1, 2, or 3 were included in the "to be" groups. Again, ideally no cases would have been included where any subject rated even one 3, but the sample would not have been adequate.

Of an initial pool of 130 cases, 69 cases were excluded by these criteria, and 61 cases were retained. The 61 represented two extreme groups with respect to intended outcomes, 16 in the "to be" group and 45 in the "not to be" category.

The two groups were markedly different from each other in terms of the details of their suicidal attempt. Of the 16 suicidal victims in the "to be" group, eleven are known to have made their attempt in the close presence of others or very shortly to have confided in friends or family so that remedial steps could be undertaken. Five of these eleven persons initiated the action toward medical care. Of the remaining five cases, two subsequently denied that they had intended to die, two were found very shortly after the attempt, and only one had isolated himself by going to a strange hotel. Not only did their social behavior reveal their intentions, but the suicidal methods were neither violent nor particularly dangerous. Six chose transverse wrist cuts, and the remaining ten ingested drugs, in severity from small numbers of aspirins to moderate doses of sedatives.

By contrast 34 of the 45 "not to be" victims were known, for certain, to have been alone; eighteen had gone to remote or isolated places, nine had registered in strange hotels, sometimes using a fictitious identity. One other person was alone with his mother; they had entered into a suicide pact, she had died, he had not. Of the eleven who were in the presence of or near to other persons, many leaped to their death, either in front of a moving vehicle or from a high place. Those who survived did so fortuitously. Three persons who had ingested drugs were recovered from comas; one person survived a serious auto wreck after he drove his car off a cliff. None of the 45 victims were known to have confided about their plans of self-destruction. Methods with swift systemic consequences were preferred–gunshot wound, usually to the head or face was elected by thirteen, and fourteen hanged themselves. Six leaped from buildings, two in front of oncoming trains. Only five chose ingestion, one of whom took potassium cyanide. The other four took sufficient barbiturates to result in coma and/or death.

These studies support the extensive demographic data that reveal differences in sex ratio and in age between persons making suicidal attempts and suicidal deaths. They suggest that there are more fundamental differences between these categories, namely that persons who commit suicide choose methods which are violent, swift, and very dangerous as contrasted with many persons making sublethal attempts who choose methods which are not violent, are slow acting, and are relatively not dangerous or not systemic in effect. They further show that many, if not most, persons who make sublethal attempts do communicate in many ways, do seek help, and do engage in social interactive behavior at the time of the suicidal attempt as compared with the secretive and social isolated behavior of persons who intentionally die. It would suggest that much of the intent and behavior of the suicide commits is life destructive, and much of the intent and behavior of suicidal attempters is life preserving. Hence statements about one group based on studying the other group appears hazardous and unwarrented.

CONCLUDING REMARKS

The purpose of this paper has been to review the research literature and to evaluate the effectiveness of the Thematic Apperception Test as a means of assessing suicidal risk. That task, narrowly undertaken, reveals that for practical purposes, the Thematic Apperception Test has not shown itself to be useful for such a purpose. This is so because the literature is very scanty, studies are not easily comparable, and the results are negative or inconclusive.

Perhaps no further considerations are warranted. However, our inquiry has led us to ask many questions about suicidal phenomena, about research problems, and about the Thematic Apperception Test as an instrument for evaluating aggression or suicidal disposition. Considering the multiple problems and the complexity of these problems, it would be rather astonishing if the TAT were an effective instrument for assessing suicidal phenomena. Some of the apparent reasons for that are:

(1) Suicidal phenomena are diverse and not easily classified; nor can it be argued persuasively, that they are unified by a common single dynamic.

(2) Persons who engage in suicidal activity are not of a typical character make-up nor are they motivated by a common single motivation.

(3) Aggression and aggressive disposition and activities are defined differently by different investigators. Aggression in human beings is complex, its causes and manifestations are variable; its relationship, if any, to suicidal phenomena is poorly understood.

(4) The Thematic Apperception Test is a somewhat structured set of stimuli. The cards themselves have an indeterminant effect upon the content and form of response. Both in studies of suicidal phenomena and aggressive disposition, results using the Thematic Apperception Test are conflicting and complex.

(5) Suicidal phenomena, particularly those with lethal consequences, pose unusually difficult methodological problems which are only partially understood and, as yet, are largely unsolved in any effective degree.

For these reasons, one cannot expect to employ the Thematic Apperception Test until these difficulties are resolved.

REFERENCES

Broida, D. C.: An investigation of certain psychodiagnostic indications of suicidal tendencies and depression in mental hospital patients. *Psychiatric Quarterly, 28:*453-464, 1954.

Coleman, J. C.: Stimulus factors in the relation between fantasy and behavior. *Journal of Projective Techniques and Personality Assessment, 31:*68-73, 1967.

Dimond, S. J.: *The Social Behavior of Animals.* London, Batsford, 1970.

Dollard, J., Dobb, L., Miller, N., Mowrer, O. H., and Sears, R. R.: *Frustration and Aggression.* New Haven, Yale University Press, 1939.

Epstein, S.: Some theoretical considerations on the nature of ambiguity, and the use of stimulus dimensions in projective techniques. *Journal of Consulting Psychology, 30:*183-192, 1966.

Farberow, N. L.: Personality patterns of mental hospital patients. *Genetic Psychology Monographs, 42:*3-73, 1950.

Fisher, S., and Hinds, E.: The organization of hostility controls in various personality structures. *Genetic psychology monographs, 44:*3-68, 1951.

James, P. B., and Mosher, D. L.: Thematic aggression, hostility-guilt, and aggressive behavior. *Journal of Projective Techniques and Personality Assessment, 31:*61-67, 1967.

Jensen, V., and Petty, T.: The fantasy of being rescued in suicide. *Psychiatric Quarterly, 27:*441-444, 1958.

Kagan, J.: The measurement of overt aggression from fantasy. *Journal of Abnormal and Social Psychology, 52:*390-393, 1956.

Lawick-Goodall, J.: *In the Shadow of Man.* Boston, Houghton Mifflin, 1971.

Lester, D.: Factors affecting choice of methods of suicide. *Journal of Clinical Psychology, 26:*437, 1970.

Levenson, M., and Neuringer, C.: Intropunitiveness in suicidal adolescents. *Journal of Projective Techniques and Personality Assessment, 34:*409-411, 1970.

Levenson, M., and Neuringer, C.: Phenomenal environmental oppressiveness in suicidal adolescents. *Journal of Genetic Psychology, 120:*253-256, 1972.

Lorenz, K.: *On Aggression.* New York, Harcourt, Brace and World, 1966.

McEvoy, T. L.: An investigation of aggressive fantasy in suicide. Unpublished doctoral dissertation, University of California at Los Angeles, 1963.

McNeil, E. B.: Aggression in fantasy and behavior. *Journal of Consulting Psychology, 26:*232-240, 1962.

Megargee, E., and Cook, P. E.: The relations of TAT and inkblot aggressive content scales with each other and with criteria of overt aggressiveness in juvenile delinquents. *Journal of Projective Techniques and Personality Assessment, 31:*73-79, 1967.

Mussen, B. L., and Naylor, H. K.: Relationship between overt and fantasy aggression. *Journal of Abnormal and Social Psychology, 49:*235-240, 1954.

Murstein, B. I.: Projection of hostility on the TAT as a function of stimulus, background, and personality variables. *Journal of Consulting Psychology, 29:*43-48, 1965.

Reimer, F.: Classification of attempted suicide. In Farberow, N. L.: *Fourth International Conference for Suicide Prevention.* Los Angeles, Del Mar, 1967,

Rosenzweig, S.: An outline of frustration theory. In Hunt, J. Mc. V. (Ed.): *Personality and the Behavior Disorders.* New York, Ronald, 1944, Vol. I.

St. John-Stevas, N.: *Life, Death, and the Law: Law and Christian Morals in England and the United States.* Bloomington, Indiana University Press, 1961.

Saltz, G., and Epstein, S.: Thematic hostility and guilt responses as related to self-reported hostility, guilt, and conflict. *Journal of Abnormal and Social Psychology, 67:*469-479, 1963.

Scodel, A., and Lipetz, M. E.: TAT hostility and psychopathology, *Journal of Projective Techniques, 21:*161-165, 1957.

Shneidman, E. S., and Farberow, N. L.: TAT heroes of suicidal and nonsuicidal subjects. *Journal of Projective Techniques, 22:*211-228, 1958.

Stengel, E., and Cook, N.: *Attempted Suicide. Its Social Significance and Effects.* London, Chapman Hall, 1958.

Stone, H.: The relationship of hostile aggressive behavior to aggressive content on the Rorschach and the Thematic Apperception Test. Unpublished doctoral dissertation, University of California at Los Angeles, 1953.

Stone, H.: The TAT aggressive content scale. *Journal of Projective Techniques, 20:*445-452, 1956.

Weismann, S. L.: Some indicators of acting out behavior from the Thematic Apperception Test. *Journal of Projective Techniques and Personality Assessment, 28:*366-375, 1964.

CHAPTER VI

SUICIDAL RISK ASSESSMENT VIA THE MINNESOTA MULTIPHASIC PERSONALITY INVENTORY (MMPI)

JAMES R. CLOPTON

D AHLSTROM, WELSH, AND DAHLSTROM (1972) state that scale 2 (D) of the Minnesota Multiphasic Personality Inventory (MMPI) measures the degree of a person's depression and that frequently this mood state is characterized by preoccupation with death and suicide. Dahlstrom et al. (1972) note that the implications of high scores on scale 2 depend upon other features of the MMPI and upon the behavior of the person taking the test. For instance, it is their conclusion that suicidal risk is greater when a person's MMPI results show a significant elevation on scale 2 but his behavior does not give any indication of depression, and he denies depressive thoughts and feelings, than when the depression indicated by a scale 2 elevation is clearly reflected in the person's behavior.

Simon and Hales (1949) examined the standard MMPI clinical scales of 50 male psychiatric patients with suicidal preoccupation and found consistent elevations on scales 2 and 7 (Pt). Similarly, Simon (1950) looked at the MMPI scale scores of 22 male psychiatric patients tested with the card form of the MMPI after attempting suicide. Except for a peak on scale 2, no predominant trends were found. An examination of the mean scale scores for the various diagnostic groups and for different methods used in attempting suicide revealed that an elevated scale 2 was most characteristic of psychoneurotic patients and patients who attempted suicide by hanging. For suicidal patients diagnosed psychopathic or alcoholic, a peak on scale 2 was not found. These findings should be viewed with caution since classification of the 22 patients by diagnosis and by suicide method resulted in very small

118

samples. Also, neither Simon and Hales (1949) nor Simon (1950) compared MMPI scale scores of suicidal patients with those obtained from nonsuicidal patients.

Farberow (1956) looked at the MMPI scale scores of psychiatric patients who attempted suicide prior to testing, patients who had threatened suicide prior to testing, and nonsuicidal patients. Each of the three groups consisted of 32 male patients tested with the short-form (373 items) of the MMPI. A psychiatrist acquainted with the suicidal patients divided them into seriously suicidal and not seriously suicidal groups on the basis of his judgment of the probability that a patient would successfully commit suicide if left to his own devices. To compare the mean scale scores of the suicide attempt group, suicide threat group, and nonsuicidal comparison group Farberow (1956) performed an analysis of variance for each scale. Pairwise comparisons with *t* tests were used for those scales producing a significant F ratio. Farberow (1956) found that for seven MMPI scales–F, 2, 4 (Pd), 6 (Pa), 7, 8 (Sc), and 9 (Ma)–the suicide threat group scored significantly higher than both the suicide attempts group and the nonsuicidal comparison group. The suicide threat group had the most elevated scale scores of the three groups; the only clinical scales having a mean T score below 70 for this group were scales 5 (Mf) and 9. Scales K, 1 (Hs), 3 (Hy), and 5 did not differentiate the groups, while on the L scale the nonsuicidal comparison group scored significantly higher than the suicide threat group. Mean scale scores for the suicide attempt and nonsuicidal comparison groups were not significantly different from each other. With regard to the division of suicidal patients according to the seriousness of suicidal intent, only scales L and 6 produced significant differences for any comparisons among the serious, nonserious, and nonsuicidal groups. The mean L scale score for the nonsuicidal comparison group was significantly higher than for the nonserious suicide group, and the mean scale 6 score for the serious suicide group was significantly higher than for the nonserious group. Farberow (1956) did not analyze his data in a manner permitting comparison of mean profiles for the various groups of patients.

Rosen, Hales, and Simon (1954) compared 50 male psychiatric

patients who had attempted suicide prior to admission and testing, 100 male patients who had thought about suicide, and 211 nonsuicidal male patients. Rosen et al. (1954) described their study as a replication of the Farberow (1956) study. However, it is not clear that their suicide thought group was comparable to Farberow's (1956) suicide threat group. At any rate, Rosen et al. (1954) analyzed the mean scale scores, both with and without K corrections, in the same manner as Farberow (1956). In general, the mean T scores for most scales were higher for the suicide thought group than for either the suicide attempt or nonsuicidal comparison groups, and the mean T scores for the latter two groups were quite similar. The suicide thought group scored significantly higher than the nonsuicidal comparison group on scales F, 6, and 8. On scale 3 the suicide thought group scored significantly higher than the suicide attempt group. On scales 2, 7, and 0 (Si) the suicide thought group scored significantly higher than both the suicide attempt and nonsuicidal comparison groups. On scale 4 both the suicide thought and the suicide attempt groups scored significantly higher than the nonsuicidal comparison group. On scale 1 both the suicide thought and the nonsuicidal comparison groups scored significantly higher than the suicide attempts group. On the K scale the nonsuicidal comparison group scored significantly higher than the suicide thought group. There were no significant differences in mean scale scores among the three groups for scales L, 5, and 9. In every comparison where a significant difference was found involving a K-corrected scale score, the comparison would have also been significant without the K correction. If the suicide thought group in the Rosen et al. (1954) study is considered comparable to Farberow's (1956) suicide threat group, a direct comparison of the results of the two studies can be made. Both Rosen et al. (1954) and Farberow (1956) found 15 pairwise comparisons to be significant, and 8 comparisons were significant in both studies.

Simon and Gilberstadt (1958) compared the MMPI results of 26 male psychiatric patients who had committed suicide with the three groups of patients included in the Rosen et al. (1954) study. The mean scale scores for the suicide group were generally similar to those for the nonsuicidal comparison group. Like the suicide attempt and the nonsuicidal comparison groups, the suicide group had significantly lower scores than the suicide thought group for scales F, 2, 6, 7, 8, and 0. For scale 9 the suicide attempt group scored significantly higher than the suicide group.

Broida (1954) compared 20 suicidal patients with 20 nonsuicidal psychiatric patients matched for diagnosis, age, education, occupation, and marital status. Ten of the suicidal patients had attempted suicide, while the other 10 were rated by the ward psychiatrist as having excessive suicidal thinking. Only the 60 items of scale 2 were administered to patients. While this may appear to be questionable (Lester, 1970a), Broida (1954) defended his procedure by pointing out that scale 2 was originally standardized separately from other MMPI items. The mean T score on scale 2 for the suicide group (74.6) was significantly higher than the mean T score for the nonsuicidal comparison group (62.9).

Lester (1970b) compared the MMPI scale scores for males who completed suicide using active methods (e.g., shooting) with those using passive methods (e.g., asphyxiation by gas). No significant differences were found. Similarly, no significant differences were found between the scale scores for persons shooting themselves and those for persons hanging themselves. These results are consistent with Simon and Gilberstandt's (1958) discovery that there was no apparent relationship between MMPI scale scores and the method chosen by persons who subsequently committed suicide.

MMPI PROFILE ANALYSIS

Some studies attempting to find ways of using the MMPI to assess suicidal risk have employed profile analysis. Marks and Seeman (1963) identified 16 common profile code types among MMPI records obtained from 1,200 psychiatric patients (inpatients and outpatients of both sexes). Each profile code type was defined by a set of explicit rules and was identified by the two or three highest scale scores for that profile. Among the information collected for each patient were suicide attempts, suicidal thoughts, and suicide threats. For each MMPI profile type Marks and Seeman (1963) reported the percentage of patients among a group of 300 female patients who displayed each of the three types of suicidal behavior. The base rates for suicide attempts, suicidal thinking, and suicide threats were 16.9 percent, 23.0 percent, and 4.7 percent respectively. Patients with either of two profile code types, 4-8-2 and 4-6-2, were found to be higher than the base rate for all three suicidal behaviors. Forty-five percent of the patients with profile type 4-8-2 had attempted suicide, 35 percent had suicidal thoughts, and 10 percent made suicide threats. For patients with profile type 4-6-2 the rates were 26 percent suicide attempts, 32 percent suicidal thoughts, and 16 percent suicide threats. Patients with profile types 2-7-8 and 2-8 were high, compared to base rates, for both suicidal thoughts and suicide threats, but not for suicide attempts. Patients with profile type 4-6 had 39 percent suicide attempts but did not have a high incidence of suicidal thoughts or suicide threats. It is interesting to note that several of the profile types with elevations on scale 2 had rates for the various suicidal behaviors that were lower than the base rates. This appears to be especially true if, in addition to an elevation on scale 2, the profile was defined by elevations on either scales 1 and 3 or scale 7.

Devries and Farberow (1967) used a multivariate discriminant analysis in attempting to differentiate a group of 80 nonsuicidal psychiatric patients, a group of 82 patients who had threatened suicide prior to testing, a group of 77 patients who had attempted suicide prior to testing, and a group of 43 patients who had completed suicide. Instead of utilizing the complete profile, only the six MMPI clinical scales (2, 4, 6, 7, 8, and 9) previously found (Farberow, 1956) to show promise in differentiating suicidal and nonsuicidal groups were considered. The mean T scores of the six scales were found to be significantly ($p < .001$) different for the four groups. The discriminant analysis showed that 52 percent, 17 percent, 59 percent, and 28 percent, respectively, of the patients in the nonsuicidal comparison, suicide attempt, suicide threat, and suicide groups were correctly classified. The efficiency of the test (number of patients correctly identified divided by the total number of patients) was 41 percent. With regard to the efficiency of the test in identifying patients who will subsequently commit sui-

cide, 25 percent (12 patients) of the 43 patients placed in the suicide group by the discriminant analysis were correctly classified
while 15 percent (36 patients) of the 239 patients in the other
three groups were misclassified as being in the suicide group.
Using the six MMPI scales to separate patients who will commit
suicide from other psychiatric patients, including those showing
other suicidal behavior, would result in 75 percent false negative
or misses and 15 percent false positives. In general, the Devries
and Farberow (1967) results were consistent with other research
(Farberow, 1956; Rosen et al., 1954; Simon and Gilberstadt,
1958) in showing that patients who threaten suicide are most easily distinguishable and patients who commit suicide are least easily
distinguishable from other groups of patients.

Ravensborg and Foss (1969) examined the MMPI profiles of
a group of patients who had committed suicide in a state hospital,
a group of patients who died of natural causes in the same hospital, and a random sample of hospital inpatients for whom test
material was available. Each group consisted of 23 patients of
both sexes. Group profiles were analyzed by profile analysis of
variance. Since the obtained F ratio was not significant, it was concluded that the MMPI profile could not be used to discriminate
psychiatric patients who would subsequently commit suicide from
comparison groups.

Devries and Shneidman (1967) obtained the MMPI records
from five suicidal patients (three males and two females) who
took the MMPI monthly for a period of a year. Each of the patients also rated the lethality of his suicidal thinking monthly on
a 9-point scale. A discriminant analysis of the five groups of profiles correctly grouped all profiles for each patient together. The
profiles were sorted by two clinicians with 75 percent accuracy.
There thus appears to be a very high degree of reliability in a suicidal individual's MMPI profile over time. Of course, the results
of this analysis may have been dependent on the degree of heterogeneity among the five patients in this study. Devries and Shneidman (1967) correlated each patient's lethality ratings with his
scores for 12 of the standard MMPI scales (scale 0 was not included). Of the 60 correlation coefficients obtained only nine were

statistically significant. No scale correlated significantly with the lethality ratings of more than two patients. Interestingly enough, scale 2 did not correlate significantly with the lethality ratings for any patient. It appears, therefore, that although each of the five patients may have shown increases and decreases in suicidal intent, these changes were not related to changes in MMPI scale scores. It would have been interesting to have also correlated MMPI scale scores and ratings of lethality made by someone other than the patient himself. Devries and Shneidman (1967) conclude that changes in degree of lethality cannot be detected by changes in MMPI scale scores, and that any changes in the MMPI profile of a suicidal patient are in terms of his own profile characteristics. As a suicidal patient becomes acutely suicidal, his MMPI scale scores do not change toward a general suicidal profile.

In a case study of an individual who had been tested three days prior to committing suicide, Holzberg, Cahen, and Wilk (1951) found the MMPI profile (scale 0 was not included) to be within the normal range.

MMPI ITEM ANALYSIS AND SPECIAL SCALE DEVELOPMENT

Simon and Hales (1949) examined the MMPI responses of a group of male psychiatric patients who were judged to be preoccupied with suicide. Although they did not compare the MMPI responses for this group with those of a nonsuicidal comparison group, they reported finding seven items in scale 2 and ten items in scale 7 that were answered in the scored direction by a majority of the suicidal patients. However, item 88 in scale 2 (I usually feel that life is worthwhile) was answered in the negative direction by less than one-sixth of the suicidal patients. Holzberg et al. (1951) found the responses of their subject to be similar to those of Simon and Hales (1949) for only one scale 2 item and four scale 7 items.

Simon and Gilberstadt (1958) compared the MMPI responses of a group of patients who committed suicide with those of a nonsuicidal comparison group in an attempt to derive an empirical scale to predict suicide. An item analysis showed 23 of the 550 items to differentiate the groups significantly. However, Simon and

Gilberstadt (1958) concluded, perhaps erroneously (Devries, 1966b), that this number of significant differences could be obtained strictly by chance. Inspection of the set of items revealed a lack of face validity. Apparently the items did not stand up under cross-validation, although no data are presented to support this. Simon and Gilberstadt (1958) did not report which 23 items were found to differentiate significantly suicidal and nonsuicidal patients, and they rejected the idea of attempting to develop a suicide prediction scale for the MMPI.

Farberow and Devries (1967) did an item analysis of the MMPI responses of 215 suicidal and 80 nonsuicidal male psychiatric patients. The suicidal patients consisted of three categories of patients. One group of 54 patients had committed suicide while in a VA neuropsychiatric hospital. The second group consisted of 79 patients admitted to the hospital as a result of a suicide attempt. The third group consisted of 82 patients admitted as a result of suicide threats. The total sample of patients was divided in half to allow for both original and replication studies. The MMPI responses of each of the four groups of patients were compared with the responses of every other group. (The .10 level of significance was used for the item analysis in both original and replication studies.) Only when the number of significant items in the various comparisons exceeded the number estimated to be expected by chance (Devries, 1966b) in both the original and replication studies was it assumed that there was a significant differentiation between the appropriate groups. It was discovered that only the suicide threat group satisfied this criterion; none of the other groups were significantly differentiated from each other in both the original and replication comparisons. The 52 items which significantly differentiated the suicide threat group from the nonsuicidal comparison group in both the original and replication studies were selected for development of an MMPI Suicide Threat scale. The standard MMPI scales represented most often among the 52 items were scales 8 (19 items), 7 (18 items), and 2 (14 items).

Farberow and Devries (1967) found 20 to be the optimum cut-off score for differentiating suicidal from nonsuicidal patients with their Suicide Threat scale. Classifying patients whose scores fell below 20 as nonsuicidal and patients whose scores were at or above 20 as threat suicidal, 80 percent of the suicide threat group and 68 percent of the nonsuicidal comparison group were correctly identified. With a new sample of 50 nonsuicidal patients and 50 suicide threat patients, the percentages of correct classifications dropped to 72 percent and 42 percent, respectively. In other words, in a psychiatric hospital with an estimated base rate for suicide threats of 26 percent, classifying the new sample of patients as nonsuicidal or threatening suicide on the basis of a Suicide Threat scale cut-off score of 20 resulted in 28 percent false negatives and 58 percent false positives.

Ravenborg and Foss (1969) scored the Suicide Threat scale for three groups of patients (suicides, natural deaths, and nonsuicidal inpatients) in a state hospital and obtained means of 21.7 for suicides and 22.9 for the other two groups. An analysis of variance was performed on Suicide Threat scale scores. F ratios for main effects were not significant, showing that the suicide group did not differ from the other two groups on this scale, and that males, as a group, did not differ from females. The Sex X Patient Group interaction, however, was significant. Inspection of means revealed that nonsuicidal female inpatients obtained the highest mean score on the Suicide Threat scale. Overall, these results indicate that the Suicide Threat scale has no value in differentiating patients who subsequently commit suicide from other state hospital inpatients.

Devries (1966c), in a follow-up study to that of Farberow and Devries (1967),[1] included a group of 72 patients who had attempted suicide, a group of 154 patients who had threatened suicide, and a group of 83 patients who had both threatened and attempted suicide, and compared these groups with a group of 283 nonsuicidal psychiatric inpatients. As in the Farberow and Devries (1967) study, the samples were divided in half to allow for both original and replication studies. For both the original and replication studies the MMPI responses of every one of the four patient groups were compared with those of every other group for all short-form MMPI items. In the same way the three suicidal groups

---

1. Despite being published later, the Farberow and Devries (1967) study is the earlier of the two.

from both original and replication studies were combined and compared with the two combined control groups. All comparisons of the various suicidal groups with each other were not significant.

In contrast to Farberow and Devries' (1967) finding that the suicide threat group was the only suicidal group which could be differentiated from nonsuicidal patients, Devries (1966c) found that in both original and replication studies every comparison of the various suicidal groups with the nonsuicidal group resulted in a greater number of differentiating items than would be expected by chance (approximately 18; Devries, 1966b). In particular, the numbers of differentiating items in the original study were 60 for the nonsuicidal comparison group versus the suicide threat group, 67 for the nonsuicidal comparison group versus the suicide threat and attempt group, and 30 for the nonsuicidal comparison groups versus the suicide attempt group. These same comparisons produced 63, 60, and 62 differentiating items, respectively, in the replication study. Devries (1966c) reports that few of the same items significantly differentiated any of the groups for both the original and the replication study. Therefore, the common item approach of Farberow and Devries (1967) was discarded, and an arbitrary decision was made to list as potentially useful those items that were significant in the comparison of all suicidal patients and nonsuicidal patients and in at least two of the other six comparisons (type of suicide versus nonsuicidal comparison group, original and replication studies). Thirty-one items seemed to constitute a general suicide scale since they significantly differentiated each suicidal group from the nonsuicidal comparison group. Twenty items significantly differentiated the suicide threat group and the suicide threat and attempt group from the nonsuicidal comparison group. Twelve items significantly differentiated the suicide attempt group and the suicide threat and attempt group from the nonsuicidal group. Fourteen items significantly differentiated the suicide threat group and the suicide attempt group from the nonsuicidal group. Of the 77 items making a significant differentiation in these four comparisons, 13, 3, 4, and 3, respectively, were among the 52 items in Farberow and Devries' (1967) Suicide Threat scale. It is possible that some of these items may even have been scored differently in the two studies since Devries (1966c) does not report the response indicative of suicidal behavior for any of the items in his study.

Devries' (1966c) results are clearly at odds with those reported by Farberow and Devries (1967). Of most importance, the two studies differ on whether enough MMPI items can be found to constitute a reliable suicide scale (i.e., significantly differentiate suicidal and nonsuicidal groups for both an original and a replication study) and on the particular items that differentiate the groups.

Devries (1967) has carried out a further study indicating that controlling appropriate variables increases the ability of the MMPI to differentiate suicidal and nonsuicidal patients. The definition of suicidal is left ambiguous in this study, however. Starting with 309 suicidal male patients and 283 nonsuicidal male patients, Devries (1967) sorted each population into categories for diagnosis, age, education, occupation, marital status, and number of hospital admissions. After first sorting both populations by diagnostic category, the subcategory with the most patients (psychosis) was selected for further subdivision on the basis of the next variable, age. Again the subcategory with the most patients (younger than 40) was retained for further sorting. Using this procedure the remaining patients were sorted in turn for subcategories of education, occupation, marital status, and number of hospital admissions. The two matched samples obtained in this manner consisted of eight suicidal patients and 13 nonsuicidal patients. These patients were all psychotic patients who were not over 40 years old, had a high school education, were single and employed as service workers or laborers, and had one VA hospital admission. The response frequencies of the two groups were compared for each of the 373 short-form MMPI items. Sixteen items were found to differentiate the two groups. Devries (1967) did not report the item numbers and direction of scoring for these items. When random samples of eight suicidal and 13 nonsuicidal patients from the original populations were compared, five items were found which significantly differentiated the groups. It was determined empirically (Devries, 1966b) that comparing suicidal and nonsuicidal groups of the size included in this study, only one or two items would be found by chance to differentiate the groups.

CONCLUSION

To date, neither standard MMPI scales, MMPI profile analysis, nor specially developed MMPI suicide scales have been found to be reliable in predicting suicide at useful levels. The one standard MMPI scale found most frequently to differentiate suicidal and nonsuicidal groups is scale 2. However, in two studies (Farberow, 1956; Rosen et al., 1954) the scale 2 scores of patients who attempted suicide did not differ from those of nonsuicidal patients. Simon and Gilberstadt (1958) found no difference in scale 2 scores for patients who committed suicides and nonsuicidal patients. Marks and Seeman's (1963) study indicated that whether patients with elevations on scale 2 were above or below the base rates for various suicidal behaviors depended upon the pattern of their other MMPI scale scores. In some studies (Broida, 1954; Simon and Hales, 1949) comparing suicidal and nonsuicidal patients on scale 2, the suicidal group included patients threatening suicide, and such patients have been found to score significantly higher than patients who either commit or attempt suicide on most MMPI scales (Farberow, 1956; Farberow and Devries, 1967; Jones, 1968; Rosen et al., 1954; Simon and Gilberstadt, 1958). While MMPI profile analysis has shown some promise (Devries and Farberow, 1967; Marks and Seeman, 1963), there is certainly no evidence for a general suicidal profile. The only MMPI study (Devries and Farberow, 1967) to demonstrate a differentiation of patients who commit suicide and other suicidal patients employed profile analysis. Of course, another study (Ravensborg and Foss, 1969) found that MMPI profile analysis could not separate patients who subsequently commit suicide from other psychiatric patient groups. With regard to special MMPI suicide scales, the disparity in the results of Devries (1966c) and Farberow and Devries (1967) is discouraging, although a later study (Devries, 1967) has offered hope that it may be possible to develop MMPI suicide scales for select groups of patients.

As noted by earlier review articles (Brown and Sheran, 1972; Lester, 1970a), many of the methodological difficulties in the area of suicide research are quite evident in studies examining the assessment of suicidal risk with the MMPI. For example, the statistical infrequency of suicide places a formidable burden on any test used to assess suicidal behavior. Even a fairly accurate test may predict no more accurately than always predicting the nonoccurrence of suicide. Given the low rate of suicide in a psychiatric hospital, even if the MMPI were found to correctly identify 80 percent of the patients, both suicidal and nonsuicidal, it would be impractical, and ethically questionable, to treat as suicidal the large number of false positives (Rosen, 1954). Any change in the criterion so as to reduce the number of false positives would also automatically reduce the detection of truly suicidal patients.

Some of the research exploring the possibility of assessing suicidal risk with the MMPI seems to lose sight of the fact that the true need is for a means of predicting which individuals will attempt or complete suicide. A successful differentiation of suicidal and nonsuicidal patient groups on the basis of statistical analysis of MMPI data may be all but useless in an applied setting if the differences between groups are quite small, even though statistically significant (e.g., Rosen et al., 1954), or the nature of the obtained differences is not made clear (e.g., Devries and Farberow, 1967). There appears to be no real need for a means of predicting which persons will threaten suicide but will not subsequently attempt or complete suicide. While researchers attempting to differentiate suicidal and nonsuicidal patients have often used patients who have threatened suicide in their suicidal groups, the most pressing need is for the detection of persons who will attempt or complete suicide.

Two alternative methods of assessing suicidal risk deserve mention. Dean, Miskimins, DeCook, Wilson, and Maley (1967) used hospital admissions data as the basis for developing a Suicide Potential scale. As Lester (1970a) notes, if the high probability group in the Dean et al. (1967) study is considered to be predicted suicides and the moderate and low probability groups are considered to be predicted nonsuicides, then the Suicide Potential scale identifies correctly 75 percent of the completed suicides and 93.8 percent of the patients not committing suicide. Although the data in a cross-validation study (Miskimins and Wilson, 1969) are not presented so a determination can be made of the percentage of correct classifications, the degree of differentiation of suicidal and comparison groups is nearly the same in both studies.

Devries (1963, 1966a) collected all characteristics of suicidal individuals found in a review of the suicide literature using the critical incident technique (Flanagan, 1954). On the basis of these characteristics, 55 true-false items (some highly similar to MMPI items) were written and administered to a group of nonsuicidal male psychiatric patients and to a group of "previously suicidal" male patients. Using a cut-off score of 7 with the 13 items found to make a significant differentiation between the groups, 56 percent of the suicidal patients could be identified at a cost of only 31 percent false positives. Lester (1967) found the 13-item Devries (1967) scale to differentiate significantly between suicidal and nonsuicidal college students and found that such differentiation was not merely an artifact of group differences in emotional disturbance (Lester, 1968).

REFERENCES

Broida, D. C.: An investigation of certain psychodiagnostic indications of suicidal tendencies and depression in mental hospital patients. *Psychiatric Quarterly, 28:*453-464, 1954.

Brown, T. R., and Sheran, T. J.: Suicide prediction: A review. *Life-Threatening Behavior, 2:*67-98, 1972.

Dahlstrom, W. G., Welsh, G. S., and Dahlstrom, L. E.: *An MMPI Handbook.* Minneapolis, University of Minnesota Press, 1972, Vol. I (Rev. ed.).

Dean, R. A., Miskimins, W., DeCook, R., Wilson, L. T., and Maley, R. F.: Prediction of suicide in a psychiatric hospital. *Journal of Clinical Psychology, 23:*296-301, 1967.

Devries, A. G.: Methodological problems in the identification of suicidal behavior by means of two personality inventories. (Doctoral dissertation, University of Southern California) Ann Arbor, Mich.: University Microfilms, 1963. No. 64-6237.

Devries, A. G.: A potential suicide personality inventory. *Psychological Reports, 18:*731-738, 1966a.

Devries, A. G.: Change expectance, sample size, replacement and non-replacement sampling. *Psychological Reports, 18:*843-850, 1966b.

Devries, A. G.: Identification of suicidal behavior by means of the MMPI. *Psychological Reports, 19:*415-419, 1966c.

Devries, A. G.: Control variables in the identification of suicidal behavior. *Psychological Reports, 20:*1131-1135, 1967.

Devries, A. G.: Prediction of suicide by means of psychological tests. In Farberow, N. L. (Ed.): *Proceedings of the Fourth International Conference for Suicide Prevention.* Los Angeles, Delmar, 1968.

Devries, A. G., and Farberow, N. L.: A multivariate profile analysis of MMPI's of suicidal and non-suicidal neuropsychiatric hospital patients. *Journal of Projective Techniques and Personality Assessment, 31:*81-84, 1967.

Devries, A. G., and Shneidman, E. S.: Multiple MMPI profiles of suicidal persons. *Psychological Reports, 21:*401-405, 1967.

Farberow, N. L.: Personality patterns of suicidal mental hospital patients. In Welsh, G. S., and Dahlstrom, W. G. (Eds.): *Basic Readings on the MMPI in Psychology and Medicine.* Minneapolis, University of Minnesota Press, 1956.

Farberow, N. L., and Devries, A. G.: An item differentiation analysis of suicidal neuropsychiatric hospital patients. *Psychological Reports, 20:*607-617, 1967.

Flanagan, J. C.: The critical incident technique. *Psychological Bulletin, 51:* 327-358, 1954.

Hathaway, S. R., and McKinley, J. C.: *Manual for the MMPI.* New York, Psychological Corporation, 1945.

Holzberg, J. D., Cahen, E. R., and Wilk, E. K.: Suicide: A psychological study of self-destruction. *Journal of Projective Techniques, 15:*339-354, 1951.

Jones, R.: Suicidal outpatients: The MMPI and case file data. Unpublished doctoral dissertation, University of Oregon, 1968.

Lester, D.: Suicide as an aggressive act. *Journal of Psychology, 66:*47-50, 1967.

Lester, D.: Suicide as an aggressive act: A replication with a control for neuroticism. *Journal of General Psychology, 79:*83-86, 1968.

Lester, D.: Attempts to predict suicidal risk using psychological tests. *Psychological Bulletin, 74:*1-17, 1970a.

Lester, D.: Personality correlates associated with choice of method of committing suicide. *Personality, 1:*261-264, 1970b.

Marks, P. A., and Seeman, W.: *The Actuarial Description of Abnormal Personality.* Baltimore, Williams & Wilkins, 1963.

Miskimins, R. W., and Wilson, L. T.: Revised suicide potential scale. *Journal of Consulting and Clinical Psychology, 33:*258, 1969.

Ravensborg, M. R., and Foss, A.: Suicide and natural death in a state hospital population: A comparison of admission complaints, MMPI profiles, and social competence factors. *Journal of Consulting and Clinical Psychology, 33:*466-471, 1969.

Rosen, A.: Detection of suicidal patients. *Journal of Consulting Psychology, 18:*397-403, 1954.

Rosen, A., Hales, W. M., and Simon, W.: Classification of "suicidal" patients. *Journal of Consulting Psychology, 18:*359-362, 1954.

Simon, W.: Attempted suicide among veterans. *Journal of Nervous and Mental Disease, 111:*451-468, 1950.

Simon, W., and Gilberstadt, H.: Analyses of the personality structure of 26 actual suicides. *Journal of Nervous and Mental Diseases, 127:*555-557, 1958.

Simon, W., and Hales, W. H.: Note on a suicide key in the Minnesota Multiphasic Personality Inventory. *American Journal of Psychiatry, 106:*222-223, 1949.

CHAPTER VII

ASSESSMENT OF SUICIDE RISK USING SELECTED TESTS

SHERMAN EISENTHAL

THIS CHAPTER DESCRIBES and evaluates the application of five selected psychological tests to the task of assessing suicidal risk. Three of these tests are commonly used in clinical assessment batteries: the Bender-Gestalt, the Rosenzweig Picture-Frustration Study, and the Sentence Completion method. The other two tests are seldom used clinically (the Hildreth Feeling and Attitude Scale and the Maslow Social Personality Inventory), but were selected because they are directed to two relevant aspects of suicidal behavior: feelings and self-concept.

Two unsettling facts emerge after a survey of the literature: first is the sparsity of work on this problem, and second is the lack of systematic evaluation-centered studies among the published research. A major element considered in systematic evaluation is the careful delineation of one's objectives (Suchman, 1967). A number of objectives in suicide assessment are discernable. For example, in mental hospitals and clinics, a common assessment objective is evaluating whether an individual's suicidal behavior should be taken seriously. The patient may be threatening to suicide or may have made a "gesture" at suicide. Should that person be placed on suicide status? A related assessment task is evaluating whether a patient who is on suicidal status should be taken off and given hospital privileges, a day pass, or a trial visit home. The patient appears to be improved, but the clinician wants further confirmation. A somewhat different assessment task in hospitals and clinics is the identification of patients who are not easily recognized as being a suicidal risk. Clinicians know that the majority of patients who will subsequently make suicide attempts either will not have been previously identified as a risk or will not be considered to be suicidal at the time of their subsequent suicidal behavior. From this analysis one can recognize two broad sets of objectives in assessment of suicidal risk: (1) screening for suicidal potential among individuals not previously or currently identified as a risk, and (2) evaluating individuals who have been identified as having suicidal potential for the degree of risk and for changes in risk. Differentiation of these very broad objectives is a first step in the direction of valid test evaluation.

The objective that is chosen sets the guidelines for evaluation of the design of research on the assessment of suicidal risk (Suchman, 1967). If, on the one hand, the assessment objective is to screen individuals entering a hospital for future suicidal risk, then proper evaluative research will require collection of test scores before the criterion behavior is manifested. Such behavior may be threats, attempted suicide, or completed suicide. If on the other hand, the assessment objective is to evaluate improvement in patients on suicidal status, the research design will require repeated test measures and an acceptable criterion measure of improvement (e.g., absence of threats or actions for a designated time that is obtained concurrently with the test scores). For a detailed discussion of some of the other methodological problems see Rosen, 1954; Neuringer 1962, 1965; Devries, 1968; and Lester, 1970.

After a careful examination of the specified objectives in the research on these five tests, no differentiation between the broadest objectives was found. The review of the research revealed that most studies were not designed to evaluate test effectiveness: some were designed to test the hypothesis that suicidal individuals are more intropunitive than others. Among those studies that had test evaluation as an objective, none were properly designed to evaluate change or screen for future suicidal behavior.

All the research on the tests under consideration compared known suicidal patients with either a matched psychiatric control group, a normal control group, or the test's norms. The criteria for inclusion in the suicidal group varied with respect to the kind of behavior (suicidal threat, serious, and non-serious attempts) and the recency of such behavior at the time of testing. Only in the case of some threat groups was there an actively suicidal group studied. In the case of attempt groups, no reference was made to the presence of suicidal ideation at the time of testing. And, in addition, in no study was data from actual suicides used. The comparability of the studies is, thus, questionable.

The purpose of this review, therefore, is not to describe the established efficiency of test indicators in assessment of suicidal risk. Past research will be presented as a source of guidance for future research on this problem.

ROSENZWEIG—PICTURE FRUSTRATION STUDY

This projective test is composed of 24 cartoons designed to tap reactions to a range of frustrating situations (Rosenzweig, 1945; Rosenzweig, Fleming, and Clarke, 1947). Responses are scored for both the direction of aggressive response [extrapunitive (E), intropunitive (I), and impunitive (M)], and type of reaction focus [obstacle-dominant (O-D), need persistent (N-P), or ego defensive (E-D)]. A variant score was devised for the extrapunitive and intropunitive directions, and a group conformity rating (GCR) was based on the deviation of responses to 12 cartoon scores from group norms.

Six studies of suicidal behavior were found that employed the PF Study covering a period of 22 years.

The earliest and most systematic study was conducted by Farberow (1950). He administered the PF study to 96 male veterans who were neuro-psychiatric patients. Sixty-four patients were on suicidal status and 32 were matched psychiatric patients who had no suicidal history. The suicidal patients were selected according to two criteria; kind of suicidal behavior (one-half were suicidal attempters and one-half suicidal threateners) and seriousness of suicidal intention (one-half were rated serious and one-half non-serious based on psychiatric judgment of the case). The research design thus permitted group comparisons on the kind and seriousness of suicidal behavior. The median age was between 35-37 and approximately one-third of each group was composed of patients with the diagnosis of neurosis and one-third with patients with a diagnosis of psychosis; the remaining third was a mixture of patients with diagnoses of character disorder and chronic brain syndrome.

Farberow employed 10 scores: E, I, M, O-D, N-P, E-D, GCR, E variant, I variant, and E plus I. No hypotheses were stated about the relationship of the scores to the kind or seriousness of suicidal behavior. His research objective was to describe and evaluate differences between the experimental and control group on the various scores.

In the comparisons between the two suicidal groups and the psychatric control group, only one statistically significant difference was found. The suicide attempt group had a higher mean percentage of the I variant scores than the control group.

Comparisons between the groups based on seriousness of intent (serious, non-serious, and control), yielded several significant findings. Compared to psychiatric controls, the serious suicidal group had a significantly lower mean percent of E variant scores and significantly lower mean differences between E-I. The mean percentage of extrapunitive scores was 35 to 39 for the serious and control groups, a non-significant difference.

The presence of differences between the suicidal attempt and threat groups was among the most important findings. The threat group had a significantly higher mean percent of E scores than the attempt group (42 versus 35) and a significantly lower E-M difference score. The suicide threat group thus appears to be significantly more extrapunitive than the suicide attempt group.

The "serious" group was also significantly less extrapunitive than the non-serious suicidal group as measured by E (35 percent to 42 percent), by E variant (2 percent to 4 percent), and by the E-I difference score.

Fisher and Hinds (1951) investigated the expression of hostility and compared a schizophrenic suicidal group with a schizophrenic non-suicidal control group and a normal control group. The suicidal group was composed of 20 patients who made a suicide attempt within three months of admission and who had not been given shock treatment. The suicidal group was composed mostly of males (85 percent) as was the psychiatric control (75 percent) in contrast with the normal controls (42 percent).

They used 12 of the PF study cartoons and scored for direction of aggression only. They used their own scoring procedures for three measures of hostility: outward, inward, and neutral which parallel the extrapunitive, intropunitive, and impunitive categories used by Rosenzweig.

The suicide group did not differ significantly from the schizophrenic control group on any of the three scoring categories, but they did have a significantly lower inward hostility score than the normal controls; a result that is opposite to expectations.

The correlation of inward and outward hostility scores was significantly negative in all three groups: suicide, $r = -.32$; schizophrenic control, $r = -.52$; and normal control $r = -.73$. The suicide group showed a relatively greater potential for reacting in both inward and outward hostile directions than the normal controls.

Winfield and Sparer (1953) investigated the hypothesis that suicidal patients would have higher intropunitive scores than a group of normals on the PF study. They compared the scores of 26 white male psychiatric patients who had made at least one serious suicide attempt with the scores for the male norms developed by Rosenzweig. The patients had a mean age of 34.4 and a mean 10th grade education. Nine of the patients were diagnosed neurotic, 16 psychotic, and 1 epileptic.

In addition to the intropunitive score (I) they scored for E, M, O-D, E-D, N-P, and GCR. The standard P-F study cartoons and procedures were used.

The hypothesis that the suicide group would have a significantly higher mean intropunitive score than the normative group was not supported; the scores were 30.8 percent versus 28 percent. However, the suicidal group was found to have a significantly lower mean E score in comparison with the normative group (37.2 percent to 45 percent) and a significantly higher M score (37.2 percent to 27 percent).

Arneson and Feldman (1968) divided suicidal attempt patients (male and female) into serious attempt ($N = 18$) and mild attempt ($N = 31$) groups and compared their scores with the PF Study norms for males and females. They used the three standard PF study scores for direction (E, I, and M) and the three standard scores for type of reaction (O-D, N-P, and E-D). No significant group differences were found in the direction of aggressive reaction. There were significant differences in type of reaction, particularly E-D.

In comparison with the norms, the mild attempt group (males) had significantly higher mean scores on E-D and lower mean scores on O-D and N-P. For females, both the mild and serious attempt groups had significantly higher mean scores on E-D and lower mean scores on O-D than the normative groups. The ego-defensive reaction to frustration thus seems to be a distinctive reaction of the suicide attempt groups and is the type of reaction score most logically linked to suicidal behavior.

The serious attempt group did not differ from the mild group on the E-D score. The serious attempt group (female) did differ significantly from the mild group in having a significantly lower O-D score.

In the only study of an adolescent population sample, Levenson and Neuringer (1970) investigated the hypothesis that intropunitive dynamics underlies suicidal behavior. They compared three groups of adolescents: a hospitalized suicide attempt group, a hospitalized non-suicidal control group, and a normal, unhospitalized control group. Each group contained 6 females and 7 males. All the suicidal patients had made a serious attempt. The normal controls were matched on age and the WAIS Information subscale. The results for the I score (only measure reported) did not support the hypothesis. The suicidal adolescents had a non-significantly higher mean I score than the other two groups.

Preston (1964) investigated the hypothesis that suicide attempters and automobile accident victims might share a common unconscious need to risk injury in accidents. Three groups were compared: 58 suicide attempters consecutively admitted to a hospital, 30 automobile accident victims consecutively admitted to a local hospital, and 30 non-accident drivers matched with the accident drivers on age, sex, and education. In the suicide attempt group there were 30 females and 19 males; and in each of the accident and non-accident groups there were 12 females and 18 males. Data analysis was performed on the following scores:

GCR, E, I, M, O-D, E-D, and N-P. The hypothesis was not supported. The suicide attempt group did not share with the accident group a common deviant direction of response to frustration or type of response focus. The suicide attempt group did not differ from the non-accident control group on any of the measures. The suicide attempt group differed from the accident drivers on four measures, suggesting (opposite to the hypothesis) that these two groups were more different than similar. The attempters were significantly more impunitive, less extropunitive, less ego-defensive, and more obstacle-dominant than the accident drivers.

Looking at the results of all these studies, one does not find distinctive and useful signs of suicidal potential. If there was a powerful relationship between the measures of direction or type of reaction to frustration and suicidal behavior, it would have shown through, despite the variations in populations studies, the kind of suicidal behavior studied, and the administration and scoring of the test. The data do not encourage one to place much confidence in using this test to screen for suicidal potential, let alone evaluate for change.

If there is a relationship between the test measures of the PF Study and suicidal behavior, it is subtle and requires more systematic investigation than has been found in the present literature. It should be noted, in this regard, that there were no item analyses reported. It would make clinical sense to expect that some stimulus situations depicted by the 24 cartoons are more prepotent than others in tapping self-destructive motivations. In addition, in no study was there a concurrent analysis of direction and type of reaction. That is, each cartoon is scored for both direction and type of reaction. It could be that there is an interaction between the stimulus situation and the combined direction and type of reaction (e.g., an intropunitive direction and ego-defensive type of response to situations threatening a loss of love). On the other hand, reactions to situations such as a car splashing a person with mud may be unrelated to suicidal motivation.

BENDER-GESTALT TEST

Three studies were found that used this test (Sternberg and Levine, 1965; Nawas and Worth, 1968; and Esler, 1964). Only one of these showed positive results (Sternberg and Levine, 1965). They investigated the relationship of suicidal behavior to a measure of the spatial relationship of Figures 5 and 6 of the Bender-Gestalt Test. According to Levine (1960) Figure 5 symbolically represents affect and Figure 6 a normally assertive mother-figure. If Figure 6 penetrates the space of the previously drawn Figure 5, then the symbolic implication is both aggressive and representative of a desire to return to the womb (i.e., a suicidal motivation). An experimental group (persons having a penetration of designs 5 and 6) was composed of psychiatric patients who were hospitalized within three years preceding the study and were later discharged. A control group (non-penetration of Figures 5 and 6) was matched with the experimental group on age, sex, and diagnosis and hospitalization period. Each group contained 25 patients, 16 female and 8 male who were mostly psychotic and 33 years old on the average. The discharge records of the two groups were rated for the presence of suicidal behavior by three judges; their inter-rater reliability was found to be high. Twenty-two of the experimental group (88%) were rated as having had suicidal ideation or a suicide attempt, whereas 11 (44%) of the controls were found to have suicidal behavior. A chi-square test of this data was found to be statistically significant. The expected figure of suicidal behavior used in the chi-square was 46 percent and was based on checking the records of a random sample of hospital patients. This percentage was quite close to the finding of 44 percent suicide behavior in the matched control. Unfortunately no statement was made regarding the relationship of the administration of the Bender-Gestalt and the appearance of suicidal behavior (i.e., whether the penetration score was a predictive or postdictive measure).

Nawas and Worth (1968) investigated whether the test could distinguish patients who had made a recent suicidal attempt from matched controls. Ten test signs of suicidality were devised to fit the five criteria they formulated of the suicidal personality. The personality traits and their respective signs are as follows: *Depression:* (1) Figure 6 had flattened lines, (2) Figure A rotated clockwise, (3) Figure 4 rotated clockwise. *Hostility:* (4) Figure 3 reversed, (5) Figure 3 rotated. *Dependency:* (6) Figure A ran to-

142   Psychological Assessment of Suicidal Risk

gether, (7) Figure 4 ran together. *Emotional Constriction:* (8) Figure sizes reduced, (9) Figure A placed in extreme upper left hand corner of paper. *Rigidity:* (10) Figures placed one right below the other.

A search of ten years of state hospital discharge records yielded a suicide attempt group of 17 individuals who made their attempt within six months of hospital admission. A matched control group of 17 patients was selected on the basis of age, diagnosis, marital status, education, and sex. In the E group there were eight males and nine females, 14 character disorder diagnoses (82%), mean age of 23, 12th grade education, and a median of 13.5 months of hospitalization.

Three judges rated the 34 test protocols and obtained non-significant reliability on signs 2, 3, and 4. On the remaining seven signs, the reliability was significant, ranging from .53 to .97. Scores for group comparisons were based on the average of the scores of the three judges. The results indicated that none of the ten signs significantly distinguished the suicidal from the nonsuicidal patients. It should be noted that the penetration of designs 5 and 6 was not one of the signs used. A number of indicators sensitive to affect were not used (Tolor, 1966).

Esler (1964) compared 20 suicidal and 20 nonsuicidal patients to test the hypothesis that two groups would differ on an object sorting task. The Bender-Gestalt Test was used to determine whether there were group differences in degree of psychopathology. Two judges rated the test protocols very reliably and found no differences in the degree of psychopathology.

Starer (1960) investigated the hypothesis that suicidal patients would be more disrupted in a psychomotor task than nonsuicidal patients by affective stimuli. The psychomotor task was to copy a complex design, presented in different positions. He did not use the Bender-Gestalt, but because of the similarity of the two tests his findings seemed relevant to its use in the assessment of suicidal risk. He compared a group of 25 chronic schizophrenic patients who had made a suicidal threat or attempt with a non-suicidal chronic schizophrenic control group matched for age (the mean was 37) and education (the mean was 10th grade). The special feature of this research was the comparison of the psychomotor performance of each subject with himself during two conditions: a neutral baseline condition and then an affective condition (asking subjects questions about past suicidal history). It was found that all of the 24 control subjects improved their performance after the affective condition, whereas only 11 of the suicidal patients improved. The performance of 14 of the suicidal patients deteriorated.

It would seem that the Bender-Gestalt has not been given a proper chance to show its utility in assessing suicidal risk. Despite the remarkably high accuracy found by Sternberg and Levine (1965) using the "penetration" score, there have been no studies either elaborating or replicating this research. The variation in the administration of the Bender-Gestalt to tap affective state would seem to be a potentially productive approach to screening in view of what Starer (1960) found when he compared production during a baseline and affective condition. The Bender-Gestalt is particularly attractive since it is easy to administer repeatedly and is sensitive to changes in the present psychological state.

HILDRETH FEELING AND ATTITUDE SCALE

The test was developed by Hildreth (1946) to measure with precision how patients feel in clinical setting. Two clusters of four scales each were constructed using a Thurstone attitude scaling methodology. One cluster tapped feeling state (mood, energy, outlook, and mental state) and yielded a feeling score. The other cluster of four scales tapped feelings or attitudes about objects (people and work) and yielded an attitude score. Farberow (1950) used the scale in his study of suicide. The threat group was found to have significantly lower scores than the control and attempt groups on both the feeling and attitude scale measures. The attempt group did not differ from the control group. The serious intention group had significantly lower scores than the control group on feeling and attitude scale measures. In addition, the serious intention group had significantly lower scores than the non-serious intention group on the attitude measure and on the total score. On the feeling score there was a trend in the predicted direction.

Kochansky (1970) compared the baseline mood state of four

groups (suicide attempt, suicide threaten, psychiatric control, non-psychiatric hospital control) as part of an experiment on risk taking and hedonic mood stimulation in suicidal patients. He used the Psychiatric Outpatient Mood Scale [POMS] (McNair and Lorr, 1964), which is composed of seven mood scales, and the depression-elation subscale of the Personal Feelings Scale (Wessman and Ricks, 1966). The two suicide groups and the psychiatric control group contained 15 subjects each, and the non-psychiatric control group contained 30 subjects. More than two-thirds of the patients in each of the three psychiatric groups carried non-psychotic diagnoses.

His findings replicate those of Farberow (1950) on the Hildreth Feeling and Attitude Scale. The threat group was most dysphoric, more so than the attempt or other groups. Both the threat and attempt groups had significantly higher scores on the POMS and Personal Feelings Scale depression subscale than the two control groups. The attempt group differed significantly from the psychiatric control group also on the Anger, Fatigue, and Confusion mood subscales of the POMS. It should be noted that the attempt group in the Farberow study did not differ from the control group, although the serious group did differ. Despite contrary appearance, these findings are actually consistent with those of Kochansky (1970) since his attempt group contained only subjects who had made a serious attempt.

Of all the approaches to the assessment of suicidal risk, the evaluation of feelings and mood would seem to be among those with the greatest potential pay-off. It is a test sensitive to the interaction of personality and present situation, properties essential for evaluation change, and also in screening for present motivational state. The findings of both Farberow (1950) and Kochansky (1970) suggest that any one of the three instruments described may be very useful. A special feature is their ease in repeated administrations.

SELF-CONCEPT

Farberow (1950) used the Social Personality Inventory (Maslow, 1940) as a measure of self-esteem in his study of suicide. No statistically significant differences were found in the group comparisons. The threat and the serious intention groups had scores in the expected direction.

Two other studies of self-concept in which different tests of self-concept were used shall be briefly described. Kamano and Crawford (1966) evaluated the hypothesis that suicidal patients would have lower self-satisfaction and higher self-abasement scores than controls. All the white female suicidal patients in a state hospital were screened for this study. Those who attained a minimum consistency score of 10 on the Edwards Personal Preference Scale (Edwards, 1959) were included. They were divided on the basis of seriousness of attempt into an attempt group (N = 18) and a gesture group (N = 28). A control group of 56 patients was formed; the basis was not specified. The determination of self-satisfaction was based on the patients semantic differential ratings of three concepts: least-liked self, real self, and ideal self. No significant group differences were found using these scores. The measure of self-abasement, derived from the Edwards Personal Preference Scale measure of abasement, yielded significant differences between the control groups, and each suicidal group but not between the two suicidal groups.

Wilson, Braucht, Miskimins, and Berry (1971) compared a group of severe suicide attempters, psychiatric controls, and normal controls for their response to the Miskimins Self-Goal-Other Discrepancy Scale (Miskimins, 1968). It was the only predictive study of attempted suicide found. There were 22 subjects in each group matched for sex, age, and education (and diagnosis for the psychiatric control). No data was presented for age, sex, diagnosis, nor the prediction time interval. The attempt group was found to differ from the normal control on four of five factor measures and on three measures from the psychiatric control—greater total tension, anxiety, and depression. They point out that the attempt group differed from the psychiatric controls in the degree of internal stress but not in interpersonal problems. Using discriminant analysis, they could correctly sort 65 percent of the attempt group, 63 percent of the psychiatric control group, and 63 percent of the normal control group. They note that the attempter tends to value himself less than he feels that others value him.

Self concept scales have not been widely used in research on suicidal risk. Their potential value has not been assessed. The Data on the Edwards Personal Preference Scale and the Miskimins SGO Discrepancy Scale are positive but not very exciting.

SENTENCE COMPLETION

Only one study of suicide was found that employed this method (Efron, 1960). He devised a 54 item test which he said was weighted with items that "pull" depressive thema. No other details were given regarding the selection of items and the construction of the test. He investigated the hypothesis that skilled clinicians could differentiate patients who had suicidal rumination from those who did not. This was a study of clinicians and not of the method. Four skilled clinicians were given test protocols of 54 mental patients and instructed to sort them into three categories: suicidal rumination, assaultive behavior, neither suicidal nor assaultive. They were told that among the 54 protocols there were 18 from suicidal patients, nine from assaultive patients, and 27 from neither category. The results revealed that only one clinician sorted the protocols with above chance accuracy; this clinician was 79 percent accurate on those cases about which he felt highly confident in his sorting. The overall average for correct identification of suicidal patients was 43 percent. Unfortunately no evaluation was made of an objective scoring approach to differentiating groups.

Efron (1960) also investigated in this study the number of false positives likely when clinicians sort test protocols without knowledge of the number of suicidal patients. He had the four clinicians sort 54 different protocols under such a condition and found that the mean percentage of false positive identifications was 33.

The results of this study suggest that routine clinical inspection of sentence completions would not be useful in screening or evaluation improvement.

CONCLUSION

The clinician shopping for tests with demonstrated utility in assessing suicidal risk will have to look elsewhere. The literature on the five selected tests is scanty and unsystematic; the findings only tentative and suggestive. One cannot help but wonder about the reasons for this gap in research. There have been some negative and inconsistent findings, but there also have been as many positive and suggestive results. At any rate, one should like to review some promising directions for future work with these tests despite the nagging feeling that not too many clinical researchers are disposed to investigate this problem.

The P-F study was the most widely researched of the five tests and produced meagre results. A surprising gap in this literature was the absence of an item analysis and also of a concurrent analysis of both direction and type of reaction to frustrating situations. Someone should do a study on items most sensitive to self-destructive motivation. On the Bender-Gestalt, an attempt should be made to replicate and extend the research of Sternberg and Levine (1965) on the "penetration" score. In addition, the work of Starer (1960) raises interesting possibilities which have not been explored (i.e., a comparison of an individual's reproductions under a baseline and an affective condition). On the Sentence Completion method, Efron (1960) demonstrated that clinical judgment of suicidal behavior was not good. However, an objective scoring approach was not tried. Since many clinicians routinely administer a sentence completion test, it would be relatively easy to run comparative studies of suicidal and non-suicidal groups using objective measures. The method that seemed most promising, at least intuitively, was a feeling or mood scale such as the Hildreth Feeling and Attitude Scale or the POMS. The results have been positive, and this method would seem to be sensitive to situational effects. An instrument sensitive to situational influences may be the best means of obtaining predictive clues to suicide.

Scales of self concept have been barely researched. Since the Edwards Personal Preference Scale is widely used with College populations, an attempt to replicate the data on the abasement scale would be feasible and interesting.

Future research on these tests will be more valid and useful to the extent that they are designed to investigate the specific decisions clinicians have to make regarding suicidal risk.

REFERENCES

Arneson, G., and Feldman, J.: Utilization of the Rosenzweig Picture-Frustration Test to distinguish gestures from suicidal attempts. Paper presented at the Annual Meeting of the American Association of Suicidology, Chicago, 1968.

Devries, A. G.: Definition of suicidal behaviors. *Psychological Reports, 22:* 1285-1302, 1968.

Edwards, A.: *Manual for the Edwards Personal Preference Schedule.* New York, Psychological Corp., 1959.

Efron, H. Y.: An attempt to employ a sentence completion test for the detection of psychiatric patients with suicidal ideas. *Journal of Consulting Psychology, 24:*156-160, 1960.

Esler, H. D.: An investigation of the causes of suicide in patients diagnosed schizophrenic. *Dissertation Abstracts, 26:*1169, 1965.

Farberow, N. L.: Personality patterns of suicidal mental hospital patients. *Genetic Psychology Monographs, 42:*3-79, 1950.

Farnsworth, P. R., and Ferguson, L. W.: The growth of a suicidal tendency as indicated by score changes in Bernreuter's personality inventory. *Sociometry, 1:*339-341, 1938.

Fisher, S., and Hinds, E.: The organization of hostility control in various personality structures. *Genetic Psychology Monographs, 44:*3-68, 1951.

Hildreth, H. M.: A battery of feeling and attitude scales for clinical use. *Journal of Clinical Psychology, 2:*214-221, 1946.

Kamano, D. K., and Crawford, C. S.: Self-evaluations of suicidal mental patients. *Journal of Clinical Psychology, 22:*278-279, 1966.

Kochansky, G.: Risk-taking and hedonic mood stimulation in suicide attempters. Unpublished doctoral dissertation, Boston University, 1970.

Levenson, M., and Neuringer, C.: Intropunitiveness in suicidal adolescents. *Journal of Projective Techniques and Personality Assessment, 34:*409-411, 1970.

Lester, D.: Attempts to predict suicidal risk using psychological tests. *Psychological Bulletin, 74:*1-17, 1970.

Levine, A.: Appraising ego strength from the projective test battery. *Journal of Hillside Hospital, 9:*228-240, 1960.

Maslow, A. H.: A test for dominance-feeling (self-esteem) in college women. *The Journal of Social Psychology, 12:*255-270, 1940.

McNair, D. M., and Lorr, M.: An analysis of mood in neurotics. *Journal of Abnormal and Social Psychology, 69:*620-627, 1964.

Miskimins, R. W.: *Manual: MSGO Discrepancy Scale.* Ft. Collins, Colorado, Rocky Mountain Behavioral Science Institute, 1968.

Nawas, M. M., and Worth, J. W.: Suicidal configurations in the Bender-Gestalt. *Journal of Projective Techniques, 32:*393-394, 1968.

Neuringer, C.: Methodological problems in suicide research. *Journal of Consulting Psychology, 26:*273-278, 1962.

Neuringer, C.: The Rorschach test as a research device for the identification, prediction and understanding of suicidal ideation and behavior. *Journal of Projective Techniques, 29:*71-82, 1965.

Preston, C.: Accident proneness in attempted suicide and in automobile accident victims. *Journal of Consulting Psychology, 28:*79-82, 1964.

Rosen, A.: Detection of suicidal patients. *Journal of Consulting Psychology, 18:*397-403, 1954.

Rosenzweig, S., Clarke, H. J., Garfield, M. S., and Lehndorff, A.: Scoring samples for the Rosenzweig Picture-Frustration Study. *The Journal of Psychology, 21:*45-72, 1946.

Rosenzweig, S., Fleming, E. E., and Clarke, H. J.: Revised scoring manual for the Rosenzweig—Picture Frustration Study. *The Journal of Psychology, 24:*165-208, 1947.

Starer, E.: The effects of two simultaneous cognitive and affective stimuli on a group of chronic schizophrenic patients with suicidal ideation. *Journal of Clinical Psychology, 16:*341-343, 1960.

Sternberg, D., and Levine, A.: An indicator of suicidal ideation on the Bender Visual-Motor Gestalt Test. *Journal of Projective Techniques, 29:* 377-379, 1965.

Suchman, E. A.: *Evaluative Research.* New York, Russell Sage Foundation, 1967.

Tolor, A.: The Graphomotor Techniques. *Journal of Projective Techniques & Personality Assessment, 32:*222-228, 1968.

Winfield, D. L., and Sparer, P. J.: Preliminary Report of the Rosenzweig P-F Study in Attempted Suicides. *Journal of Clinical Psychology, 9:* 379-381, 1953.

Wilson, L. T., Braucht, G. N., Miskimins, R. W., and Berry, K. L.: The severe suicide attempter and self-concept. *Journal of Clinical Psychology, 27:*307-309, 1971.

Wessman, A. E., and Ricks, D. F.: *Mood and Personality.* New York, Holt, 1966.

CHAPTER VIII

COGNITIVE CORRELATES OF SUICIDAL RISK

Marvin Levenson

ONE OF THE MOST DIFFICULT decisions for the clinician to make is the assessment of suicidal risk. The potential repercussions for the client, clinician, and community are wide ranging in that such decisions involve issues of life and death, responsibility, and the mobilization of resources. How is this most vital of decisions to be made? For the moment the answer does not appear to lie in the vast array of clinical instruments available to the psychologist. Lester's (1970) review of the literature systematically highlighted the inadequacies of clinical instruments such as the Rorschach, TAT, and MMPI, etc., in accurately assessing suicidal risk. This raises the need for the development of new and unique assessment techniques. One such attempt is the utilization of admission and personal history data. It is in the spirit of looking for new methods of assessment that the ideas in this paper are put forth. This new means of assessment emanates from the cognitive approach to suicide and is based on the belief that suicidal phenomenon can best be understood by examining the cognitive characteristics of suicidal individuals. Briefly, the approach focuses on the thinking processes and conceptualizes the suicidal person as being confused and incorrect in his logic (Shneidman, 1957) as well as being rigid, inflexible, and dichotomous in his thinking (Neuringer, 1961, 1964a). Thus the suicidal person is seen as possessing some unique thinking style or certain cognitive characteristics which diminish his ability to find viable solutions to life's problems and to diminish his capacity to cope with the stresses of life. It is possible that these cognitive characteristics so profoundly affect the suicidal person's view of the world and his ability to cope with it that when he is placed in a state of disequilibrium or crisis, he does not have the necessary coping or cognitive problem solving processes to reorient his relationships to his environment or to adequately cope with the source of stress. If the potentially suicidal person can only know his world in a very limited way, he is very poorly prepared to cope with the vagaries of an ever changing environment. Because of this he is doomed to extinction unless he receives external support and intervention. What is basic here is the belief that cognition is a vital determinant in suicidal behavior. Although this notion has received relatively little attention, there has been an increasing number of studies (Levenson and Neuringer, 1971; Neuringer, 1961, 1964a, and 1967; Neuringer and Littieri, 1971; and Shneidman, 1957) which indicate that the suicidal individual possesses unique cognitive characteristics. From this, one might speculate that suicide as a problem solving behavior is likely to occur when an individual's cognitive capacities are so impoverished that he is unable to cope with his problem. At this point it might be prudent to examine this point of view and present some of the more important research in this area in the hope that one may be able to devise assessment techniques based on this approach. The cognitive approach to suicide has shown suicidal individuals to be characterized by thinking processes which are rigid and inflexible (Binswanger, 1958; Cavan, 1928; Dublin and Bunzel, 1933; Levenson and Neuringer, 1971; Muhl, 1927; Neuringer, 1964a, 1964b; and Shneidman, 1957) and dichotomous (Brockhaus, 1922; Cavan, 1926; Farrar, 1951; Neuringer, 1961 and 1967; and Westcott, 1885) as well as fostering fallacious assumptions in their patterns of logic (Shneidman, 1957).

The view that suicidal individuals can be characterized as thinking in a rigid and inflexible manner is one which has received much attention from both a theoretical and empirical point of view (Binswanger, 1958; Cavan, 1928; Dublin and Bunzel, 1933; Levenson and Neuringer, 1971; Muhl, 1927; Neuringer, 1964a; and Shneidman, 1957). One of the basic tenets of suicidology is that suicidal individuals are very rigid and inflexible (Binswanger, 1938; Cavan, 1928; Dublin and Bunzel, 1933; Menninger, 1938; and Shneidman, 1957, 1961). These theorists have generally felt that the suicidal person, as a result of his very rigid and inflexible manner of thinking, is restricted in his ability to develop new or alternative solutions to his immediate and pressing emotional problems. As a result he feels very helpless and hopeless because he is unable to escape from a current intolerable situation except through death. Although this notion has been a widely accepted clinical observation, it remained for Neuringer (1964a) to empirically demonstrate that rigidity is present to a significantly greater extent in suicidal individuals than in other emotionally disturbed and normal groups. It has only been within the last decade that these types of variables have begun to be empirically investigated. Neuringer (1961) was the first to systematically examine dichotomous thinking in suicidal individuals. In exploring this variable to determine if it is a distinguishing characteristic of suicidal individuals, he used three groups of subjects comprised of serious suicide attempters, nonsuicidal psychiatric subjects, and normal subjects respectively. In order to measure dichotomous thinking, he had his subjects rate various concepts on the evaluative factor of Osgood's Semantic Differential Scale (1957). His results indicated that suicidal individuals were significantly more dichotomous on rated concepts than normals, but they did not differ significantly from nonsuicidal psychiatric patients. From these results Neuringer concluded that dichotomous evaluative thinking is a characteristic of emotionally disturbed people but not a unique characteristic of suicidal individuals. However, in a more recent study (Neuringer, 1967) utilizing the same design as above, Neuringer was able to demonstrate that suicide attempters were significantly more dichotomous on the evaluative as well as the activity and potency factors of the semantic differential than their non-suicidal peers when lethality was taken into account.

More recent research (Levenson, 1972) has focused on the suicidal individual's narrowed thinking or narrowed range of conceptualization. The suicidal person is very often clinically perceived as being unable to look at his environment in a broad manner. Consequently, his view of the world is narrow to the extent that he probably has difficulty coping with problem situations which require the generation of new and different alternatives to his problems. In brief, he conceptualizes within very limited and restricted bounds. In an attempt to empirically examine this quality in suicidal individuals, three groups of subjects consisting of serious suicide attempters (S), non-suicidal psychiatric patients (P), and normal subjects (N) were tested. Each group of subjects was administered the Unusual Uses Test (Getzel and Jackson, 1962) and the Word Association Test (Getzel and Jackson, 1962). The Unusual Uses Test consisted of five common objects –bricks, pencils, paper clips, toothpicks, and newspaper. The subjects were instructed to write down as many different uses for each object as they could, with the test then being scored for the number of different uses for each item. The Word Association Test is comprised of 25 words that have more than one meaning (e.g. arm). Each subject was required to write down as many meanings for each word as he could. The test was then scored for the number of different meanings used.

The range of scores for all subjects on the Unusual Uses Test was from 5 to 32. The means and standard deviations for each group are presented in Table VIII-I.

In addition, an analysis of variance was performed on the data to determine if there were any significant differences between the three groups. Table VIII-II presents these results.

The F ratio of 10.98 for 2 and 45 degrees of freedom showed that there were significant differences between the groups beyond the .01 level. In order to assess the differences between the means, Tukey's method (1949) was used. It revealed that the S group scored significantly lower than the P group at the .01 level and significantly lower than the N group at the .01 level. Furthermore,

TABLE VIII-I

MEAN SCORES AND ACCOMPANING STANDARD DEVIATIONS ON THE UNUSUAL USES TEST FOR THE PSYCHIATRIC SUICIDE ATTEMPTER (S), PSYCHIATRIC NON-SUICIDE ATTEMPTER (P), AND NORMAL (N) GROUPS

	S	*P*	*N*
Mean	10.25	16.81	20.19
S.D.	4.51	7.21	6.26

TABLE VIII-II

ANALYSIS OF VARIANCE OF SCORES ON THE UNUSUAL USES TEST
FOR THE PSYCHIATRIC SUICIDE ATTEMPTER (S), PSYCHIATRIC
NON-SUICIDE ATTEMPTER (P), AND NORMAL (N) GROUP

Source	df	MS	F
Between	2	408.56	10.98**
Within	45	37.20	
Total	47		

** $p < .01$

the P group scored significantly lower than the N group at the .05 level.

Turning to the Word Association Test, it was found that the range of scores for all subjects in the study was from 6 to 134. The means and standard deviations for each group are presented in Table VIII-III.

Similarly an analysis of variance was performed on the data (Table VIII-IV) which resulted in an F ratio of 9.11 which was found to be significant beyond the .01 level.

A closer examination of the results (Tukey, 1949) showed the S group to have scored significantly lower than the P group (beyond the .05 level) and was significantly lower than the N group (beyond the .01 level). The P group was also found to be significantly lower than the N group (beyond the .05 level).

If indeed these tests measure a person's ability to shift frames of reference within an organized structure as well as an ability to use the environment in a broad and flexible manner (Getzel and Jackson, 1962), the S group can be characterized by a cognitive rigidity, one in which the world is viewed as very fixed in that it

TABLE VIII-III

MEAN SCORES AND ACCOMPANYING STANDARD DEVIATIONS
ON THE WORD ASSOCIATION TEST FOR THE PSYCHIATRIC
SUICIDE ATTEMTPER (S), PSYCHIATRIC NON-SUICIDE
ATTEMPTER (P), AND NORMAL (N) GROUPS

	S	P	N
Means	38.37	54.38	70.94
S.D.	12.34	30.60	17.54

TABLE VIII-IV

ANALYSIS OF VARIANCE OF SCORES ON THE WORD ASSOCIATION
TEST FOR THE PSYCHIATRIC SUICIDE ATTEMPTER (S),
PSYCHIATRIC NON-SUICIDE ATTEMPTER (P), AND
NORMAL (N) GROUPS

Source	df	MS	F
Between	2	4,241.69	9.11*
Within	45	467.57	
Total	47		

* p < .01

cannot be readily restructured. For the suicidal person, the world
seems to be one in which he views things in a very limited and
stereotypic manner. If one assumes that this is a pervasive cognitive characteristic, one is then faced with the view of the suicidal
person as not possessing a certain diversity or ability to look at
things in a new light. Implied here is that his view of the world is
very stereotyped and limited, with little chance of coping with
problems except in a very set manner. This is consistent with the
reports of Binswanger, 1958; Cavan, 1928; Dublin and Bunzel,
1933; Levenson and Neuringer, 1971; Muhl, 1927; Neuringer,
1964; and Shneidman, 1957, who feel that the suicidal person, because of his very rigid and inflexible manner of thinking, is restricted in his ability to develop new or alternative solutions to his
immediate and pressing emotional problems. Thus when he is confronted with a crisis situation in which he is placed into a state of
disequilibrium, he has few avenues or alternatives for placing himself in a balanced state. In a real sense he has come to the end of
his rope. The expressed feeling of "I don't know what to do" or
"I can't see any other solution" is probably a very accurate appraisal in terms of the individual's own resources. For him the
number of response alternatives that he can produce is limited,
and this perhaps reduces the chances of his reaching an acceptable
and viable solution.

As an extension of prior work (Neuringer, 1967), the current
finding would seem to suggest that these cognitive processes in
suicidal individuals are not simply limited to or operative only
along an affective dimension, but rather seems to be representative

of a general cognitive organization or cognitive style. Add to this the debilitating aspects of stress on cognitive processes in general and it is not difficult to conceptualize how the suicidal choice is seized upon as a vehicle of escape from a dismal, despairing, and hopeless situation.

What may be emerging is a tripartite model of cognition as it relates to psychopathology in general and suicide in particular. It may be that as one's range of conceptualization becomes narrowed, a psychopathological level is reached followed by a suicidal level at a higher point. If this is the case it would seem that it would be fruitful to explore this variable as a measure for predicting suicidal behavior. One possibility is that there may be some threshold level beyond which the likelihood of suicidal behavior would be very high. It would seem that assessment techniques based on this premise would hold great promise.

Shneidman (1957) has presented the most comprehensive approach of relating different types of logic to suicide. Within his scheme he has four different types of logic. The first of these is *catalogic* which is destructive in that it confuses the self as experienced by the self, with the self as experienced by others. Individuals who feel lonely, helpless, fearful, and pessimistic about making meaningful personal relationships are found in this group and Shneidman calls their act referred suicide. The second kind of logic is *normal logic* which follows the principles of Aristotelian logic. The suicidal person with this type of logic is usually older, widowed, or in physical pain. This form of death has been referred to as surcease suicide in which the individual wishes for the surcease from pain that death can afford. The third kind of logic is *contaminated logic* in which the logical or semantic error is in the emphasis on the self as experienced by others. This is found among individuals whose beliefs allow them to look at suicide as a transition to another life. This has been associated with cultural suicides in which the concept of death plays a primary role. The final type of logic is *paleologic* in which logical identifications are made in terms of attributes of the predicates rather than of the subjects. This form of death is referred to as psychotic suicide in which the individual is delusional and/or hallucinatory.

Although researchers in suicide have looked at various cognitive characteristics of suicidal individuals (Neuringer, 1961, 1964a, 1967; Neuringer and Littieri, 1971; Shneidman, 1957), no study as of yet has been carried out to explore the general perceptual-cognitive style of suicidal persons (Farberow, 1969). Research has tended to be piecemeal in looking at various cognitive characteristics (e.g., rigidity, dichotomous thinking, etc.) rather than studying the overall cognitive style of suicidal individuals. However, some research (Levenson and Neuringer, 1971) has indicated that suicidal individuals have difficulty in problem solving.

The exploration of characteristic, self-consistent ways of functioning that people exhibit in their perceptual and intellectual behavior (i.e., cognitive style) has received much attention in this century (Asch and Witkin, 1948; Bauman, 1951; Gibson and Mowrer, 1938; Wertheimer, 1912; Witkin, 1950; Witkin, Lewis, Hertzman, Machover, Mussiner, and Wapner, 1954; Witkin, Dyk, Faterson, Goodenough, and Karp, 1962). Perhaps the most prolific worker in this field has been Witkin who, in using a conceptual framework derived from Gestalt Psychology, has examined cognitive styles by focusing on perceptual processes and space orientation responses of individuals. The basic construct for Witkin (1954) has been field dependence which he defines as the extent to which a person in making his determinations adheres to the axes of the visual field or resists the influence of the field, through reference to sensations of the body. Thus a person with this mode of perception is strongly controlled by the overall organization of the field with its parts experienced as "fused." The converse of this is the field independent mode of perception in which parts of the field are experienced as discrete from the organized background. These particular styles are not just restricted to an individual's perceptions but also express themselves in intellectual activities as well. Thus field dependent individuals do less well in problem solving situations which require the isolation of necessary parts from the context in which they are presented (Witkin et al., 1962). In addition, field dependence has also been found to be related to rigidity (Fenechel, 1958; Guetzkon, 1947) and impulsivity (Witkin et al., 1962). These latter factors have been shown to be related to suicidal behavior through a long line of research (Binswanger, 1938; Cavan, 1928; Dublin and Bunzel, 1933;

Menninger, 1938; Shneidman, 1957 and 1961; Levenson and
Neuringer, 1971; Muhl, 1927; and Neuringer, 1964a) which
views suicidal behavior as more prevalent in individuals who are
rigid and inflexible and who are unable to adjust or shift their
thinking to meet the demands of a changing environment. As a result of this rigid way of thinking, the suicidal individual is unable to develop alternative solutions for dealing with his problems.
When an individual who has this particular mode of thinking is
placed in an intolerable situation in which he feels helpless, he
may see no way to escape except by death. Various studies and
clinical descriptions (e.g., Jacobziner, 1960; Kessel, 1967; and
Lourie, 1966) have characterized the suicidal person as being
more impulsive than his nonsuicidal peers. The thrust of the research in this area is that the suicidal person has less control over
his fantasies and thoughts, a condition that puts him at the mercy
of his inner impulses and which sometimes results in self-destructive actions. Thus the suicidal person has relatively poor impulse
control, and when faced with the pressures of the moment he may
suddenly react to a stressful situation by engaging in suicidal behavior.

In an attempt to measure this variable, the Rod and Frame Test
(Witkin, Lewis, Hertzman, Machover, Mussiner, and Wapner,
1954), which is a measure of one's spatial orientation or level of
field dependence, was administered to three groups (suicidal, psychiatric nonsuicidal, and non-patient). The resulting means and
standard deviations are presented in Table VIII-V.

An analysis of variance on the data produced an *F* ratio of
12.59 (See Table VIII-VI) which was found to be significant beyond the .01 level. A closer investigation of the groups (Tukey,

TABLE VII-V

MEAN SCORES AND ACCOMPANYING STANDARD DEVIATIONS ON
THE ROD AND FRAME TEST FOR THE PSYCHIATRIC SUICIDE
ATTEMPTER (S), PSYCHIATRIC NON-SUICIDE ATTEMPTER
(P), AND NORMAL (N) GROUPS

	S	P	N
Means	15.33	6.32	5.98
S.D.	9.28	3.23	3.19

TABLE VIII-VI

ANALYSIS OF VARIANCE OF SCORES ON THE ROD AND FRAME
TEST FOR THE PSYCHIATRIC SUICIDE ATTEMPTER (S),
PSYCHIATRIC NON-SUICIDE ATTEMPTER (P), AND
NORMAL (N) GROUPS

Source	df	MS	F
Between	2	481.59	12.59*
Within	45	35.57	
Total	47		

*p < .01

1949) showed the S group to be significantly different than the P and N groups at the .01 level.

These findings suggest the emergence of a group of serious suicide attempters with a cognitive style which furnishes them with a view of the world which is highly undifferentiated, inarticulate, and global. Perception for them is controlled by the overall organization of the field as well as experiencing parts of it as being fused. Thus one may think of the field dependent person as locked into his environment in that his actions for the most part are dependent on the environment maintaining a certain stability in order for him to function optimally. When environmental stability breaks down as it does in time of acute stress or crisis, he may not have the necessary wherewithal to look within himself for the solution. It is quite conceivable that this could be the fatal flaw in predisposing a person to making the suicidal choice. If such a person is confronted with a world that requires him to make choices, decisions, find solutions to problems, adequately cope with stress and the nuances of life, etc., and at a very fundamental level he does not have the inner resources, then he may seize upon suicide as the only viable choice. This would be consistent with viewing the suicidal act as problem solving behavior which is geared towards coping with highly emotionally laden conflict or crisis. The suicidal solution becomes highly feasible because the individual's problem solving abilities are not up to dealing with the crisis situation. Thus the potentially suicidal person, once placed in a state of crisis or disequilibrium, may not have the necessary coping or cognitive problem solving processes to reorient his relationship to his environment in order to actively cope with the source of stress. This would be consistent with the characterization of the suicidal person as possessing thinking processes which are dichotomous, rigid, and inflexible. These factors contribute to his ambivalance and inability to develop alternative solutions to deal with his problems. However, it should be pointed out that not all field dependent individuals are overtly suicidal. A case in point is the alcoholic. A common finding (Chess, 1969; Goldstein and Chotlos, 1965, 1966; and Klappersack, 1968) is that alcoholics as a group tend to be field dependent, yet what is of interest is that theorists (e.g., Menninger, 1938) have viewed the alcoholic as being self-destructive but in a very slow and deliberate manner. At this point one wonders if it is not the use of alcohol which prevents the alcoholic from seeking a quick demise. Another observation is that the S group has been found to exhibit a higher degree of field dependency than any of the alcoholic groups reported in the studies cited above. Perhaps one could discover some absolute degree of field dependency which is suicidogenic. Self-destructive people may have reached a point at which the environment can give them no more support or clues for dealing with their difficulties, and at this point they are lost and suicide is seen as the only way of coping.

One final means of assessment to be presented here is the measurement of diminished problem solving capacity in suicidal individuals (Levenson and Neuringer, 1971). Various writers have attempted to link self-destructive behavior to diminished problem solving capacity (Binswanger, 1958; Cavan, 1928; Dublin and Bunzel, 1933; Menninger, 1938; Neuringer, 1964; Shneidman, 1957, 1961, 1969). It is generally felt that the suicidal individual, because of either temporary or permanent cognitive deficiencies, finds it difficult to generate new or alternative solutions to debilitating emotional problems. Such constricted problem solving ability may be lethal since the person could well feel that there is no way out of an anxiety-laden situation except as escape into death. In a study using the WAIS Arithmetic Subtest and the Rokeach Map Test, Levenson and Neuringer (1971) found that suicidal adolescents had diminished problem solving capacity as compared to their nonsuicidal peers.

The notion that cognition is a vital determinant in suicidal behavior is one which has been receiving increasing support (Levenson and Neuringer, 1971; Neuringer, 1961, 1964, 1967; Neuringer and Littieri, 1971; and Shneidman, 1957). What appears to be emerging is that there are certain cognitive characteristics or a particular cognitive style which is more prevalent among individuals who engage in suicidal behavior than others who do not. Granted, these characteristics are not solely restricted to suicidal individuals but are found also in other psychopathological conditions and to lesser degrees in normal populations. The vital difference here may be one of degree in that as these characteristics become more extreme, the possibility of self-destructive behavior increases. In a like manner, within self-destructive individuals, as these processes become more accentuated, lethality increases. Theoretically one may be moving toward an assessment model which measures suicidal risk in terms of the prevalence and degree of these cognitive processes. It may be that as the cognitive structure becomes increasingly restricted, the possibility of suicidal behavior (as a coping or problem solving strategy) may increase. Given this particular cognitive structure, what are the necessary ingredients which ultimately culminate in the suicidal act? Assuming that this cognitive structure is the result of a developmental history, at what point does the person become suicidal? Is it the result of stress or of complex, multifaceted forces which interact with these cognitive processes in a unique fashion? These are issues that future research should deal with. For the moment it seems that cognition is a variable which is of importance in better understanding the suicidal phenomenon. It is felt that suicidal behavior is more likely in those individuals who are characterized by cognitive capacities that are so impoverished that the person cannot intellectually cope with the stress of his life. It is almost as if the cognitive factors are analogous to the loaded gun, but what is unknown is what exactly causes it to fire.

REFERENCES

Asch, S. E., and Witkin, H. A.: Studies in space orientation. *Journal of Experimental Psychology, 38:*325-337, 1948.

Bauman, G.: The stability of the individual's mode of perception, and of perception-personality relationships. Unpublished doctoral dissertation, New York University, 1951.

Binswanger, L.: The case of Ellen West. In May, R., Angel, E., and Ellenberger, H. F. (Eds.): *Existence*. New York, Basic Books, 1958.

Brockhaus, A. T.: Zur psychologie des selbstmordes der psychopathem. *Mschr. Kriminal-psychologie, 13:*290, 1922.

Cavan, R.: *Suicide*. Chicago, University of Chicago Press, 1928.

Chess, S.: The relationship between arousal level and rod and frame performance. Unpublished doctoral dissertation, University of Kansas, 1963.

Dublin, L. I., and Bunzel, B.: *To Be or Not To Be*. New York, Smith & Hass, 1933.

Farberow, N. L.: *Bibliography on Suicide*. Washington, D.C., Government Printing Office, 1969.

Farrar, C. B.: Suicide. *Journal of Clinical and Experimental Psychopathology, 12:*79-88, 1951.

Fenechel, G. H.: Cognitive rigidity as a behavioral variable manifested in intellectual and perceptual tasks by an outpatient population. Unpublished doctoral dissertation, New York University, 1958.

Getzel, J. W., and Jackson, P. W.: *Creativity and Intelligence*. New York, Wiley, 1962.

Gibson, J. J., and Mowrer, O. H.: Determinants of the perceived vertical and horizontal. *Psychological Review, 45:*300-323, 1938.

Goldstein, G., and Chotlos, J.: Dependency and brain damage in alcoholics. *Perception and Motor Skills, 21:*135-150, 1965.

Guetzkow, H.: An analysis of the operation of set in problem solving behavior. Unpublished doctoral dissertation, University of Michigan, 1947.

Jacobziner, H.: Attempted suicide in children. *Journal of Pediatrics, 56:* 519-525, 1960.

Klappersack, B.: Sources of field dependence. Unpublished doctoral dissertation, University of Kansas, 1968.

Lester, D.: Attempts to predict suicidal risk using psychological tests. *Psychological Bulletin, 74:*1-16, 1970.

Levenson, M.: Cognitive and perceptual factors in suicidal individuals. Unpublished doctoral dissertation, University of Kansas, 1972.

Levenson, M., and Neuringer, C.: Intropunitiveness in suicidal adolescents. *Journal of Projective Techniques and Personality Assessment, 34:*409-411, 1970.

Lourie, R. S.: Clinical studies of attempted suicide in childhood. *Clinical Proceedings in Children's Hospital of the District of Columbia, 22:*163-173, 1966.

Menninger, K.: *Man Against Himself*. New York, Harcourt, Brace & World, 1938.

Muhl, A. M.: America's greatest suicide problem: A study of over 500 cases in San Diego. *Psychoanalytic Review, 14:*317-325, 1927.

Neuringer, C.: Dichotomous evaluations in suicidal individuals. *Journal of Consulting Psychology, 25:*445-449, 1961.

Neuringer, C.: Rigid thinking in suicidal individuals. *Journal of Consulting Psychology, 28:*54-58, 1964a.

Neuringer, C.: Reaction to interpersonal crisis in suicidal individuals. *Journal of General Psychology, 71:*47-55, 1964b.

Neuringer, C.: The cognitive organization of meaning in suicidal individuals. *Journal of General Psychology, 76:*91-100, 1967.

Neuringer, C., and Littieri, D.: Affect, attitude, and cognition in suicidal persons. *Journal of Life Threatening Behaviors, 1:*106-124, 1971.

Osgood, C. E., Suci, G. J., and Tannebaum, P. H.: *The Measurement of Meaning.* Urbana, University of Illinois Press, 1957.

Shneidman, E. S.: The logic of suicide. In Shneidman, E. S., and Farberow, N. L. (Eds.): *Clues to Suicide.* New York, McGraw-Hill, 1957.

Shneidman, E. S., and Farberow, N. L.: *The Cry for Help.* New York, McGraw-Hill, 1961.

Shneidman, E. S.: *On the Nature of Suicide.* San Francisco, Jossey-Bass, 1969, pg. 9.

Speigel, D. E., and Neuringer, C.: Role of dread in suicidal behavior. *Journal of Abnormal and Social Psychology, 66:*507-511, 1963.

Tukey, J. W.: Comparing individual means of the analysis of variance. *Biometrics, 5:*99-114, 1949.

Wertheimer, M.: Experimentelle studien uber das Seben von Bewlgung. *Z. Psychology, 61:*161-265, 1912.

Westcott, W. W.: *Suicide: Its History, Literature, Jurisprudence, Causation, and Prevention.* London, 1885.

Witkin, H. A.: Perception of the upright when the direction of the force acting upon the body is changed. *Journal of Experimental Psychology, 40:*93-106, 1950.

Witkin, H. A., Lewis, H. B., Hertzman, M., Machover, K., Meisner, P. B., and Wapner, S.: *Personality Through Perception.* New York, Harper, 1954.

Witkin, H. A., Dyk, R. B., Faterson, H. R., Goodenough, D. R., and Karp, S. A.: *Psychological Differentiation.* New York, Wiley & Sons, 1962.

CHAPTER IX

CLINICAL AND SOCIAL PREDICTORS OF REPEATED ATTEMPTED SUICIDE: A MULTIVARIATE ANALYSIS[1, 2]

CHRISTOPHER BAGLEY AND STEVEN GREER

ALTHOUGH THE SUICIDE RATE in England and Wales is declining (Fox, 1970), the rate of parasuicide is increasing rapidly (Aitken et al., 1969; Stanley, 1969; Bagley, 1970). There is an obvious clinical interest in knowing the extent to which medical and other agencies can prevent such behavior, or its repetition, and in being able to predict high risk individuals. Progress in the evaluation of the prevention agencies has been reviewed by Bagley (1971), and in the field of prediction a number of studies have been published using British material. These studies usually take the form of an examination of the traits and characteristics of a group of completed or attempted suicides, and follow-up studies are less common (W.H.O., 1968). The present study, so far as we can discover, is the first follow-up study which includes patients who were not seen by a psychiatrist at the time of their key attempt.

The aims of our research design were:

1. To ascertain the effects of psychiatric intervention in parasuicide;

2. To identify clinical and social predictors of repeated parasuicide;

---

1. Reprinted from the *Brit. J. Psychiat.*, *119*:515-521, 1971, by permission of the author and the Royal College of Psychiatrists.

2. In the present study we use the terms "parasuicide" and "attempted suicide" synonymously. See, however, Kreitman et al., *Brit. J. Psychiat.*, *116*:465-73, 1969, and the subsequent correspondence in this *Journal* on the meaning and use of these terms.

3. To delineate the characteristics of responders and non-responders to psychiatric treatment.

With these aims in view we carried out a follow-up study of 204 patients admitted to a casualty department. We have shown in a previous paper (Greer and Bagley, 1971) that psychiatric treatment is associated with a significant fall in the incidence of subsequent parasuicide. In the present paper we report results pertaining to the identification of factors which predict repeated parasuicide; and the identification of patients who repeat an attempt despite psychiatric treatment.

THE PREDICTION OF PARASUICIDE

Lester (1970) has reviewed studies which used psychological tests to predict suicidal risk and concludes that such tests have not been fruitful. He suggests that what is needed for prediction is a battery of demographic and clinical variables. Scales for the prediction of repeated attempted suicide, based on the study of Edinburgh patients, have been constructed by Buglass and McCulloch (1970). This study of 511 patients, 25 percent of whom repeated a suicide attempt, indicated that the best predictive factors for men were: violence in key relationships, a diagnosis of alcoholism, and having taken alcohol at the time of the act. The best predictive factors for women were: previous suicide attempt, previous psychiatric treatment; psychopathy; drug addiction; four or more dwelling changes in the past five years; father absent when patient less than 10; and mother absent when patient less than 10. The variables identified as predicting risk successfully identified 83 percent of repeaters within a year of the key attempt.

An earlier study by Kessel and McCulloch (1966) of these same 511 patients found that 29 percent had repeated the attempt within a year of initial admission. Significantly more repeaters had a marriage broken by death or desertion, and had a diagnosis of psychopathic personality disorder. The most prone to repeat, these authors concluded, were young adults with poor work records and unstable living circumstances, often with an emphasis on alcoholism and addiction. Greer and Lee (1967) followed up 52 patients admitted to King's College Hospital, London, after a suicide attempt which seriously endangered life and found that the medical danger bore no relationship to subsequent outcome, a conclusion similar to that of Kessel and McCulloch (1966). A study of 378 parasuicides in an epidemiological study in South London (Bagley, 1970) found that repeaters had significantly less contact with psychiatric services in the three months following the key attempt, and were significantly more likely to be either seriously depressed or to have a diagnosis of antisocial personality than nonrepeaters.

McDowall and his colleagues (1968) examined factors which might predict suicide in depressed patients admitted to hospital, and compared 37 patients who subsequently killed themselves with 37 controls. The successful predictive items for both men and women were: previous attempted suicide; hysterical personality; and being widowed, separated, or divorced. The cut-off points suggested by the authors indicate that the variables identified could successfully predict suicide in 70 percent of the cases studied.

METHODS

A search was made of the records of the 25,000 patients admitted to the Casualty Department of King's College Hospital, London, in the first six months of 1968; 211 cases of parasuicide were located. It was found that despite official hospital policy, 22 percent of these patients had not been referred to a psychiatrist at the time of the attempt. The main reason for this was that the attending doctor had discharged the patient when he was medically recovered without making such a referral; a second reason was that the patient had discharged himself before such a referral could be made, or had refused such a referral.

Patients were followed up retrospectively 12 to 24 months after the key attempt, the mean follow-up period being 18 months for each group. Detailed clinical and social data were obtained by means of structured interviews with patients, and where possible, from relatives as well as from hospital records. The seriousness of the suicidal attempts was rated according to Kessel's Index of Endangering Life (1966) in terms of (1) the medical consequences (rated: potentially lethal; some danger; no danger), and (2) the patient's action in avoiding or ensuring discovery (rated: tried to avoid discovery, action ambivalent or no positive action, ensured discovery).

RESULTS

Of the original sample, 204 patients (97%) were traced. A study of repeat rates (Greer and Bagley, 1971) indicated that 53 patients (26%) had made a further attempt in the follow-up period, while a further four patients (2%) had killed themselves, giving an overall repeat rate of 28 percent. Four patients had died of natural causes.

The subjects were divided into an untreated group of 44 patients; a briefly treated group (psychiatric contact limited to a maximum of two interviews) of 74 patients; and a more prolonged psychiatric treatment group of 87 patients. Of the untreated patients 39 percent had made a repeat attempt, compared with 26 percent of the briefly treated and 20 percent of the patients receiving more prolonged treatment. Two of the suicides occurred in the untreated group, and one each in the two treatment groups. The differences in repeat rate between the untreated group and the group receiving prolonged psychiatric treatment are statistically significant.

Thirty clinical and social variables were measured, and the possible interrelationships between the effects of treatment and the effects of other variables are examined below. We present, first of all, the relationship between psychiatric diagnosis and outcome (Table IX-I).

It will be seen that the proportion repeating declines with treatment in most diagnoses, and to a significant extent in the case of depressive reactions. The most notable exception is the diagnosis of antisocial personality and addiction, which does not respond to the amount of psychiatric treatment. In the multiple regression analyses which follow, diagnosis has been rated on a three-point scale: primary diagnosis; secondary diagnosis; and absent.

A multiple regression analysis of the data has been carried out (Table IX-II) using 29 social and clinical variables to predict the remaining variable, viz. subsequent suicidal behavior. The technique of multiple regression (described by Hope, 1968) analyses step by step the correlation of each variable with the dependent

TABLE IX-I

OUTCOME ACCORDING TO DIAGNOSIS AND TREATMENT

	None		Psychiatric Treatment Brief Only		More Prolonged		Total*	
	Total No.	% S.A.	Total No.	% S.A.	Total No.	% S.A.	No.	% S.A.†
Personality and neurotic disorders	13	54	24	38	18	22 + S‡	55	36
Antisocial personality, alcoholism, drug dependence	7	57 + S	12	50 + S	12	50	31	52
Affective psychosis	—	—	1	—	21	15	22	14
Depressive reaction	11	27	22	9	19	—	52	10
Situational disturbance	8	13	11	9	5	20	24	12.5
Schizophrenia	1	(100)	—	—	9	(22)	10	(30)
Organic brain disorder	1	(100)	1	(100)	2	(50)	4	(75)

* Diagnosis unknown (6 patients) excluded.
† % who made further suicidal attempts; ‡: suicide.
Percentages in brackets should be treated with caution because of the small numbers involved.
Effect of Treatment on Outcome
Depressive reaction: No treatment v. All treatment $t = 2.24 \pm .1$, p $< .05$
            No treatment v. More prolonged $t = 2.39 \pm .1$, p $< .025$
Other diagnoses: No significant differences.

TABLE IX-II

Variable	Original r With Further Attempt	r With Further Attempt After m.r.	t
Amount of psychiatric management of key attempt ..	−.24	−.25	3.58
Antisocial personality, alcoholism or drug dependence	.29	.22	3.16
Diagnosis of organic brain disorder	.20	.21	2.91
Previous suicide attempt	.25	.21	2.91
Separated or divorced	.13	.18	2.48
Diagnosis of hysterical personality	.16	.14	1.95
Occupational class (high to low)	.03	−.14	1.94
Variables not in the regression set			
Acute situational reaction	−.14	−.12	1.73
Psychiatric treatment sometime after the key attempt	−.18	−.10	1.45
Diagnosis of moderate depression	−.23	−.10	1.34
Sex of patient (male)	.14	.08	1.10
Failed to keep psychiatric appointment after key attempt	.15	.08	1.08
Born of European parents outside U.K.	−.02	−.08	1.08
Single	−.05	−.07	1.00
Married	−.02	.07	0.99
Born in U.K.	−.03	−.06	0.88
Hospitalized after key attempt	.13	.06	0.88
Diagnosis of schizophrenia	.01	.06	0.87
Age	.07	.06	0.85
Diagnosis of psychotic depression	−.09	−.06	0.84
Amount of action taken to conceal key attempt	.04	.06	0.78
Born in coloured Commonwealth	.02	.05	0.75
Widowed	−.09	−.05	0.70
Medical seriousness of suicide attempt	.05	.03	0.47
Diagnosis of personality or neurotic disorder	.04	.03	0.35
Discharged self against medical advice	.11	.03	0.35
Method (drugs/mixed/gas or cutting or hanging) ..	.05	.02	0.28
Index of seriousness of attempt	.04	.02	0.25
Length of follow up	−.03	−.01	0.11
Multiple correlation with further suicide attempt (using variables (1)-(7) which make up the regression set)	—	.504	—

variable. At each step an additional variable is included in the regression analysis, and the correlation among the predictor variables are partialled out before calculating the correlation with the dependent variable. The cut-off point (when the regression analysis is terminated) was chosen at the point where the correlation between the predictor and the dependent variable fell below the 5 percent level.

Seven variables have been included in the regression set. The variable with the strongest predictive power is the amount of psychiatric management during the key attempt, the correlation of this item with repeated attempt increasing from −.24 to −.25 after controlling on all other variables.

Is this relationship between psychiatric treatment and good outcome in parasuicide a causal one? It cannot be explained by the failure of patients who subsequently repeat an attempt to keep a psychiatric appointment, nor by the fact of such patients discharging themselves from hospital against medical advice, nor by the fact of hospitalization after the key attempt, nor by the index of seriousness of the attempt; since all these factors have been controlled in the regression analysis. One possibility which we have not directly controlled for is that casualty officers might tend to discharge without referral to a psychiatrist those patients who were unpleasant and aggressive. If this were so, however, we would expect patients with antisocial personality disorders to be particularly likely to be discharged without psychiatric referral. This is not in fact the case, the correlation between such a diagnosis and the amount of treatment being close to zero. Our conclusion is that the relationship between psychiatric treatment and a relatively favorable outcome is a real one.

Three of the diagnostic categories considered—antisocial personality, organic brain disorder, and hysterical personality—were related to adverse outcome. It should be mentioned that the correlation for organic brain disorder is based on eight cases only (primary or secondary diagnosis). Six of these patients made a further attempt. Occupational class made the interesting transformation from being a very weak predictor to a significantly inverse predictor of parasuicide. This indicates that when the effect of other variables is taken into account, members of Registrar General's social classes III, II, and I (i.e., skilled, clerical and professional classes) are more likely to repeat. The multiple correlation based on the seven variables in the regression set is .504.

Our next consideration is the extent to which clinical and social variables can predict repeated parasuicide within the treatment categories, and to see in particular what kinds of patients repeat despite the psychiatric treatment they receive. The results of the three multiple regression analyses for the untreated, briefly treated, and prolonged treatment groups are presented in Tables IX-III to IX-V. Because of the reduced N, correlations which have a t value of 1.5 and above (approximately the 1 in 10 level of probability) have been included in the regression set.

It will be seen at once that the size of the correlations in these separate regression analyses has markedly increased in comparison with the analysis (Table IX-II) which included all three treatment categories together. It looks as if these three categories are to some extent phenomenologically different groups. In the untreated group the strongest correlation with a repeated attempt, after the effect of other variables has been taken into account, is the medical seriousness of the key attempt.

The amount of action taken to conceal discovery is also strongly related to outcome. However, the correlation of these two variables with outcome is in opposite directions. The untreated patients who repeat have made a medically trivial threat to their lives; but they have taken pains to conceal this attempt. Now, the doctor who attended these patients in the casualty department based his enquiry and subsequent action on medical grounds, and only rarely enquired about the other circumstances of the attempt. The patient who has taken a dozen sleeping tablets has not, in medical terms, endangered his life. But the patient himself is often not possessed of the technical knowledge about the sufficiency of dosage necessary to kill himself. Patients who, despite the smallness of the dosage they have taken nevertheless try to conceal the attempt, do appear to be making a serious attempt on their lives. Yet they are often discharged by medical staff without being referred to a psychiatrist.

Other variables which are significantly related to repeated attempts in the untreated group are previous suicide attempts and being separated or divorced. Patients who discharge themselves against medical advice are relatively unlikely to repeat an attempt, when all other factors have been taken into account. It is the patient who does not discharge himself, but who is sent home by the casualty department doctor who is more at risk in this untreated category. The multiple correlation based on the seven variables

TABLE IX-III

VARIABLES PREDICTING REPEATED SUICIDE ATTEMPTS IN THE UNTREATED GROUP (N = 43)

| Variable | Correlation With Repeated A.S. | | |
	Before Multiple Regression	After Multiple Regression	t
Medical seriousness of the attempt	−.44	−.54	3.78
Amount of action taken to conceal discovery	.30	.53	3.65
Previous suicide attempt	.40	.43	2.75
Separated or divorced	.29	.43	2.81
Discharged self against medical advice	−.09	−.28	1.72
Born in coloured Commonwealth	.12	.28	1.69
Occupational class (high to low)	.13	−.25	1.51
Multiple correlation	—	.794	—

TABLE IX-IV

VARIABLES PREDICTING REPEATED SUICIDE ATTEMPTS IN THE BRIEFLY TREATED GROUP (N = 74)

| Variable | Correlation With Repeated A.S. | | |
	Before Multiple Regression	After Multiple Regression	t
Diagnosis of antisocial personality, alcoholism, or addiction	.45	.48	4.42
Diagnosis of organic brain disorder	.40	.47	4.27
Separated or divorced	.39	.37	3.24
Diagnosis of personality disorder	.38	.33	2.85
Discharged self against medical advice	.43	.33	2.82
Psychiatric treatment sometime following key attempt	−.27	−.25	2.12
Diagnosis of hysterical personality	.07	.23	1.88
Multiple correlation	—	.770	—

TABLE IX-V

VARIABLES PREDICTING REPEATED SUICIDE ATTEMPTS IN THE PROLONGED TREATMENT GROUP (N = 87)

| Variable | Correlation With Repeated A.S. | | |
	Before Multiple Regression	After Multiple Regression	t
Diagnosis of antisocial personality, alcoholism, or addiction	.40	.39	3.87
Married	.24	.24	2.21
Diagnosis of moderate depression	−.19	−.22	1.99
Occupational class (high to low)	−.07	−.20	1.83
Multiple correlation	—	.529	—

in the regression set is .794, which explains some 60 percent of the variance.

Some of the variance in predicting repeated attempts in the two treatment groups (Tables IX-IV and IX-V) has been accounted for by the fact of treatment itself, and for this reason the multiple correlation is lower than in the untreated groups. Two clinical variables (antisocial personality or addiction and organic brain disorder) are the best predictors of repeat in the briefly treated group, and the multiple correlation based on seven variables is .770. The variables which best predict repeat in the prolonged treatment group are antisocial personality or addiction, and being married. The multiple correlation, based on four variables, is .529.

It is interesting to note that being married is a predictor of poor prognosis[3] in the prolonged treatment group. The reason for this is not clear, but it may be that conventional psychiatric treatment does not help individuals with profound and unresolved marital problems. Some support for this view has been provided by Kessel and McCulloch (1966); they identified a group of patients ". . . who, without much, if any, abnormality themselves, are trapped in an unbearable social situation, for instance with abnormal or excessively difficult relatives." By contrast, being separated or divorced predicts repeat in the untreated and in the briefly treated groups. Obviously, combining the groups (which was necessary in order to examine the effects of treatment) tends to obscure relationships such as these.

Nevertheless, in attempting to make use of these findings for the prediction of repeated parasuicide, we have no alternative but to apply the variables we have identified to clinical populations without this differentiation. The present division of cases into treatment groups is based on a set of clinical and organizational circumstances which are probably unique to the institution studied. We have attempted a prediction study using the variables which are positively related to repeated attempted suicide in the multiple regression using all cases (Table IX-II).

A combination of the following variables was considered: anti-

---

3. These patients were more likely to make more than one subsequent attempt than the repeaters in the briefly and untreated groups.

social personality; addiction; organic brain disorder; a previous attempt; or being widowed, separated, or divorced; or membership of Registrar General's classes I to III. One or more of these variables was applicable to 46 of the 57 repeaters in our study. We are thus able to successfully predict 81 percent of the repeaters, which is an acceptable proportion when compared with the predictive success of the variables identified by McDowell et al. (1968) and Buglass and McCulloch (1970). When similar methods of calculating the proportion of repeaters are employed, these two studies identified 70 and 83 percent of cases respectively which had an outcome of suicide or attempted suicide.

It is interesting to note the predictive variables identified by at least two of these studies, including the present one. These are: psychopathy (or antisocial personality); addiction to drugs or alcohol; previous suicide attempt; being widowed, separated, or divorced; and hysterical personality. These variables appear to be particularly important in identifying individuals who are at risk for further parasuicide.

SUMMARY

Two hundred and four patients presenting at a casualty department following deliberate self-poisoning or self-injury (97% of the total sample) were traced after an average interval of 18 months. In contrast to other studies, the present sample included patients (44) who had not been seen by a psychiatrist. Comparison of outcome among treated and untreated patients, reported in a previous paper, demonstrated that psychiatric intervention was associated with a significant reduction in subsequent suicidal behavior.

In the present paper, we report the results of a multiple regression analysis:

1. The correlation between psychiatric treatment and outcome remained significant when all other variables, including those associated with outcome, were controlled.

2. Five variables were identified which in combination successfully predicted 80 percent of repeaters in the total sample: (a) antisocial personality, (b) organic brain disorder, (c) previous attempt, (d) widowed, separated or divorced, (e) membership of Registrar General's classes I to III.

3. Among patients who received prolonged psychiatric treatment, the best predictors of further parasuicide were (a) a diagnosis of antisocial personality, alcoholism, or drug dependence and (b) being married; the variables of diagnosis and marital state were independent of each other.

4. Among patients who received brief psychiatric treatment, the best predictors of further parasuicide were (a) antisocial personality, alcoholism or addiction; (b) organic brain disorder; (c) separated or divorced; (d) personality disorder.

5. Among untreated patients, the best predictors of further parasuicide were (a) attempts by the patient to conceal his parasuicide and avoid discovery, (b) the lack of medical seriousness of the attempt, (c) previous suicide attempt, (d) separated or divorced.

REFERENCES

Aitken, R., Buglass, D., and Kreitman, N.: The changing pattern of attempted suicide in Edinburgh 1962-1967. *British Journal of Preventive and Social Medicine, 23:*111-15, 1969.

Bagley, C.: Causes and prevention of repeated attempted suicide. *Social and Economic Administration, 4:*322-30, 1970.

Bagley, C.: The evaluation of agencies concerned with suicide prevention. *Life-Threatening Behavior, 1:*245-259, 1971.

Buglass, D., and McCulloch, J.: Further suicidal behavior: The development and validation of predictive scales. *British Journal of Psychiatry, 116:*483-91, 1970.

Fox, R.: Consultant psychiatrist's report. *In Annual Report of the Samaritans,* London, 1969-70.

Greer, S., and Lee, H.: Subsequent progress of potentially lethal attempted suicides. *Acta Psychiatrica Scandinavia, 43:*361-71, 1967; and Bagley, C.: The effect of psychiatric intervention in attempted suicide: A controlled study. *British Medical Journal, 1:*310-12, 1971.

Hope, K.: *Methods of Multivariate Analysis.* London, London University Press, 1968.

Kessel, N.: The respectability of self-poisoning and the fashion of survival. *Journal of Psychosomatic Research, 10:*29-36, 1966; and McCulloch, W.: Repeated acts of self-poisoning and self-injury. *Proceedings of the Royal Society of Medicine, 59:*89-92, 1966.

Kreitman, N., Philip A., Greer, S., and Bagley, C.: Parasuicide. *Bristish Journal of Psychiatry, 115:*746, 1969.

Lester, D.: Attempts to predict suicidal risk using psychological tests. *Psychological Bulletin, 74:*1-16, 1970.

176   *Psychological Assessment of Suicidal Risk*

McDowall, A., Brooke, E., Freeman-Browne, D., and Robin, A.: Subsequent suicide in depressed in-patients. *British Journal of Psychiatry, 114:*749-54, 1968.
Stanley, W.: Attempted suicide and suicidal gestures. *British Journal of Preventive and Social Medicine, 23:*190-95, 1969.
W.H.O.: *The Prevention of Suicide.* World Health Organization Public Papers No. 35. Geneva, 1968.

CHAPTER X

MODELS FOR PREDICTING SUICIDE RISK

ROBERT E. LITMAN

CLINICIANS ARE CONSTANTLY evaluating patients for degrees of suicide risk. To assist clinicians in this task, a number of suicide risk assessment schedules or rating scales have been published. An abbreviated list of references includes Litman and Farberow (1961); Tuckman and Youngman (1963); Cohen, Motto, and Seiden (1966); Poeldinger (1967); and Van De Loo and Diekstra (1970).

These scales are being applied to different populations in different settings. Results are usually evaluated as "high," "moderate," or "low" risk. The question arises, does "high risk" mean the same thing in different settings? Can the suicidal population in a Los Angeles clinic be compared to patients at facilities in Mexico, London, or Stockholm? In order to clarify the question of what is meant by "high" suicide potential, an attempt has been made to conceptualize a quantitative measure or index of suicidal potentiality. Since the purpose is to plan interventions and evaluate outcomes, the "risk" concept is used, not so much as a measure of past intention, as, for example, in a past suicide attempt, but rather as a guide for predicting future behavior. A successful model of suicidal behavior will assign a suicide probability to individuals and to groups according to certain well-defined traits, characteristics, and behaviors. The model "fits" together, and compares the distribution of, suicide potentiality in various populations and subpopulations and in various contexts. A subsidiary goal is to develop and validate potential-suicide risk scales. These scales are used to assign numerical ratings of self-destructive potentiality to individuals or groups.

We have conceptualized "risk" as a *prediction of suicide prob-*

ability using certified committed suicides as the definition of "suicide." Suicide potential is an expression of expected suicide risk based on past experience. This concept is borrowed directly from actuarians who are customarily making probability predictions about mortalities on the basis of past experiences and use the concept for the practical purpose of setting insurance rates.

An illustration of data which are clarified by this point of view is provided in Table X-I by the known suicide experiences for the first 1,000 Los Angeles Suicide Prevention Center cases, 1959-1962. The follow-up survey extended to January, 1968.

What is the significance of these suicide rates? Mortality statements have relevance chiefly for the purpose of comparing different individuals or different groups. The average suicide mortality for the United States is 11 suicides per year per 100,000 population. Compared with the general population, all members of the Suicide Prevention Center population are pathologically elevated in suicide risk. There is a greater than one order of magnitude jump in suicide probability between groups of individuals who are identified at suicide prevention centers, and the general population, even when the general population is in a "suicide capital" (San Francisco, suicide rate 30). It makes sense to distinguish be-

TABLE X-I

FOLLOW-UP OF 1,000 CONSECUTIVE LOS ANGELES
SUICIDE PREVENTION CENTER CASES

Time Period	Number of Suicides
Within one month	3
One month to six months	7
Six months to one year	4
One year to two years	7
Two years to six years	12

The suicide rate (suicides per year per 100,000 people at risk) for this cohort was as follows:

Time Period	Suicide Rate
During the first month	3,600
During the first six months	2,000
During the entire first year	1,400
During the second year	700
During the first two years	1,050
During the last four years of follow-up	300
Over the entire six years	550

TABLE X-II

RISK DEFINED AS SUICIDE PROBABILITY

Suicide Probability	*"Risk"*
A rate of 10,000 (10,000/100,000)	High risk
A rate of 1,000 (1,000/100,000)	Moderate risk
A rate of 100 (100/100,000)	Low risk
A rate of 10 (10/100,000)	Subclinical or normal minimal risk
A rate of 0 to 1	Non-risk

An alternative classification is as follows:

Suicide Probability	*"Risk"*
0-5/100,000	Non-risk
5-50/100,000	Normal (minimal) risk
50-500/100,000	Suicidal with low risk
500-5,000/100,000	Suicidal with moderate risk
Over 5,000/100,000	Suicidal with high risk

tween the population at large, where the individual potentiality for suicide is "unrecognized" and special individuals or groups in whom the suicide possibility is "clinical" or "recognized." Moreover, it makes clinical sense to distinguish degrees of risk among potential suicides.

For heuristic purposes, Table X-II has had constructed in it the following definitions of suicide risk corresponding to suicide probability, categorized by orders of magnitude so that each category is at ten times greater risk than the next lower or less lethal category.

According to this classification scheme, unselected Suicide Prevention Center (SPC) cases are "moderate" suicide risks, clustering around an average predicted suicide mortality of 1,000 per 100,000 per year for several years. If one knew nothing more about a person except that he had called the SPC recently, his suicide probability would be 100 times that of the ordinary unselected United States citizen. SPC cases evaluated as "high risk" are 1,000 times more lethal than the ordinary citizen (Litman, 1970). Currently, high risk cases are being identified at the SPC, Los Angeles, in large numbers, about 1,000 a year. Follow-up reports from suicide prevention centers in other cities indicate that they too have encountered a subcategory of high risk cases.

It is quite appropriate to compare the expected suicide rates of suicide prevention center cases with that of suicide attempters. The two groups are similar in such characteristics as age, sex, and marital status. A review by Wold (1970) of 26,000 SPC cases emphasized the overlapping since it was found that 51 percent of SPC cases had made a suicide attempt at some time in the past. This group includes the 31 percent of SPC cases who had made a recent suicide attempt which was a main reason for being referred to the Suicide Prevention Center. There have been a number of excellent studies of suicide attempters, for example by Stengel (1969), Rosen (1970), and Motto (1965). On the average, suicide attempters who injure themselves seriously enough or dramatically enough to be hospitalized commit suicide at a rate of about one percent a year (1,000 per 100,000); hence, they are "moderate" suicide risks. Certain subcategories of suicide attempters are "high risks." A "highest risk" sample was described by Moss and Hamilton (1956). They selected patients who were in a psychiatric hospital because of "high risk" suicide attempt and had in addition obvious mental illness. The suicide mortality of this group was 22 percent, with a majority of the deaths occurring in the first year of follow-up. Both Moss and Hamilton and Motto agree that it is possible to identify potential high risk suicide cases. The big problem is how to reach these patients with effective treatment. Both authors stress the importance of maintaining long-term therapeutic contacts with high risk individuals.

Patients in psychiatric treatment have in general a "low" suicide risk amounting to an expectation of a mortality of 100 over 100,000, which is about ten times that of the unselected population, according to reports from Pokorny (1964) and Babigian and Odoroff (1969). There are at least two types of moderate risk psychiatric patients: those who have a diagnosis of depression or manic-depressive illness (Pokorny, 1964; Thomson, 1970), and veterans who have had psychiatric hospitalization with special attention drawn to their suicidal status (Pokorny, 1966; Eisenthal, Farberow, and Shneidman, 1966). A history of chronic alcoholism carries with it a suicide risk comparable to being a psychiatric patient, namely, "low" (Kessel and Grossman, 1961; and Rushing, 1967). In England, male heroin addicts have a suicide rate 50 times the normal rate (James, 1967). Certain social indicators provide a special clue to suicidal lethality in suicide attempters. An outstanding example is the living arrangement "alone" for suicide attempters as reported by Tuckman and Youngman (1963). The combination of these two features, namely suicide attempt and living alone, predict a suicide rate of 7,140.

Examples of predicted suicide risk are presented in Table X-III. This table illustrates that it is possible to place many individuals in the low to moderate clinical risk groups on the basis of brief history and demographic data. It is even possible to diagnose high risk in a few persons on demographic data alone. However, for diagnosing high lethality, usually some sort of clinical report on the current and recent status of the individual is needed. This clinical evaluation might include, for example, answers to questions such as, "How long have you been thinking about hurting yourself?"

It is concluded that in order to identify high-risk suicidal indi-

TABLE X-III

EXAMPLES OF PREDICTED SUICIDE RISK

Type of Case or Group	1 "Non-Risk"	10 "Minimal"	100 "Low"	1,000 "Moderate"	10,000 "High"
SPC Cases (unselected)				x	
Selected "high risk" SPC cases					x
Suicide attempters seen in hospitals				x	
Psychiatric patients			x		
Suicidal psychiatric patients				x	
Manic-depressive psychiatric patients				x	
Young men		x			
College students		x			
Age under 12	x				
Young female with no obvious turmoil	x				
Old females		x			
Young females suicide attempters			x		
Female, repeated suicide attempts				x	
Old man, lives alone			x		
Heroin addicts			x		
Chronic alcoholics			x		
Depressed alcoholic middle-aged male, SPC					x
Suicide attempter, lives alone					x
"Serious" suicide attempter in a mental hospital					x

viduals, a two-stage screening process is called for. What is needed is, first, a "general screening" scale which can be given to any group in the general population, for example college freshmen or members of a union. The goal of this first screening instrument is to pick out from a general type of population the upper 2 percent in lethality. This recognized potentially suicidal group is then suitable subjects for a "clinical" scale, a second type of instrument which evaluates the degree of suicidal potentiality that is present and serves as a guide to treatment and prognosis. In practice, psychiatric hospitals, medical emergency treatment rooms for suicide attempters, and the telephone service of the SPC act as effective primary screening stations.

At the Suicide Prevention Center in Los Angeles continuing efforts have been made to describe and clarify distinctive cues or signs which discriminate between high risk suicidal patients and lower risk suicidal patients. In one such study, a sample of 500 randomly selected Suicide Prevention Center cases who had not killed themselves two years after being seen at the Center was compared with a group of 52 Suicide Prevention Center callers who did commit suicide with a median time period of nine months elapsed between the call to the SPC and the death by suicide. Table X-IV presents 15 items which discriminated between the two groups.

TABLE X-IV

DISCRIMINANT FUNCTION ANALYSIS

Variable in Rank Order	Content of Item	Direction for Suicide
1 .... Age		Older
2 .... Alcoholism		Yes
3 .... Irritation-rage-violence		No
4 .... Lethal prior behavior		Higher
5 .... Sex		Male
6 .... Accept help now		No
7 .... Duration of current episode		Longer
8 .... Prior inpatient psychiatric treatment		No
9 .... Recent loss-separation		No
10 .... Depression-somatic		Yes
11 .... Loss of physical health		Less
12 .... Occupational level		Higher
13 .... Depression-affective		No
14 .... Repeatedly discarded		No
15 .... Family available		Less

TABLE X-V
COMMITTED SUICIDES COMPARED TO NONSUICIDES
ON PREDICTION TEST SCORES

Score	Committed Suicides	Nonsuicides	Total
14.0+	2	1	3
13.0-13.9	1	2	3
12.0-12.9	7	7	14
11.0-11.9	13	32	45
10.0-10.9	17	71	88
9.0- 9.9	6	143	149
8.0- 8.9	5	132	137
7.0- 7.9	1	58	59
6.0- 6.9	0	17	17
5.0- 5.9	0	2	2
Total	52	465	517

Weights were assigned to each of the items according to the results of discriminant function analyses and scores on the weighted scale for 465 nonsuicide committers were compared to scores of 52 suicide committers. The outcome is shown in Table X-V.

In this scale, the cutting score for high risk is approximately 11. At this level, the scale designates 12 percent of the SPC contacts as "high risk," and this group includes 44 percent of those who subsequently go on to commit suicide. The expected lethality of this high risk group is 10.2 percent spread out over two years follow-up. The score range from 9.0 to 10.9, designated as moderate risk, picks up about 45 percent of the population, and included in that are about 45 percent of the suicides. The predicted low risk range below nine falls somewhat over 40 percent of the population, and a little more than 10 percent of the suicides. These results derived from scales constructed from empirical data are strongly in agreement with theoretical expectations derived from clinical models. Brown (1972) reported and discussed this research.

In summary, efforts to quantify the concept "suicidal risk" as part of a mathematical model of suicidal behaviors has been reported in this paper. It appears that a two-stage screening process is effective in identifying high risk suicidal individuals. It is felt that suicide is probably too complex and variable a problem to be handled by any general or unitary scale or testing device. One would not expect specific signs or groups of signs effective in predicting suicide risk in the Suicide Prevention Center population to be readily generalizable to either the general population or to all varieties of special populations (e.g., psychiatric patients, offenders in prison, or medical school graduates). Presumably the best prediction results from using scales consisting of different combinations of signs or cues that are found to be appropriate for each specific setting. For the purpose of evaluating and planning the treatment of suicidal individuals, the scales should supplement, but not replace, the clinical judgment of people with experience in any particular setting. Probably the greatest value of suicide prediction scales and prediction models and instruments for the measurement of suicidal behaviors, at the present time, is their use as guides in research leading toward developing new treatment facilities and in evaluating the effectiveness of anti-suicide programs (Litman and Farberow, 1970).

REFERENCES

Babigian, H. M., and Odoroff, C. L.: The mortality experience of a population with psychiatric illness. *American Journal of Psychiatry, 126:*470-480, 1969.

Brown, T. R.: Evidence for the importance of a holistic view of suicide. Paper read at the American Association of Suicidology Annual Meeting, Detroit, 1972.

Cohen, E., Motto, J. A., and Seiden, R. H.: An instrument for evaluating suicide potential: A preliminary study. *American Journal of Psychiatry, 122:*886-891, 1966.

Eisenthal, S., Farberow, N. L., and Shneidman, E. S.: Follow-up of neuropsychiatric hospital patients. *Public Health Reports, 81:*977-990, 1966.

James, I. P.: Suicide and mortality among heroin addicts in Britain. *British Journal of Addiction, 62:*391-398, 1967.

Kessel, N., and Grossman, G.: Suicide in alcoholics. *British Medical Journal, 2:*1671-1672, 1961.

Litman, R. E., and Farberow, N. L.: Emergency evaluation of self-destructive potentiality. In Farberow, N. L., and Shneidman, E. S. (Eds.): *Cry for Help.* New York, McGraw-Hill, 1961.

Litman, R. E., and Farberow, N. L.: Evaluating the effectiveness of suicide prevention. In Farberow, N. L. (Ed.): *Proceedings of the Fifth International Conference for Suicide Prevention.* Los Angeles, Delmar, 1970.

Litman, R. E.: Suicide prevention center patients: A follow-up study. *Bulletin of Suicidology, 6:*12-17, 1970.

Moss, L., and Hamilton, D.: The psychotherapy of the suicidal patient. *American Journal of Psychiatry, 112:*814-820, 1956.
Motto, J. A.: Suicide attempts. *Archives of General Psychiatry, 13:*516-520, 1965.
Pokorny, A. D.: Suicide rates in various psychiatric disorders. *Journal of Nervous and Mental Disease, 139:*499-506, 1964.
Pokorny, A. D.: A follow-up study of 618 suicidal patients. *American Journal of Psychiatry, 112:*1109-1116, 1966.
Poldinger, W.: Psychologie und prophylaxe des suizids. (Psychology and prevention of suicide.) *Monatskurse fur die Arztliche Fortbildung, 3:* 127-129, 1967.
Rosen, D. H.: The serious suicide attempt: Epidemiological and follow-up study of 886 patients. *American Journal of Psychiatry, 127:*764-770, 1970.
Rushing, W. A.: Individual behavior and suicide. In Gibbs, J. P. (Ed.): *Suicide.* New York, Harper, 1967.
Strengel, E.: *Suicide and Attempted Suicide.* England, Penguin, 1969.
Thomson, I. G.: Suicide and mortality in depression. In Farberow, N. L. (Ed.): *Proceedings of the Fifth International Conference for Suicide Prevention.* Los Angeles, Delmar, 1970.
Tuckman, J., and Youngman, W. F.: Identifying suicide risk groups among attempted suicides. *Public Health Reports, 78:*763-766, 1963.
Van De Loo, K. J. M., and Viekstra, R. W. F.: A questionnaire for the prediction of subsequent suicidal attempts. In Farberow, N. L. (Ed.): *Proceedings of the Fifth International Conference for Suicide Prevention.* Los Angeles, Delmar, 1970.
Wold, C. I.: Characteristics of 26,000 suicide prevention center patients. *Bulletin of Suicidology, 6:*24-28, 1970.

CHAPTER XI

PREDICTION OF SUICIDE IN NEUROPSYCHIATRIC HOSPITAL PATIENTS

NORMAN L. FARBEROW AND DOUGLAS MacKINNON

PREDICTION AND CONTROL are fundamental aspects in the scientific appraisal of any phenomenon. These often remain only aspirations in mental health, where psychological data are complex and influenced by a wide variety of independent variables. This is especially true for hospital neuropsychiatric patients where the suicidal aspects are integral in a picture of pervasive emotional disturbance, and where differentiation of subgroups must be based on relatively more subtle clues. Nevertheless, there has been a number of efforts not only to understand better the many facets of its occurrence among hospitalized mental patients but also to predict and, hopefully, to prevent it. This chapter presents a survey of those efforts and reports the progress in a recent project aimed at developing a scale to predict suicidal potentiality in hospitalized neuropsychiatric patients.

Brown and Sheran (1972) appraise the results of all efforts at prediction as equivocal to date. Research has been conducted on predictive signs derived from attributes of the suicidal person's behavior, surroundings, and person. The research has employed single signs, standard psychological tests, specially devised tests, clinical judgments, and scales, and has found difficulty in predicting suicide at useful levels. Of the various approaches, however, scales have seemed to offer the best potential. Brown and Sheran identify the primary methodological problems as being in the definition of committed suicide, the low base rates, the methods of data collection (e.g., substitute subjects, such as attempt and threat suicides for committed suicides), and the necessary use of residuals, or material indicating the state of mind, mood, and health of the subject before his death. Brown and Sheran urge that we stop looking for signs expected to be generalizable (as from persons attempting suicide to those committing it) and turn instead to the determination of situation-specific signs. "Instead of general population studies, a more useful approach may be to compare committers and noncommitters by means of the pre-facto method of residuals, in specific settings where suicide prediction is of major concern" (p. 93).

Neuringer (1965) and Lester (1970), reviewing investigations of suicide by means of the Rorschach, felt that the problems in prediction resulted from difficulties in methodology, especially the conceptualizations of suicide. Lester also looked at other tests and concluded that one difficulty lay in the fact that the studies were more often oriented around the test rather than the task, that is, they tried to validate the test rather than predict suicide.

Diggory (1971) has stated forcibly that one of the reasons why efforts to predict suicide have been so meager is that the researchers have not been using the most powerful methods of analysis available. He suggests multiple regression analysis for several reasons: it determines the maximum correlation between a team of predictors and the criterion, it eliminates redundant variables, it discovers suppressor or facilitator effects, it can deal with nonlinear correlations, and it is open-ended, that is, more variables can be added.

Suicide prevention of hospitalized neuropsychiatric suicidal patients is an excellent example of a problem requiring the consideration of the above-listed concerns. The data have shown that by far the majority of such suicides have occurred while the patient is out of the hospital, generally while an out-patient, or when on leave (Farberow, Ganzler, Reynolds, and Cutter, 1972). One major objective would be to develop a predictive scale focused on a specific group from a particular setting (neuropsychiatric hospital patients considered for discharge), using sophisticated statistical techniques (stepwise discriminant function analysis) with sufficient power to obtain variables with maximum discriminatory power.

PREVIOUS WORK

Previous work in the area of suicide prediction among neuropsychiatric hospital patients has been relatively sparse. The studies were primarily aimed at deriving characteristics which distinguished persons who committed suicide from those who did not. Some attempts were made to differentiate among subgroups of suicidal persons, such as suicide commits from attempts and threats as well as from those not considered self-destructive. Using nonsuicidal neuropsychiatric patients as controls made the problem more difficult, inasmuch as emotional disturbance was so much a characteristic of both the suicidal persons and the mentally ill. In the early work there was relatively little effort to incorporate those distinctive characteristics into any predictive scale.

Research into Identifying Characteristics

Among the earlier efforts were the exploratory studies by the Central Research Unit which focused on the characteristics which differentiated neuropsychiatric suicides from neuropsychiatric controls (Farberow, Shneidman, and Neuringer, 1966), and schizophrenic suicides (Farberow, Shneidman and Leonard, 1962) and anxiety-depressive suicides (Farberow and McEvoy, 1966) from matched controls. The first study compared the case history and hospitalization factors of 218 neuropsychiatric hospital patients who had committed suicide with 220 patients who had not. The control group was first compared with the total neuropsychiatric population of the V.A. on their distributions of age, race, and diagnosis with no significant differences found. The suicidal patient, in comparison with the controls, seemed to be more seriously psychiatrically ill and with wide fluctuations between extremes, and to show characteristic behavior, such as restlessness, hyperactivity, pacing and agitation at one extreme and severe depression, muteness, and withdrawal at the other. They made more demands, complained and criticized more often, and showed marked ambivalence about leaving the security of the hospital. Early history items showed marked disturbance in the dependence-independence area, usually stemming from strong ungratified dependency needs. They had extremely strong need to please and needed support from others more often. As adults, the suicidal patients were over-strivers with intense need to achieve.

The study of suicidal schizophrenics revealed at least three sub-types–dependent-satisfied, -dissatisfied, and unaccepting. Along the dependency continuum, the satisfied group liked the hospital, presented few problems in adjustment to the hospital, wanted to stay, and were sorely upset when it seemed they might be forced to leave. The dissatisfied group needed the hospital too but showed it by constant demands, great need for attention and reassurance, and frequent complaints and criticisms. Both groups showed rest-lessness, anxiety and depression, and frequently expressed feelings of guilt, inadequacy, or worthlessness. The unaccepting patient re-sisted the hospital and did not admit his disturbance or his illness, although his behavior included restlessness, hyperactivity, and im-pulsivity. Unlike the other two groups, there was an absence of feelings of guilt, inadequacy, and somatic complaints.

Suicides among patients with diagnoses of anxiety or depression or both (Farberow and McEvoy, 1966) were found to fall into three main groups: (1) *Object-loss.* This was primarily an inter-personal group with the patient feeling he was in danger of losing a love object. In some cases the threatened loss was for a job in which he had overinvested himself. (2) *Involutional.* This group was made up primarily of older men reacting to a threat to their psychological integrity, centered mostly around industrial or occu-pational failures and the fear of losing economic independence. Other threats included sudden illness or failing health and recent changes in the marital or family relationship. (3) *Egoistic.* This group was characterized mainly by the small degree of integration into the community, with few or no important relationships. They were chronically anxious and depressed, with character-disorder symptoms. They showed obsessive health concern, bodily preoccu-pations, and self-pity.

The interaction of tranquilizers with suicide was investigated (Cohen, Leonard, Farberow, and Shneidman, 1966) and found to be minor, with no one drug specifically capable of inducing de-pression or suicide. The attitude of the staff toward the use of the drugs as measures for control, manipulation, or detachment was considered to be much more important. Beisser and Blanchette (1961) also felt this to be more important in their study.

The results of two additional studies might be included although they were conducted on general medical and surgical patients rather than neuropsychiatric hospital patients. Suicidal patients with diagnoses of malignant neoplasms and with cardiorespiratory illnesses were compared with matched controls (Farberow, Shneidman, and Leonard, 1963; Farberow, McKelligott, Cohen, and Darbonne, 1966) and were found to contain in marked degree the dependent-dissatisfied patients encountered in the neuropsychiatric study populations. In addition, the concept of the "implementer" emerged as someone who had an active need to control his environment. In the hospital he tried to control treatment by refusing some, demanding others, requesting changes in wards and, in many ways, indicating an active interest in directing and controlling his situation. To some degree, these behaviors were also shown by the dependent-dissatisfied patients.

Levy and Southcombe (1953) found the diagnosis itself to be a distinguishing feature, with 50 percent of the patients who committed suicide classified as schizophrenic and 10 percent as manic-depressive, depressed. There was no evidence of depressive features either during the psychotic episode nor in the premorbid personality make-up. Banen (1954) also felt that more psychotics than nonpsychotics committed suicide. This does not necessarily make suicide a psychotic act, but rather that psychotics who are governed more by primitive and infantile drives without the benefit of a strong controlling ego, would be more likely to carry out a suicidal act impulsively.

Beisser and Blanchette (1961) compared suicidal patients in a state hospital with a control group and found schizophrenia plus depression to be the greatest danger signs. They also found a lack of response to hospital treatment to be discriminatory. Chapman (1961) felt that dependency rather than depression, along with severe disorganization, were the central issues in hospitalized patients. Fourteen of his 16 patients were diagnosed as having schizophrenic reactions. In 1966, Achté, Stenback, and Teravainen, investigating suicidal deaths among Helsinki mental hospital patients, found depressive symptoms, paranoid trends, and aggressive character trends. Rotov (1970) felt an important clue lay with the patient's projected concern over the death and well-being of his relatives. Rotov divided the factors affecting a patient's suicide potential into two groups, "necessary causes," or those causes that make the suicide possible, and "sufficient causes," or those that make the suicide probable. In Rotov's model, outside or environmental influences could increase or decrease the possibility of a patient killing himself.

Patrick and Overall (1969) used a multivariate analysis of the clinical symptoms of neuropsychiatric patients with suicidal behavior, checking the profiles of all patients admitted and comparing them with nonsuicidal patients. They found more severe anxiety, fewer severe schizophrenic symptoms, and more neurotic than psychotic diagnoses. They concluded that computer analysis of symptom-rating profiles based on brief clinical interviews was an efficient method, but only after identification and group placement had been made. However, identifying suicidal patients on the basis of their symptom profiles alone was very limited.

Ravensborg and Foss (1969), on the other hand, compared the admission complaints of three groups–completed suicides in a state hospital, natural deaths (primarily from circulatory and respiratory causes), and inpatients–and found no significant differences among the groups. Depression was the most frequent admission complaint for all three groups. In addition, comparison of the three groups on MMPI profiles and the recently developed threat suicide scale (Farberow and Devries, 1967) revealed no differences. The suicides were found to be younger, more intelligent, and better educated when comparisons were made on social competence variables. Singer and Blumenthal (1969) listed 14 clues they felt were important, derived from their reading of the literature. They were (1) suicide ideation, (2) verbalization of aggesssion, (3) strong feeling tones of recrimination or self-accusation in hallucinations, (4) despair following the realization of functional incapacity, (5) loss of *élan vital,* and clinical symptoms such as (6) anorexia, (7) doubts regarding the worth of existence, (8) loss of a previously introjected loved one, (9) loss of emotion in sexual fantasies, (10) psychosomatic delusions with morbid content, (11) emergence of a "smiling depression," (12) breakthrough of latent homosexual trends, (13) statements in correspondence of underlying morbid trend, and (14) changes in attitude toward personal possessions. The authors did not apply their clues to any population group, but urged that when the clues appeared in any combinations the patient should be carefully watched for possible depressive trends.

Yufit, Benzies, Fonte, and Fawcett (1971) developed the Time Questionnaire because they had been impressed in some of their prior research by the person's feelings about his future as a predictive clue for suicide. They found that suicidal patients consistently showed less projection into the future and elaborated less on future fantasies. Greaves (1971) examined the verb tense of incomplete sentence responses by suicidal and nonsuicidal controls and found the suicidal patients were more present- and less future-oriented. Melges and Weisz (1971) also found an inability to view the future objectively as well as feelings of helplessness and powerlessness to characterize suicidal patients.

Directly related to the above reported feelings about the future are investigations of Miller and Goleman (1970) who attempted to predict the suicidal risk of 16 hospitalized attempters after they were released. They found support for their hypothesis (derived from symbolic interaction theory) that the person's positive or negative feelings about the hospital would be most significant in differentiating high risk from low risk suicidal patients, especially when the "significant others" had the same opinions as the patients and reinforced them. Beck, Minkoff, Bergman, and Beck (1972) also focused on the role of hopelessness in suicide (no future) and found their highest positive correlation occurring between hopelessness and seriousness of suicide intent. They suggested that hopelessness was a much more sensitive sign for suicide than depression. The feeling of hopelessness and the patient's consideration of the hospital as a continuing resource both reflect the patient's feeling about his future.

Psychological Tests in Prediction of Suicide

Prediction of suicide in neuropsychiatric hospital populations by means of established psychological tests has been singularly unrewarding. Devries (1968) lists the various tests which have been used to differentiate suicidal from nonsuicidal persons and indicates that the Rorschach has been used most often (25 out of the separate 75 studies examined). Next most often investigated was the MMPI with 14, followed by the TAT with nine, and the Rosenzweig Picture Frustration test with five. Despite the consistently negative results, Devries tends to be optimistic, summarizing that with better control of independent variables, suicidal behavior could probably be identified through the use of projective and nonprojective personality tests. He feels especially that MMPI item analysis and the suicidal configuration or checklist of suicide signs on the Rorschach hold promise. Farberow (1972) discussed the use of the Rorschach since the Neuringer (1965) and Lester (1970) reviews and agreed there was need for better conceptualizations. He urged that a major objective be the prediction of the probability of an *acting out* rather than of an *act,* and of predicting for particular groups at specified times.

Efforts to use the Rorschach to identify and predict suicidal behavior are too voluminous to itemize in detail. In general, the results have been "equivocal, inconsistent, and contradictory" (Neuringer, 1965). The problems have been *temporal,* that is, the protocol groups have been drawn at varying intervals in relation to the event, with some before, as in committed suicide, and other after, as in attempts and threats, and many varying as much as ten years before or after the act. The *definition* of suicide has included behavior of the widest variety, with some groups containing within a single classification persons with only a suggestion of depressive rumination along with persons with very serious self-injuries. The groups have also reflected great differences in the *psychodynamic and motivational* factors among the individual subjects, especially along the continuum of *intention,* with some persons using self-destructive behavior despite no intention of dying, others fully intending to do so, while still others often initiating lethal behavior along with rescue actions and then leaving it up to fate to determine survival.

Most of the work done with the Rorschach and suicide can be grouped into either configurational or sign studies. Some start theoretically, deriving Rorschach signs from hypothesized personality traits, attitudes, or dynamics of suicidal people, while others proceed empirically by comparing groups of persons identified as suicidal with control groups who are nonsuicidal.

In the configurational approach, the three persons who have contributed most have been Hertz (1948), Beck (1945), and Piotrowski (1950). Hertz hypothesized 14 configurations: (1) neurotic structure, (2) deep anxiety, (3) depressed states, (4) constriction, (5) active conflict, (6) obsessive-compulsive personality components, (7) hysterical features, (8) ideation symptomatology, (9) agitation phenomena, (10) resignation, (11) sudden emotional outbursts, (12) withdrawal from the world, (13) paranoid tendencies, and (14) chaotic sexuality. She reported six or more signs correctly identified 92 percent of her suicidal subjects. In a later validation study (1949) she analyzed unselected protocols using a cut-off score of five and correctly identified 95 percent.

Beck looked for oppressive anxieties, strenuous inner conflict in a neurotic structure of compulsive form, and rumination over deeply personal life experiences by an individual of superior intelligence. He hypothesized shading shock on Card IV and a high number of M responses on Cards II, VIII, and IX. Beck did not use any control groups in his studies.

Piotrowski looked for a high number of dark shading responses indicating tendencies toward intermittent depressive moods, a low F plus percent indicating poor conscious control over thought processes, a high W representing quality and intensity of drive for difficult achievement, and a high color response reflecting impulsive emotionality. He also makes much of the response in which animals behave like humans. In 1970, Piotrowski used the Rorschach to explore the differences between patients who committed suicide and those who attempted. He found 14 out of 28 signs to be significant–R less than 20, at least one failure, shading shock on IV, sex shock on VI or VII, delay of first meaningful color response, at least one shaded color response, percentages of responses with human content below ten, at least one food response, at least one mention of death, at least one M expressing unhampered dancing, at least one M or A expressing a pleasant or joyful activity, no constructive whole responses, spontaneous criticism, and more than two white spaces (the last two signs are negative signs). With patients who had attempted suicide at least twice, a scale score of plus four points indicated chances of 90 in 100 the patient would succeed in taking his life in the future.

Some investigators have used a single sign approach, such as Rabin (1946), who emphasized a combination of color and shading shock; Lindner (1950), who identified Card IV as the "suicide card" and looked for responses with decayed, burned, or rotting elements; White and Schreiber (1952), who also looked for morbid content, such as blood, mutilation, death, and decay, etc.; Berk (1949) and Fisher (1951), who looked for various proportions of color and anatomy responses; Broida (1954), who felt suicidal patients produced significantly fewer animal responses than controls; Crasilneck (1954), who reported a "deep depression" sign (F plus percent plus TRT, plus ShWt) and a "histrionic" sign (FC-(CF plus C)wt); and Appelbaum and Holzman (1962) and Appelbaum and Colson (1968), who felt that the combined color and shading response indicated a patient's heightened sensitivity and vulnerability to his affect and that the combination of color and shading indicating isolation of affect was a defensive maneuver. Neuringer, McEvoy, and Schlesinger (1964) were not able to corroborate the color shading sign in female suicidal patients. Sapolsky (1953) found support in the Rorschachs of suicide attempters for his hypothesis that suicidal patients would be attracted to the lower center on Card VII because of their wish to return to the womb. However, attempts by other investigators to replicate Sapolsky's results were unsuccessful. Sakheim (1955) attempted to validate many of the indicators suggested by other investigators up to that time but found only dark shock on IV and M responses in which animals behaved like humans to differentiate significantly between the two groups. He also found that five of Hertz' suicidal configurations identified a significant number of the suicidal individuals.

Martin (1960) used a multiple sign approach and derived 16 signs significant at the 10 percent level or better, five of which continued to differ at the .05 level in a replication. These five signs were concerned with color and/or shading responses, showing poor affect, control, and insensitivity to internal and external control. Daston and Sakheim (1960) found that a cut-off of seven signs correctly identified 62 percent of the suicide commit records. Cutter, Jorgensen, and Farberow (1968) used some of the signs from Martin's checklist, but introduced ratings of the variable of suicide intention in their committed suicide group. They also controlled in part for temporal factors by dividing the subjects into equal subgroups on the basis of long or short intervals between the Rorschach administration and suicide. They found that differentiating the cases on the basis of time interval yielded results which were inconclusive, but that the use of ratings of intention provided more possibility of obtaining Rorschach signs with statistical significance than the use of a single dichotomy.

Costello (1958) used Rorschach content by tabulating responses that occurred at least 25 percent of the time in suicide attempts and matched control subjects. Using as a group-identifying-criterion any response occurring twice as often in one group as compared with the other group, he found seven types of responses to the cards which he considered typical of suicidal persons: maps on Cards I and VII, passive posture M on III, winged whole on V, object response to top D on VI, man's head response to bottom pink on IX, and a whole plant response on X. Other studies, however, have failed to validate the content approach.

A new application of the Rorschach to suicide has been the use of the consensus Rorschach by Cutter (1968). He obtained consensus Rorschachs on suicidal persons and their families and found that the roles played in relationship to each other (revealed by comparisons of the responses produced on individual and consensus Rorschachs) were clinically significant in evaluating suicidal potentiality. Cutter and Farberow (1968) extended the application of the technique to other groupings besides family, such as subject and friends, roommate, wife, high-low status pair, and others.

Four studies have explored the TAT and suicide. Fisher and Hinds (1951) tested suicidal schizophrenics, a control group of nonsuicidal schizophrenics, and a sample of the normal population for test signs such as neutral feeling, positive favorable feeling, hostility, ambivalence, and others. They found only that the control schizophrenics showed less overt hostility and more hostility turned inwards than did the suicidal schizophrenics. McEvoy (1963) hypothesized more themes expressing especially aggressive content or dysphoric aspects in suicidal patients, but found no differences between patients who had attempted suicide and a control group. Broida (1954) looked at the responses to Cards 3BM of ten psychiatric patients who had attempted suicide before testing, of ten patients with thoughts about suicide, and of 20 matched nonsuicidal control patients. Thematic analysis showed no differences for suicide themes, depression, parental pressure, fatigue, aggression, and other "unclassifiable" themes. There also were no significant differences in the length of the stories.

Shneidman and Farberow (1958) compared TAT's by patients after a suicide attempt, TAT's administered prior to a completed suicidal act, and TAT's from a comparable nonsuicidal neuropsychiatric group. Using a technique proposed by Friedman (1955), they rated heroes of the TAT stories with a Q-sort but found few significant differences in the between-group comparisons.

Farberow (1950) used the Rosenzweig–Picture Frustration Test with groups of attempts, threats, and controls and found higher E and E minus M scores for the threats over the attempts. He also obtained ratings of "seriousness" of the suicidal patients and found the more serious had lower E and E minus I than the controls and less serious patients. Winfield and Sparer (1953) found that his group of attempted suicides scored significantly higher on the M scale and significantly lower on the E scale. Arneson and Feldman (1968) compared 31 patients after a mild suicide attempt and 18 patients after a serious attempt against the norms of the test given by Rosenzweig. There were no significant differences for the males. For the females the only significant difference was that the mild attempts had significantly higher O-D than the serious attempts. Males with mild attempts had significantly lower O-D and N-P scores, and significantly higher E-D scores, when compared with the test norms. Both mild and serious female attempts had significantly lower O-D scores and significantly higher E-D scores when compared with the norms for the test.

The MMPI studies at first dealt mainly with profiles or with separate scales (Simon and Hales, 1949; Simon, 1950; Rosen, Hales, and Simon, 1954; Farberow, 1950) and found a small measure of success in differentiating the groups of suicides from the nonsuicidal controls. Farberow and Devries (1967) conducted an item analysis of the MMPI using groups of threatened, attempted, committed, and nonsuicidal controls and found that the threatened suicides was the only group which could be significantly differentiated from the controls. A threat suicide scale containing 52 items from the MMPI was constructed using 15 items significant at the .01 level or better, 24 items at the .05 level, and 13 items at the .10 level. Devries (1966b) refined the study by separating the threat and attempt suicide group into those whose history showed only threats, those who showed only attempts, and those who showed both. This seemed to increase the discriminatory power of the MMPI, allowing the differentiation of attempted suicides and the threat-and-attempt suicide group from the neuropsychiatric controls.

Devries and Farberow (1967) used a multivariate discriminant analysis on the MMPI profiles (using the Pa, Sc, Pt, Ma, Pd, and D scales only) of threats, attempts, commits, and controls and found that the groups could be distinguished from each other with greater accuracy than without the tests. Devries and Shneidman (1967) looked at the MMPI profiles of five subjects who took the test monthly over a period of one year. The subjects also evaluated themselves monthly on a 9-point scale on the lethality of their suicidal preoccupation. A discriminant analysis correctly grouped all the profiles by each of the patients together. The authors concluded that when patients become acutely suicidal, changes in the MMPI profile were more related to their own pre-acute profile than to a "general suicidal" profile. They felt that it was not possible to identify general trends for all suicidal patients nor to detect in an MMPI profile changes in the degree of suicidal syndrome.

Devries (1966a) developed a 55 item inventory predicting potential suicide by reviewing the literature for "critical incidents" and constructing MMPI-like items from them. He found that a group of threats, a group of attempts, and a group of threats plus attempts could all be differentiated from a nonsuicide control group, although not from each other.

Efron (1960) made up a sentence completion test with 54 items, almost a third weighted with items of depressive themes. With 104 psychiatric subjects, correct identifications varied from 30 percent to 43 percent. However, false positives were 33 percent. Efron felt that the primary factor in the ratings was severity of illness rather than specific suicidal traits.

Sternberg and Levine (1965) tried a sign approach in the Bender Visual Motor Gestalt, hypothesizing that the vertical element of Figure 6 penetrating or running into the open semicircle of dots of Figure 5 indicated suicidal ideation. When they compared two groups of patients, one suicidal and the other control, they found significantly more suicidal ideation in the patients showing the sign (88%) than in those not showing the sign (44%).

Nawas and Worth (1968) asked three clinicians experienced in the use of the Bender-Gestalt to rate the presence or absence of ten signs relating to depression, dependency, emotional constriction, and rigidity in the protocols of 34 hospitalized mental patients, 17 of whom had attempted suicide. None of the indices distinguished between the groups. The authors wondered if the suicidal attempt, because of its abreactive effect, might have produced measurable changes sufficient to reduce the differences between the groups.

Blau, Farberow, and Grayson (1967) compared male psychiatric patients after an attempt or a threat with a group of nonsuicidal patients on the Semantic Differential Test. Thirteen concepts were rated on ten scales, but only eight reached significance at the .05 level or better, no more than would be expected by chance alone. No significant differences were found when attempted sui-

cides were compared with threatened suicides. Neuringer (1968)
looked at the ratings of concepts of life and death by persons after
a suicide attempt, by a group of psychosomatic patients, and by
a control group of normals. No differences in the groups for the
ratings of the concepts on each of the scales were reported. He did
find that the suicidal patients showed a greater amount of diver-
gence between their evaluation of life and death than did the other
two groups.

In general, except for a few indications of possible usefulness
of the Rorschach and the MMPI, the effectiveness of any of the
common psychological tests in the prediction of suicide is yet to
be demonstrated.

Scales and Schedules

There are a few studies of scale development which relate most
closely to the task in the present research. Cutter, Jorgensen, Farberow, and Ganzler (1968) modified the Suicide Potentiality
Scale in use at the Los Angeles Suicide Prevention Center and developed ratings of intention to die which could be applied to hospitalized suicidal patients. These consisted of ratings from 0 to 6
for each of three aspects of any suicide attempt: adequacy of the
planning, effectiveness or lethality of the method used, and the
provisions for rescue effected by the patient. The sum of the
ratings on each of the three subscales provided an evaluation of
the individual's future lethal potentiality. Poeldinger (1967) examined suicide attempters admitted to psychiatric hospitals in
Switzerland and devised a schedule listing 35 factors in the psy-
chopathologic, psychodynamic, and sociological areas. The factors
are weighted 0, 1, or 2 depending upon sex, age, and other aspects. The sum of the scores allows an evaluation of serious, moderate, or no suicide potentiality.

Three articles reported the development of a prediction scale
in Fort Logan, Denver. Dean, Miskimmins, DeCook, Wilson, and
Maley (1967) compared presuicidal behavior and personality
characteristics of matched committed suicide and nonsuicidal mental hospital patients, using information available from admission
data, and developed a Suicide Potential Schedule. Miskimmins
and Wilson (1969) later validated the schedule with two new

groups of committed suicide and nonsuicidal hospital populations and refined the schedule originally obtained. The final list of variables, weighted from 0 to 6, included: sex and age, admitting diagnosis, times admitted, marital status, years of education, preoccupation with problems of self, slowing of thought processes, use of language, anger, depression, apathy, inappropriate behavior, social pattern against (people), impairment of effectiveness, external precipitating stress, and danger to self. They found, in general, that the more symptoms of overt psychotic behavior, the lower the suicidal potential. Applying the new schedule to all of the original subjects and their new validation subjects, they were able to differentiate significantly the suicidal groups from the nonsuicidal groups. In 1970, Braucht and Wilson used a discriminant function analysis on the same subjects and found each group differentiated from the other at a highly significant statistical level. They reported their total prediction accuracy as 58 percent.

More recently, Beck, Herman, and Schuyler (1971) reported on the development of a Suicidal Intent Scale, using patients admitted to the Philadelphia General Hospital and the Hospital of the University of Pennsylvania. While these patients enter the general medical hospitals, they are evaluated by a psychiatric team and treated for the most part in psychiatric wards. The scale focuses on suicide attempters at present, but separate forms for completed suicides and suicidal ideation are planned. The scale is now being tested in a five-year longitudinal study of 500 suicide attempts. The scale contains 15 items, the first nine items related to the circumstances surrounding the act, and the second six items provided information about the communication around suicide, that is, the subject's own expectations and conceptions of his self-destructive behavior. The authors differentiate between medical lethality, which they consider resides in the specific method used, and the intent of the person, defined as seriousness or intensity of the wish to terminate one's life.

Weisman and Worden (1971) have also developed a measure for evaluating the lethality of a recent suicide attempt. Their schedule, an assessment of Risk-Rescue factors, was developed working with patients admitted to a general hospital. They state that their schedule, taken by itself, is primarily a descriptive and quantitative assessment of a specific attempt. However, if the two other posited dimensions of lethality, intentionality, and involvement, are considered, the Risk-Rescue rating acquires more predictive significance. They are currently developing assessments for these other aspects of lethality.

Zung (1971) has developed an Index of Potential Suicide with a two-part schedule made up of 19 variables in a social scale and 50 variables in a clinical scale. Zung applied his scale to all mental hospital patients admitted to a V.A. neuropsychiatric hospital for nine consecutive months and found that his clinical scores differentiated the nonsuicidals from the suicidals but did not differentiate within the suicide groups, made up of ruminators, threateners, and attempters. Another form of the clinical scale, using self-ratings, did differentiate the ruminators from the threateners and attempters. Analysis statistically was by means of analysis of variance, multiple tests, and factor analysis on both the social and the clinical scales. The specific items which appeared most useful in discriminating between the groups of attempters and nonsuicidal patients were those in depression, anxiety, and emotional status categories.

Three additional studies are included in our survey although they are not based upon neuropsychiatric hospital populations. However, they do use multivariate analysis and indicate the strength of these procedures in deriving predictive variables. Bagley and Greer (1971) traced 204 patients out of 211 cases of attempted suicide after they had been treated at the emergency room of Kings College Hospital. The group included those who had been treated subsequently by a psychiatrist and those who had not. A previous study had compared the outcome among the treated and untreated patients and indicated that psychiatric intervention was usually associated with a significant reduction in subsequent suicidal behavior. Using multiple regression analysis in the later study the authors identified five variables which in combination, successfully predicted 80 percent of the repeaters in the total sample: (1) anti-social personality, (2) organic brain disorder, (3) previous attempt, (4) widowed, separated, or divorced, and

(5) membership of Registrar General Classes I, II, and III. Two variables were the best predictors of repeated suicide attempts among patients who had received prolonged psychiatric treatment. These were: (1) diagnosis of anti-social personality, alcoholism, or drug dependence, and (2) married. The best predictors of repeated suicide attempts among patients who received brief psychiatric treatment were: (1) anti-social personality, alcoholism, or addiction; (2) organic brain disorder, (3) separated or divorced; and (4) personality disorder. Among the untreated patients the best predictors of further suicide attempts were: (1) attempts by the patient to conceal his suicidal attempt and to avoid discovery, (2) the lack of medical seriousness of the attempt, (3) the previous suicide attempt, and (4) separated or divorced.

Brown (1972) and Lettieri (1971) applied a discriminant function analysis in deriving a predictive scale of long-term suicide potentiality, using patients from the Los Angeles Suicide Prevention Center. Both used the same two groups of 52 suicide commit cases and 465 callers who were still alive from among the population using the Center, but Brown derived his scale from the two groups as a whole while Lettieri divided the population into four subgroups. Brown found 11 items which discriminated at the .10 level or better, eight of them at or beyond the .05 level. The most predictive item was age, with increasing age more indicative of higher risk. Second was alcoholism and, in order, no recent irritation, rage, or violence; lethality of prior suicidal episodes; no prior psychiatric inpatient experience; no current loss by separation; somatic indicators of depression; and no recent loss of physical health. Four cues were reversed in direction from what had been assumed to be indicators of acute high lethality. These were: no recent irritation, rage, or violence; no prior psychiatric inpatient experience; no current loss by separation; and no recent loss of physical health. Brown indicates, however, that caution must be used in interpreting the meaning of the discriminant function analysis, especially the importance of the specific items or areas. This is because the ordering of the items, the level of significance of the individual cues, and the number of significant items from each level can be changed either with the addition of new cues or the removal of some items which are used, even if the added or removed cues are ones which are not highly discriminative.

Lettieri (1971) split the subject sample into four age-by-sex groupings, using 40 years of age as the dividing point, giving him older and younger males and older and younger females. He then performed four separate stepwise discriminant functions analyses and derived a long and a short form of scales for each subgroup. The short form allowed quick appraisal with relatively little loss of variance-explaining power. For older males the long forms contained 13 items of which the first seven items made up the short form; for younger males, the long and short forms contained nine, or the first five items respectively; for older females, there were 10, or the first four items for the long and short forms respectively; and for younger females there were eight, or the first three items for the long and short forms respectively. Weights are provided for each of the items which, when added, provide a rating of high, moderate, or low lethality. Where the lethality rating is high, the prediction is that the patient will commit suicide within the next two years.

For older males the variables are: divorce status; somatic aspects of depression; irritation, rage, and violence; accepts help now; loss through divorce, repetition of attempts; role failure; dual suicidality; family available, repeatedly discarded; thinking; anxiety; panic; and dependence versus independence. Reversals appear in the variables of irritation, rage, and violence; role failure; dual suicidality; repeatedly discarded; thinking; and more inclined to be independent. The long form correctly classified 94 percent of the deaths and 93 percent of those still alive.

The scale for younger males included: marital status, race (Caucasian), thinking, omnipresent suicidal feelings, homicide component, dual suicidality, loss through divorce, criminal behavior and culture trap (in traditionally defined sex role). The reversals were Caucasian race, homicide component, dual suicidality, and actual loss through divorce. The percentage of correct classifications for the long form was 77 percent for death and 84 percent for controls.

The scale for older females consisted of: single status, socioeconomic status, time, family available, drinking currently, prior psychiatric treatment, alcoholism, living arrangement, lethality of prior suicidal behavior, and repeatedly discarded. Reversals occurred in prior psychiatric treatment, living arrangement, and repeatedly discarded. The long scale correctly identified 82 percent of those who were dead and 88 percent of those who were still living.

For younger females, the items were: friends in the vicinity; dependent-independent; warm interdependent relationships; occupation; irritation, rage, and violence; lethality of prior suicidal behavior; and criminal behavior. The reversals were: irritation, rage, and violence, and criminal behavior. The percentages of successful classification by the long form were 72 percent and 90 percent for those who committed suicide and the controls, respectively.

The next section of this chapter presents a prediction scale for the potentiality of a suicide death among psychiatric patients who have been hospitalized and treated for suicidal behavior and are about to be released from the hospital.

NP HOSPITAL SUICIDE PREDICTION SCALE

Procedures

Selection of Population

The population used in the study was composed of two groups of neuropsychiatric hospital patients, committed suicides, and non-committed suicide controls. The suicide population consisted of all ($N = 187$) the reported suicides of neuropsychiatric patients in V.A. neuropsychiatric hospitals for the calendar years 1966-1968 reposited in the Central Research Unit, while the controls were neuropsychiatric patients hospitalized during the same years who had not committed suicide as of 1971. The control group patients were obtained by a stratified random procedure which assured that the diagnostic distribution in the sample reflected the relative proportions of diagnostic categories within the general population of all neuropsychiatric patients residing in V.A. hospitals. The majority of these controls were also hospitalized during the years 1966-1968. Although the total neuropsychiatric population for those years of approximately 40,000 includes the suicides, there

TABLE XI-I

DISTRIBUTION OF DIAGNOSTIC CATEGORIES IN SUICIDAL AND
NONSUICIDAL (CONTROL) GROUPS AND IN TOTAL
VA NP POPULATION

Diagnostic Categories	VA NP Population[a]		Control Population		Suicide Population	
	N	%	N	%	N	%
Psychotic	28,775	60.6	114	58.7	139	75.1
Brain syndromes	9,395	19.6	36	18.5	17	9.2
Psychoneurotic	3,645	7.6	14	7.2	19	10.3
Alcoholism	4,550	9.5	23	11.8	4	2.2
Personality disorders	1,335	2.7	7	3.6	6	3.2
Total	47,700	100.0	194	99.8	185	100.0

[a] From Table 40, VA Annual Report, 1969, giving population figures for November 1968.

are so few suicides relative to the total neuropsychiatric population (approximately 0.25 percent), their distribution plays no appreciable role in the distribution of the total population. Therefore, the diagnostic distribution of the control cases is essentially the same as the diagnostic distribution of the total neuropsychiatric population. Table XI-I gives the distributions for the total neuropsychiatric population, the suicides, and the control cases.

Each group of suicides and controls was divided into two subgroups by taking a random sample within each, stratified by diagnosis. This permitted a validation procedure, with the first population used to derive the scale, and the second population used to assess its reliability on a new group not previously involved. This gave us an original population of 93 suicides and 94 controls, and a replication population of 92 suicides and 100 controls.

Preparation of Rating Schedule

A rating schedule consisting of 71 items was prepared by deriving items from various publications identifying characteristics of suicidal behavior of psychiatric patients in hospitals. Most of the items were taken from the studies of the Central Research Unit in which comparisons were made between groups of suicidal patients compared with matched nonsuicidal patients (Farberow, Shneidman, and Leonard, 1962; Farberow and McEvoy, 1966; and

TABLE XI-II

ROBINSON'S A MEASURE OF AGREEMENT AMONG RATERS

Raters	A	B	C	D
		Objective Items Raters		
A	—	.96	.96	.94
B			.99	.97
C				.98
D				—
		Subjective Items Raters		
Raters	A	B	C	D
A	—	.83	.90	.88
B			.81	.87
C				.88
D				—

Farberow, Shneidman, and Neuringer, 1966). In addition, significant items deemed appropriate to hospitalized patients were selected from the scales derived for suicidal patients in the community who called a suicide prevention center (Lettieri, 1971).

The schedule was used to rate 50 cases, 25 suicides and 25 controls, by the authors and two experienced research associates of the Central Research Unit.[1] Discussions among the four raters on items which were divergent, confusing, or variously interpreted eliminated items on which there was no agreement. Other items were added from a study by Motto (1971) identifying suicidal persons admitted to a general hospital. The final form consisted of 81 variables.

Reliability of Raters

As a check on the reliability of rating, each rater was required to rate one suicide and one control in common. The items were divided into objective and subjective categories, and the level agreement for each computed separately. Robinson's[2] measure of agreement (A) for the objective items ranged between .94 and .99. The measure of agreement for the subjective items ranged be-

1. Mary Jorgensen and Bruce Tapper.
2. Unlike the coefficient of reliability, r, Robinson's A requires equal means and standard deviations and thus is a truer measure of agreement.

tween .81 and .90 (Table XI-II). Using the squares of the obtained measures to indicate the percent agreement, the range of agreement among the raters for the objective items was 88 to 98 percent, and for the subjective items was 66 to 81 percent. The rater (B) with poorest percent agreement on the subjective items was not used in rating the total sample. The percent agreement for A, C, and D thus ranged from 88 to 96 percent on the objective items and from 77 to 81 percent on the subjective items. These levels were considered satisfactory.

Results

Ratings

The possible responses within each of the items were rank ordered where a rationale existed for doing so. Where no rationale existed for rank ordering the responses, a dummy variable was constructed (permitting yes-no responses). Ratings of the first group, consisting of 93 suicides and 94 controls, were made, using the 81 item schedule, and a stepwise discriminant function analysis was performed.[3] F-ratios were computed for all variables, the item with the highest F-ratio was extracted, and new F-ratios for the remaining variables were computed. This was repeated at each step until 15 items were extracted. A minimum F-ratio of .01 was specified. The number of items extracted was stopped at 15 in order not to end up with a scale which would be either too cumbersome for clinical use or too methodologically suspect. Past an optimal point, the longer the scale, the more likely it is to predict fluctuations of the sample rather than the actual differences for the population as a whole. The fifteen items and their scoring direction showing increased suicidal risk, follow:

---

3. Discriminant function analysis is preferred over standard multiple linear regression analysis in cases where one has a dummy dependent variable because multiple linear regression analysis is not sufficiently "robust" in situations where a dummy dependent variable is used. The discriminant function determines coefficients of the linear combinations of variables which best discriminate between groups of subjects. It maximizes the between-group sum of squares relative to the within-group sum of squares. Thus, for two groups within which there is usually considerable overlap, the weights will help in differentiating between them by establishing the maximum difference for each variable relative to the variance within each group.

1. Was the subject depressed most of the time while in the hospital?   Yes.

2. The subject had shown life-long good or moderate ability to maintain warm, mutually interdependent relationships.   No.

3. During his most recent hospitalization, did the subject have any hope that things would be better for him?   No.

4. Were somatic problems, such as disturbed appetite, sleep disorders, or excessive fatigue significant symptoms leading to the subject's last hospitalization?   No.

5. The subject's age at final summary or release was younger (negative correlation with age).   Yes.

6. During the current hospitalization, was the subject under the influence of either drugs or alcohol?   No.

7. During the last hospitalization, did the subject ever return unusually early to the hospital from either passes or leaves?   Yes.

8. Did the subject ever elope during either his previous or current hospitalizations?   Yes.

9. During the current hospitalization, did the subject experience an actual divorce from his wife?   Yes.

10. Did the subject have a history of suicidal behavior of any kind?   Yes.

11. Either just before or during the subject's most recent hospitalization, had the patient been more nervous, anxious or agitated than usual?   No.

12. The subject has worked fairly steadily.   No.

13. The subject had serious physical injury.   No.

14. During the last hospitalization, the subject was experiencing the actual death of a loved one.   Yes.

15. During the last hospitalization, was the subject reluctant to leave the hospital (feels safer in the hospital)?   Yes.

Utilizing the discriminant function analysis to fix the weights or coefficients for each variable, eleven sub-scales were constructed with varying numbers of items, 5 through 15. Table XI-III shows the variables and their varying weights in each of the nine scales.

Of most concern clinically are the cases misclassified among the suicides as false negatives and among the controls as false positives. Using a cutoff point which produces an approximate 50 per-

TABLE XI-III

RANKED DERIVED VARIABLES AND THEIR COEFFICIENTS FOR SCALES WITH FIVE TO FIFTEEN VARIABLES

			Scales with Indicated Number of Variables										
Rank	Scale Items	Item No.	5	6	7	8	9	10	11	12	13	14	15
1.	Hospital depression	54	.00938	.00976	.00963	.00966	.00959	.00893	.00891	.00974	.00976	.00987	.00991
2.	Relationship with others	20	-.00515	-.00488	-.00421	-.00297	-.00338	-.00305	-.00273	-.00132	-.00211	-.00145	-.00175
3.	Hope	40	.00651	.00644	.00713	.00661	.00680	.00704	.00692	.00674	.00712	.00704	.00687
4.	Somatic problems	28	-.00270	-.00272	-.00316	-.00283	-.00279	-.00254	-.00211	-.00205	-.00206	-.00209	-.00239
5.	Age	1	-.00126	-.00126	-.00145	-.00148	-.00149	-.00151	-.00141	-.00164	-.00136	-.00148	-.00158
6.	Under influence of drugs/or alcohol	47		-.01001	-.01141	-.01274	-.01327	-.01383	-.01428	-.01443	-.01474	-.01438	-.01453
7.	Early return from pass	59			.00954	.01180	.01254	.01274	.01371	.01386	.01274	.01333	.01209
8.	Elope?	60				.00289	.00293	.00275	.00328	.00291	.00264	.00288	.00293
9.	Current divorce	69					.01276	.01431	.01611	.01686	.01788	.01785	.01810
10.	Suicidal history	33						.00266	.00301	.00318	.00361	.00357	.00368
11.	Anxiety	53							-.00402	-.00408	-.00532	-.00394	-.00473
12.	Job history	18								-.00274	-.00308	-.00281	-.00321
13.	Recent illness	16									-.00361	-.00375	-.00360
14.	Death of loved one	70										.01418	.01530
15.	Reluctant to leave	62											.00736

cent error split for both groups, relative distributions between predicted and actual cases are obtained. The use of a 50 percent error
split indicates greater concern for the errors among the suicide
cases because of the small number of suicides compared to the total population from which the control cases are sampled. Thus,
each percentage error among the controls represents a population
approximately 400 times greater than each percentage error in the
suicide population and each misclassified suicide is represented as
400 times more important than each misclassified control.

TABLE XI-IV

PERCENT ACTUAL AND PREDICTED SUICIDES AND CONTROLS
FOR SCALES OF VARYING LENGTHS IN INITIAL AND
VALIDATION SAMPLES

| | | | Predicted Percentages | | | |
| | | | Initial Sample | | Validation Sample | |
Number of Items in Scale			Suicide (N = 93)	Control (N = 94)	Suicide (N = 92)	Control (N = 100)
Five	Actual	S	84	16	74	26
		C	15	85	31	69
Six	Actual	S	86	14	73	27
		C	14	86	28	72
Seven	Actual	S	85	15	78	22
		C	15	85	28	72
Eight	Actual	S	85	15	79	21
		C	16	84	29	71
Nine	Actual	S	84	16	75	25
		C	16	84	23	77
Ten	Actual	S	85	15	77	23
		C	15	85	25	75
Eleven	Actual	S	85	15	79	21
		C	16	84	25	75
Twelve	Actual	S	87	13	75	25
		C	16	84	24	76
Thirteen	Actual	S	88	12	76	24
		C	12	88	25	75
Fourteen	Actual	S	87	13	71	29
		C	14	86	25	75
Fifteen	Actual	S	89	11	70	30
		C	12	88	25	75

Validation Procedures

All the scales were applied to the second subgroup consisting of 92 suicides and 100 controls in a validation procedure. Each subscale was again evaluated to see how well it differentiated between the two groups. Table XI-IV presents the predicted and actual percentages of suicides and controls for the initial and validation populations on scales of varying numbers of items, from 5 through 15 items. The 11 item scale is seen to produce the least number of false positives and negatives in the validation population and is considered the most efficient.

Variable Weights

The weights for the 11 item schedule were recomputed by dividing each coefficient by the smallest coefficient, giving the lowest weight a value of 1. By adding 11 to each weight for the variables, negative weights were eliminated and new weights for each of the additional variables in relative proportion were established.

Risk Ratings

For clinical use, cutoff points have been established for the purpose of categorizing subjects at various levels of suicide risk. These are:

1. High suicide risk, 130.0 and above,
2. Moderately high suicide risk, 117.45 to 129.99,

TABLE XI-V

PERCENT ACCURACY IN PREDICTIONS WITH ELEVEN-ITEM SCALE
ON INITIAL AND VALIDATION SAMPLES

Suicide Risk	Initial		Predicted Percent Accuracy	Validation		Percent Accuracy
	Suicides	Controls		Suicides	Controls	
High	35	0	100.0	35	5	87.5
Moderately high .	44	15	74.6	38	20	65.5
Moderately low .	14	39	73.6	17	44	72.1
Low	0	40	100.0	2	31	93.9

3. Moderately low suicide risk, 107.67 to 117.44,
4. Low suicide risk, 107.66 and below.

In the original sample, the high and low cut-off points predicted suicide and nonsuicide with 100 percent accuracy, and the moderately high and moderately low suicide risk with 74.6 percent and 73.6 percent accuracy, respectively (see Table XI-V). In the validation sample, the prediction accuracies are reduced. The high risk group was predicted with 87.5 percent accuracy, the low risk, or nonsuicide group, with 93.9 percent accuracy, and the moderately high and moderately low suicide risk with 65.5 percent and 72.1 percent accuracy, respectively.

DISCUSSION

Diggory's (1971) recommendation that more powerful statistical procedures be used in the efforts at prediction is important for research in suicide. In the problem of suicide we are undertaking the task of predicting a relatively rare event which is complex in nature and has many variables both facilitating and preventing its appearance. Diggory suggested using multiple regression analysis because it would eliminate redundant variables and determine the best predictors working in conjunction with each other for predicting the dependent variable. Subtle factors, not statistically significant of themselves, might thus emerge as important. The researcher must keep in mind some important considerations in the use of multiple linear regression, inasmuch as multiple regression analysis is most suited for ordinal or ranked data, while most information about suicide (the independent variables) is comprised of both nominal and ranked data. Thus, there are nominal categories such as sex and race, etc., along with items relating to distributions, such as anxiety and depression. In addition, the dependent variable, suicide, is frequently comprised of two nominal categories, such as suicide and nonsuicide, which, in form, is also referred to as a dummy variable. The use of a dummy variably as the dependent variable often exceeds the "robustness" of a multiple regression analysis, inasmuch as predicting with a dummy dependent variable, can avoid neither negative probabilities nor probabilities greater than one, and also cannot assume error terms of equal variances.[4] In addition, Neter and Maynes (1970) and Stevens (1966) outline empirical and theoretical reasons to expect curvilinearity when some variable such as suicide is measured as a dummy dependent variable.

A substitute and similar statistic is the discriminant function analysis which, when combined with a stepwise procedure (which chooses the "best" variables in a series of steps without regard to theory), is a powerful means of predicting nominal categories from multivariate analysis. Of all the scales in use, or currently being developed for use, with neuropsychiatric hospital suicidal patients, none used the stepwise discriminant function analysis nor the linear multiple regression analysis to arrive at their scales (Beck, Herman, and Schuyler, 1971; Weisman and Worden, 1971; Zung, 1971; Cutter, Jorgensen, Farberow, and Ganzler, 1968; Poeldinger, 1967; and Dean, Miskimmins, Cook, Wilson, and Maley, 1969). However, Braucht and Wilson (1970) used a discriminant function analysis to test their scale after its development and found each of the groups readily differentiated from the other. Their 58 percent total prediction accuracy seems to indicate, however, that a large number of misclassifications continue to occur, compared with the 77 percent level accuracy in total predictions of our 11 item scale.

In our study a minimum F-ratio of .01 was specified for the stepwise algorithm. Other researchers have recommended a significance level of from .10 to .15 as most applicable for suicide research due to the greater probability of Type II errors with small Ns (Neuringer and Kolstoe, 1966; Brown, 1971; and Lettieri, 1972). There is question whether it is appropriate to establish a constant level of significance for any one kind of research. Skipper, Guenther, and Ness (1968) have presented strong arguments against establishing such conventional levels and Labovitz (1968) has suggested a number of potential dimensions which the re-

---

4. See Bohrnstedt and Carter (1971) for a discussion of robustness in regression analysis. It should be noted, however, that Boyle (1970) and Cohen (1968) accept the application of multiple regression to independent variables measured as nominal categories as well as ordinal and interval independent variables.

searcher may employ as an aid in establishing a meaningful error rate. Among those, four were felt to be most useful for this study. These were: sample size, size of true difference, degree of control in design, and the robustness of the statistical test. In addition, the power of the statistical technique was appraised. These five criteria were evaluated together and established the .01 level as the error rate which would be most meaningful for this study.

When we construct a predictive instrument or scale, our prime concern is how well it will perform in general use. Testing the instrument upon the data set which generated it tends to overestimate the scale's accuracy. The algorithm which produced the scale optimally selects the variables and their respective coefficients from a large number of possible combinations and capitalizes on any idiosyncracies of the data set. Consequently the predictive instrument will perform more accurately for this data set than for almost any other data set. The need for the validation of any scale is emphasized by the results in this study which show not only the usual drop in efficiency from an average of 15.5 to 24.5 percent misclassifications with scales of varying lengths, but also indicate the 11 item scale to be most efficient rather than the 15 item scale, even though the latter uses a greater quantity of information.

Clinically, the 11 item scale provides interesting contrasts with other schedules, especially those used to predict short-range acute suicidal potential (Farberow, Heilig, and Litman, 1968; Tuckman and Youngman, 1968; Cohen, Motto, and Seiden, 1966). Bock and Haggard (1968) have pointed out some of the difficulties in interpreting discriminant function coefficients, that is, the coefficients do not always closely indicate either direction or magnitude of the effects of the corresponding variables. Sometimes a weight is equally divided between two highly correlated variables, or a variable may act as an "error suppressor," that is, it contributes to discriminations primarily by removing error from another variable. Such a variable may have an algebraic sign in the discriminant function contrary to that of the component for the variables in the standardized contrast.

With these cautions in mind, the items may be looked at to

note their contributions to the derived 11 item scale. Item 4, somatic problems leading to last hospitalization seems contrary to expected direction, for the symptoms described are mostly somatic symptoms of depression, and their presence leading to a hospitalization for suicidal behavior would have been expected. Item 5, current age at release from hospital, is also contrary to expectation, inasmuch as the usual relationship is one of increased suicide risk with older age. However, the subjects in our population are veterans, and there is a possibility that younger aged veterans are, on discharge, going to more stressful interpersonal situations. The sixth item, indicating lower risk if the patient had been seen to be under the influence of alcohol or drugs during his current hospitalization, is a moot point. In some studies, alcohol has been found to be a facilitating factor for suicide, while in others it may be a substitute behavior. The eleventh item describing nervousness and anxiety also correlates negatively with later committed suicide, again a factor usually expected to be present in suicidal patients. These factors, however, may well be "error suppressor" variables in this scale, removing errors which tend to be confabulated by the use of a control group made up of such "similar" patients as neuropsychiatric hospital patients albeit nonsuicidal.

Table XI-VI presents the final version of the schedule. As indi-

TABLE XI-VI

NEUROPSYCHIATRIC HOSPITAL SUICIDE PREDICTION SCHEDULE

Name .... Hospital .... Date ....
Sex ..... Age ..... Race ..... Marital S. ..... Diagnosis: ....
....
Admis. date of current hospitalization .... Length of stay ....
Prediction: High ..... Moderately high ..... Moderately low ..... Low .....

[Check the appropriate level within each item and note its assigned weight in the column on the right. Add the weights assigned and check where subject falls in prediction.]

Item No.	Item Title	Check One	Scores	Weight	Assigned Weight
1.	Depressed in hospital most of the time	0	No	11.00	....
		1	Slightly	17.32	....
		2	Moderately	23.64	....
		3	Severely	29.96	....

Item No.	Item Title	Check One	Scores	Weight	Assigned Weight
2.	Warm interdependent relation-	1	Inability	9.06	....
	ship	2	Limited	7.12	....
		3	Good	5.18	....
3.	Hope	0	Yes	11.00	....
		1	Slightly hopeless	15.91	....
		2	Moderately	20.82	....
		3	Severely	25.73	....
		4	None despite opportunities	30.64	....
4.	Somatic problems leading to	0	No	11.00	....
	last hospitalization	1	Slight	9.50	....
		2	Moderate	8.00	....
		3	Severe	6.50	....
		4	Delusional	5.00	....
5.	Age at release from hospital	0	25	11	....
		1	26-30	10	....
		2	31-35	9	....
		3	36-40	8	....
		4	41-45	7	....
		5	46-50	6	....
		6	51-55	5	....
		7	56-60	4	....
		8	61-65	3	....
		9	65+	2	....
6.	Under influence of drugs or	0	No	11.00	....
	alcohol during last hospitaliza-	1	Yes	0.87	....
	tion				
7.	Returned early to hospital after	0	No	11.00	....
	leaves or visits	1	Yes	20.72	....
8.	Ever elope	0	No	11.00	....
		1	Previously	13.33	....
		2	Currently	15.66	....
		3	Both	17.99	....
9.	Going through divorce during	0	No	11.00	....
	last hospitalization	1	Yes	22.43	....
10.	History of suicidal behavior	0	No	11.00	....
		1	Once	13.13	....
		2	Twice	15.26	....
		3	Three or more	17.39	....
11.	Anxiety during last hospitaliza-	1	About usual	8.15	....
	tion	2	High	5.30	....
				Total	....

	High	Moderately High	Moderately Low	Low
Sum of assigned weights	189.36 to 130.00	129.99 to 117.45	117.44 to 107.67	107.66 to 84.35

cated previously, weights for each item were computed by dividing each coefficient by the smallest coefficient and adding 11, permitting elimination of negative weights. New weights have then been determined for each interval within the variables. The final score is obtained by summing the assigned weights for each variable and this final score is then compared with the cut-off points to determine whether the subject is a member of a group characterized as high, moderately high, moderately low, or low risk for a future death by suicide.

While this 11 item scale is the result of application of sophisticated statistical procedures to both original and replication populations and there is guarded optimism about its capability for predicting self-destructive behavior, the true worth of the schedule will emerge as it is applied to still other populations. The plan is to collect prospective ratings by applying the schedule to identified suicidal neuropsychiatric hospital patients who will be observed for a period of several years in follow-up studies after they are released from the hospital. Further modification and sharpening of the schedule is foreseen.

REFERENCES

Achté, K. A., Stenback, A., and Teravainen, H.: On suicides committed during treatment in psychiatric hospitals. *Acta Psychiatrica Scandinavica, 42:*272-284, 1966.

Appelbaum, S. A., and Colson, D. B.: A reexamination of the color-shading Rorschach test response and suicide attempts. *Journal of Projective Techniques & Personality Assessment, 32:*160-164, 1968.

Appelbaum, S. A., and Holzman, P. S.: The color-shading response and suicide. *Journal of Projective Techniques, 26:*155-166, 1962.

Arneson, C., and Feldman, J.: Utilization of the Rosenzweig Picture-Frustration Test to distinguish gestures from suicidal attempts. National Conference on Suicidology, Chicago, Illinois, 1968.

Bagley, C., and Greer, S.: Clinical and social predictors of repeated attempted suicide: Multivariate analysis. *British Journal of Psychiatry, 119:*515-522, 1971.

Banen, David M.: Suicide by psychotics. *Journal of Nervous and Mental Disease, 120:*349-357, 1954.

Beck, A. T., Herman, I., and Schuyler, D.: Development of suicidal scales. Paper for Workshop on the Prediction and Management of Suicidal Behavior. Philadelphia, Pennsylvania, October, 1971.

Beck, A. T., Minkoff, K., Bergman, E., and Beck, R.: Hopelessness, depression, and attempted suicide. Paper presented at Annual Meeting of American Psychiatric Association, Dallas, Texas, May, 1972.

Beck, S. J.: *Rorschach's Test, Vol. II: Variety of Personality Pictures.* New York, Grune & Stratton, 1945.

Beisser, A. R., and Blanchette, J. E.: A study of suicides in a mental hospital. *Diseases of the Nervous System, 22:*365-369, 1961.

Berk, N.: A personality study of suicidal schizophrenics. Unpublished Doctoral Dissertation, New York University, 1949.

Blau, Kim P., Farberow, N. L., and Grayson, H. M.: The semantic differential as an indicator of suicidal behavior and tendencies. *Psychological Reports, 21:*609-612, 1967.

Bock, R. D., and Haggard, E. A.: The use of multivariate analysis of variance in behavioral research. In Whitla, R. D. (Ed.): *Handbook of Measurement and Assessment in Behavioral Sciences.* Reading, Addison, 1968.

Bohrnstedt, G. W., and Carter, T. M.: Robustness in regression analysis. In Costner, H. L. (Ed.): *Sociological Methodology.* San Francisco, Jossey-Bass, 1971.

Boyle, R. P.: Path analysis and ordinal data. *American Journal of Sociology,* 75:461-480, 1970.

Braucht, G. N., and Wilson, L. T.: Predictive utility of the Revised Suicide Potential Scale. *Journal of Consulting and Clinical Psychology, 35:*426, 1970.

Broida, D. C.: An investigation of certain psychodiagnostic indications of suicidal tendencies and depression in mental hospital patients. *Psychiatric Quarterly, 28:*453-464, 1954.

Brown, T. R.: Evidence for the importance of a holistic view of suicide. Paper presented at Annual Meeting, American Association of Suicidology, Detroit, Michigan, 1972.

Brown, T. R., and Sheran, Tamera J.: Suicide prediction: A review. *Life-Threatening Behavior, 2:*67-98, 1972.

Chapman, R. F.: Suicide during psychiatric hospitalization. *Bulletin of the Menninger Clinic, 29:*35-44, 1961.

Cohen, E., Motto, J. A., and Seiden, R. H.: An instrument for evaluating suicide potential: A preliminary study. *American Journal of Psychiatry, 122:*886-891, 1966.

Cohen, J.: Multiple regression as a general data-analytic system. *Psychological Bulletin, 70:*426-445, 1968.

Cohen, S., Leonard, Calista V., Farberow, N. L. and Shneidman, E. S.: Tranquilizers and suicide in the schizophrenic patient. *Archives of General Psychiatry, 11:*312-321, 1964.

Costello, C. G.: The Rorschach records of suicidal patients: An application of a comparative matching technique. *Journal of Projective Techniques, 22:*272-275, 1958.

220   *Psychological Assessment of Suicidal Risk*

Crasilneck, H. B.: An analysis of differences between suicidal and pseudo-suicidal patients through the use of projective techniques. Unpublished doctoral dissertation, University of Houston, 1954.

Cutter, F.: Role complements and changes in consensus Rorschachs. *Journal of Projective Techniques and Personality Assessment, 32:*338-347, 1968.

Cutter, F., and Farberow, N. L.: Serial administration of consensus Rorschachs to one patient. *Journal of Projective Techniques and Personality Assessment, 32:*358-374, 1968.

Cutter, F., Jorgensen, Mary, and Farberow, N. L.: Replicability of Rorschach signs with known degrees of suicidal intent. *Journal of Projective Techniques and Personality Assessment, 32:*428-434, 1968.

Cutter, F., Jorgensen, Mary, Farberow, N. L., and Ganzler, S.: Ratings of intention of suicidal behavior. *Newsletter for Research in Psychology, 10:*36-37, Veterans Administration Center, Hampton, Virginia, May, 1968.

Daston, P. G., and Sakheim, G. A.: Prediction of suicide from the Rorschach test using a sign approach. *Journal of Projective Techniques, 24:*355-361, 1960.

Dean, R. A., Miskimmins, R. W., DeCook, R., Wilson, L. T., and Maley, R. F.: Prediction of suicide in a psychiatric hospital. *Journal of Clinical Psychiatry, 23:*296-301, 1967.

Devries, A. G.: A potential suicide personality inventory. *Psychological Reports, 18:*731-738, 1966a.

Devries, A. G.: Identification of suicidal behavior by means of the MMPI. *Psychological Reports, 19:*415-419, 1966b.

Devries, A. G.: Prediction of suicide by means of psychological tests. In Farberow, N. L. (Ed.): *Proceedings: Fourth International Conference for Suicide Prevention.* Los Angeles, Suicide Prevention Center, 1968.

Devries, A. G., and Farberow, N. L.: A multivariate profile analysis of MMPI's of suicidal and nonsuicidal neuropsychiatric hospital patients. *Journal of Projective Techniques and Personality Assessment, 31:*81-84, 1967.

Devries, A. G., and Shneidman, E. S.: Multiple MMPI profiles of suicidal persons. *Psychological Reports, 21:*401-405, 1967.

Diggory, J. C.: Predicting suicide: Will-of-the-wisp or reasonable challenge? Paper for Workshop on the Prediction and Measurement of Suicidal Behavior, Philadelphia, Pennsylvania, October, 1971.

Efron, H. Y.: An attempt to employ a sentence completion test for the detection of psychiatric patients with suicidal ideas. *Journal of Consulting Psychology, 24:*156-160, 1960.

Farberow, N. L.: Personality patterns of suicidal mental hospital patients. *Genetic Psychology Monographs, 42:*3-79, 1950.

Farberow, N. L.: Use of the Rorschach in predicting and understanding suicide. *Journal of Personality Assessment.* (In press)

Farberow, N. L., and Devries, A. G.: An item differentiation analysis of MMPI's of suicidal neuropsychiatric hospital patients. *Psychological Reports, 20:*607-617, 1967.

Farberow, N. L., Ganzler, S., Cutter, F., and Reynolds, D. K.: *Status of Suicide in the Veterans Administration: Report II.* Washington, D.C., Veterans Administration Central Office, April, 1969.

Farberow, N. L., Heilig, S. M., and Litman, R. E.: *Techniques in Crisis Intervention: A Training Manual.* Los Angeles, Suicide Prevention Center, 1968.

Farberow, N. L., and McEvoy, T. L.: Suicide among patients with diagnoses of anxiety reaction or depressive reaction in general, medicine, and surgical hospitals. *Journal of Abnormal Psychology, 71:*287-299, 1966.

Farberow, N. L., McKelligott, J. W., Cohen, S., and Darbonne, A.: Suicide among patients with cardiorespiratory illnesses. *Journal of the American Medical Association, 195:*422-428, 1966.

Farberow, N. L., Shneidman, E. S., and Leonard, Calista V.: Suicide—evaluation and treatment of suicidal risk among schizophrenic patients in psychiatric hospitals. *Veterans Administration Medical Bulletin 8,* Washington, D.C., February, 1962.

Farberow, N. L., Shneidman, E. S., and Leonard, Calista V.: Suicide among general medical and surgical hospital patients with malignant neoplasms. *Veterans Administration Medical Bulletin 9,* Washington, D.C., 1963.

Farberow, N. L., Shneidman, E. S., and Neuringer, C.: Case history and hospitalization factors in suicides of neuropsychiatric hospital patients. *Journal of Nervous and Mental Disease, 142:*32-44, 1966.

Fisher, S.: The value of the Rorschach for detecting suicidal trends. *Journal of Projective Techniques, 15:*250-254, 1951.

Fisher, S., and Hinds, Edith: The organization of hostility controls in various personality structures. *Genetic Psychology Monographs, 44:*3-68, 1951.

Friedman, I.: Phenomenal, ideal, and projected conceptions of self. *Journal of Abnormal and Social Psychology, 51:*611-615, 1955.

Greaves, G.: Temporal orientation in suicidal patients. *Perceptual and Motor Skills, 33:*1020, 1971.

Hertz, Marguerite R.: Suicidal configurations in Rorschach records. *Rorschach Research Exchange, 12:*1-56, 1948.

Hertz, Marguerite R.: Further study of "suicidal" configurations in Rorschach records. *Rorschach Research Exchange, 13:*44-73, 1949.

Labovitz, S.: Criteria for selecting a significance level: A note on the sacredness of the .05. *American Sociologist, 30:*220-222, 1968.

Lester, D.: Attempts to predict suicidal risk using psychological tests. *Psychological Bulletin, 74:*1-17, 1970.

Lettieri, D. J.: A suicidal death prediction scale. Paper presented at the Workshop on the Prediction and Measurement of Suicidal Behavior, Philadelphia, Pennsylvania, October, 1971.

Levy, S., and Southcombe, R. H.: Suicide in a state hospital for the mentally ill. *Journal of Nervous and Mental Disease, 117:*504-514, 1953.

Lindner, R. M.: The content of the Rorschach Protocol. In Abt, L. E., and Bellak, L. (Eds.): *Projective Psychology.* New York, Knopf, 1950.

Martin, H.: A Rorschach study of suicide. *Dissertation Abstracts, 20:*3837, 1960.

McEvoy, T. L.: A comparison of suicidal and nonsuicidal patients by means of the TAT. *Dissertation Abstracts, 24:*1248, 1963.

Melges, F. T., and Weisz, A. E.: The personal future and suicidal ideation. *Journal of Nervous and Mental Disease, 153:*244-250, 1971.

Miller, Dorothy, and Goleman, D.: Predicting post-release risk among hospitalized suicide attempters. *Omega, 1:*71-84, 1970.

Miskimmins, R. W., and Wilson, L. T.: The revised suicide potential scale. *Journal of Consulting and Clinical Psychology, 33:*258, 1969.

Motto, Jerome: Refinement of variables in assessing suicide risk. Paper presented at the Workshop on the Prediction and Measurement of Suicidal Behavior. Philadelphia, Pennsylvania, October, 1971.

Nawas, M. M., and Worth, J. W.: Suicidal configuration in the Bender-Gestalt. *Journal of Projective Techniques and Personality Assessment, 32:*392-394, 1968.

Neter, J., and Maynes, E. S.: On the appropriateness of the correlation coefficient with a 0, 1 dependent variable. *Journal of the American Statistical Association, 65:*501-509, 1970.

Neuringer, C.: The Rorschach test as a research device for the identification, prediction, and understanding of suicidal ideation and behavior. *Journal of Projective Techniques and Personality Assessment, 29:*71-82, 1965.

Neuringer, C.: Divergencies between attitudes toward life and death among suicidal, psychosomatic, and normal hospital patients. *Journal of Clinical and Consulting Psychology, 32:*59-63, 1968.

Neuringer, C., and Kolstoe, R. H.: Suicide research and non-rejection of the null hypothesis. *Perceptual and Motor Skills, 22:*115-118, 1966.

Neuringer, C., McEvoy, T. L., and Schlesinger, R. J.: The identification of suicidal behavior in females by the use of the Rorschach. *Journal of General Psychology, 72:*127-133, 1965.

Patrick, J. H., and Overall, J. E.: Multivariate analysis of clinical rating profiles of suicidal psychiatric inpatients. *Journal of Projective Techniques and Personality Assessment, 33:*138-145, 1969.

Piotrowski, Z. A.: *A Rorschach Compendium.* Utica, State Hospital Press, 1950.

Piotrowski, Z. A.: Test differentiation between effected and attempted suicides. In Wolff, K. (Ed.): *Patterns of Self-destruction: Depression and Suicide.* Springfield, Thomas, 1970.

Poeldinger, W.: *Die Abschätzung der Suizidalität. (Evaluation of Suicidality).* Hans Huber, Bern and Stuttgart, 1967.

Rabin, A. I.: Homicide and attempted suicide: A Rorschach study. *American Journal of Orthopsychiatry, 16:*516-524, 1946.

Ravensborg, M. R., and Foss, Adeline: Suicide and natural death in a state hospital population: A comparison of admission complaints, MMPI profiles, and social competence factors. *Journal of Consulting and Clinical Psychology, 33:*466-471, 1969.

Rosen, A., Hales, W. M., and Simon, W.: Classification of "suicidal" patients. *Journal of Consulting Psychology, 18:*359-362, 1954.

Rotov, Michail: Death by suicide in the hospital: An analysis of 20 therapeutic failures. *American Journal of Psychotherapy, 25:*216-227, 1970.

Sakheim, G. A.: Suicidal responses on the Rorschach test: A validation study. Protocols of suicidal mental hospital patients compared with those of nonsuicidal patients. *Journal of Nervous and Mental Disease, 122:*332-344, 1955.

Sapolsky, A.: An indicator of suicidal ideation on the Rorschach test. *Journal of Projective Techniques and Personality Assessment, 27:*332-335, 1963.

Shneidman, E. S., and Farberow, N. L.: TAT heroes of suicidal and nonsuicidal subjects. *Journal of Projective Techniques, 22:*211-228, 1958.

Simon, W.: Attempted suicide among veterans. *Journal of Nervous and Mental Disease, 111:*451-468, 1950.

Simon, W., and Hales, W. M.: Note on a suicide key in the MMPI. *American Journal of Psychiatry, 102:*222-223, 1949.

Singer, R. G., and Blumenthal, I. J.: Suicide clues in psychotic patients. *Mental Hygiene, 53:*346-350, 1969.

Skipper, J. K., Guenther, A. L., and Ness, G.: The sacredness of the .05: A note concerning the uses of statistical levels of significance in social science. *The American Sociologist, 2:*16-19, 1967.

Sternberg, D., and Levine, A.: An indicator of suicidal ideation on the Bender Visual-Motor Gestalt test. *Journal of Projective Techniques and Personality Assessment, 29:*377-379, 1965.

Stevens, S. S.: A metric for the social consensus. *Science, 151:*530-541, 1966.

Tuckman, J., and Youngman, W. F.: Suicide risk among persons attempting suicide. *Public Health Reports, 78:*585-587, 1963.

Weisman, A., and Worden, J. W.: Risk-rescue rating in suicide assessment. *Archives of General Psychiatry, 26:*553-560, 1972.

White, Mary A., and Schreiber, Hanna: Diagnosing "suicidal risks" on the Rorschach. *Psychiatric Quarterly Supplement, 26:*161-189, 1952.

Winfield, D. L., and Sparer, P. J.: Preliminary report of the Rosenzweig P-F Study in attempted suicides. *Journal of Clinical Psychology, 9:*379-381, 1953.

Yufit, R. I., Benzies, Bonnie, Fonte, Mary E., and Fawcett, Jan A.: Suicide potential and time perspective. *Archives of General Psychiatry, 23:*158-163, 1970.

Zung, W. W. K.: Index of potential suicide (IPS). Paper for Workshop on the Prediction and Measurement of Suicidal Behavior, Philadelphia, Pennsylvania, October, 1971.

CONCLUSION

THE READER WILL FIND it difficult to close this volume with the feeling that he has read the chronicle of an unalloyed scientific triumph. There have been some successes in the attempts to assess suicidal risk. The lethality schedules seem to show the greatest amount of promise for future prediction of suicidal behavior. It is hoped that consequent research and cross validation studies will substantiate the early promise. The traditional psychological tests have not proved to be of great use. This appears to be particularly true of the projective personality tests. However, there are some grains of wheat among the chaff. Martin's Checklist, the MMPI, and some of the cognitive psychological tests may, if appropriately developed and used, prove to be outstanding contributions to the psychological assessment of suicidal risk. Studies of behavioral clues gathered from survey and demographic studies of suicidal persons may also prove to be of great use, but the data presentations from these studies are still somewhat unsystematic. Organizing the results of these studies into a systematic catalog would be of great help to suicidology.

It appears that the procedures that focus on the use of overt behavior (the lethality schedules and the survey researches) are more effective than those techniques that depend on hypothesized intervening mediational constructs. Techniques utilizing behavior (without reference to mediational, motivational, or personality states) in a direct comparison procedure between suicidal and nonsuicidal individuals seem to yield more conclusive results than do procedures that derive their starting points from hypothesized mediational concepts. That this should be so may be due to the nature of the concepts used in suicidology. This is especially true of the concept which we have called "suicide."

SUICIDE AS A UNITY

It is interesting to note that the noun "suicide" is of comparatively recent origin. It was not a word that existed in the classical age. It was coined in the 18th century, and its birth coincided with the height of the Age of Reason, when men tried to discover the essential unitary lawfulness of all things. At that time the scientific-philosophers searched for unity, and "suicide" was invented to meet the need for single unitary classification and description of a diverse set of phenomena. Previously, the behaviors that we now classify as suicide were not described as a unity. Men did not conceive of these various disparate acts as belonging to a family. The birth of "suicide" forced men to search for the core which would unite divergent acts and also to ignore the relevance of the divergencies. Theories were molded, not by the facts, but by the idea of a suicide unity. The unity conceptualization has done suicidology a great disservice. It fixed in us the belief that suicide was a singular specifiable and identifiable phenomenon. It has led to conceptualization, description, and measurement problems that have only recently been recognized and which are now in the process of being unraveled.

The writer recently conducted an interesting casual experiment. He asked one of his classes to phenomenally describe the "size and shape" of suicide. An overwhelming number of students described it as some sort of black, solid, heavy, immovable object which resembled a huge and very solid block of granite. Our cultural conceptualization of suicide has trapped us into a mode of thinking from which it is difficult to escape. The students rejected the concept of suicide as diffuse, fragile, insubstantial, and having an elusive will-of-the-wisp character. And yet this latter characterization may be more valid than that of the pall-draped monolith. Suicide researchers have only recently begun to grasp the inadequacy of treating suicide as a unitary monolith. As can be seen in the papers in this volume, more and more warnings are directed against accepting suicide as a unifying psychodynamic paradigm. Instead of a homogeneous phenomenon, suicidologists may be confronted with a varigated melangé which is masquerading as a unity.

The fallacy of a suicide entity has had particularly devastating effects on those who would assess suicidal risk. If suicide were one behavior, with one dynamic, with one set of antecedent conditions and with one set of circumscribed responses, then the task of the predictor of suicidal risk would indeed be simple. If suicide were a circumscribed entity, then psychologists, mathematicians, actuaries, diagnosticians, etc., with their vast armory of sophisticated evaluation techniques could solve the job of predicting suicide within a matter of months. It is the elusive character of self-destructive behavior which makes reliable and valid suicidal evaluation difficult. As long as we cling to the illusion that suicide is a unity, very little progress will be made towards the goal of adequately forecasting when a person will act in such a way as to produce a premature cessation of his existence. That progress has actually been made under these conditions is a tribute to the dedication and tenacity of many suicidologists.

A NON-THEORY OF SUICIDE

What is being suggested here is that suicidal risk evaluation should be based only on observed and compared behaviors rather than actively derived from mediational concepts. There are dangers connected with perceiving suicide as anything else than an empirical behavioral event. The unity conceptualization of suicide has led us to believe that it plays the role of mediator between input events (stimuli) and as a determinor of behavioral outcomes (responses). Because of our biomechanical-scientific training, one tends to conceive of suicidal theories in terms of a simple S-R theory paradigm. It may be more productive to think of suicide not as the arbiter of behavior, but of it as the behavior itself; a behavior that may be invoked by any of a large class of stimuli and mediators. I am proposing that suicidal behavior ought to be thought of as a general response tendency having in different people a differential place in the response tendency heirarchy, and which can be evoked by a wide variety of conditions.

Anxiety will serve as an analogy. The experience of anxiety is a generalized unlearned reaction to any number of conditions. Fear of death, impotency, loss of a limb, failure, etc., have the capacity to evoke an anxiety experience. Anxiety itself is not connected to only one antecedent condition. It is associated with an immeasurably large class of stimuli, any one of which can provoke an anxiety attack. Anxiety stands as a general response to perceived psychological danger. If our histories and natural endowments have led us towards greater coping ability, self-confidence, rational perceptions, etc., then anxiety is lower in the response tendency hierarchy and is resistant to behavioral expression. It then takes very intense stimuli to provoke an anxiety attack. The term "ego-strength" has been utilized to describe the resistance of anxiety reactions towards rising above threshold. If anxiety experiences have a place high in the response tendency hierarchy because of fragile intellectual development, underdevelopment of coping behavior, poor self-concept, lack of trust in others, autistic perceptions of the world, etc., they may appear very readily when evoked by stimulus events of very low strength.

Suicide behavior needs to be treated in the same way as anxiety. It is a generalized response tendency (existing in all people) which can be provoked by an immeasurably large class of stimuli. Whether it will appear will depend on its place in the response tendency hierarchy (ego-strength) and on the intensity of the stress situation. The mode (threat, attempt, or commit) is probably related to the tendency-towards-suicidal-behavior's place in the hierarchy. The higher in the hierarchy, the greater the tendency towards action. Suicidal behavior methods may be based on cultural training (e.g., this is a firearm using and drug taking society) or on expediency (using whatever method is most handy).

The preceding does not imply that suicidal behaviors are themselves innate and unlearned. However, they are learned behaviors which have their basis in unlearned responses. The basic inborn parent response for suicidal behavior is the avoidance reflex. The avoidance reflex can be seen in the quick withdrawal of the hand from a painful stimulus and is as much an unlearned response as is the anxiety reaction. The avoidance reflex gives rise to a host of more complex responses (e.g., denial, avoidance, retreat, and flight). These complex responses may be further elaborated into even more complicated response patterns (hysterical blindness, excessive sleeping, schizophrenic withdrawal, etc.). Suicidal behavior is only one member of the family of descendants of the avoidance reflex elaborations. A large number of the other avoidance reflex based responses seem to be concurrently evoked along with the suicidal behaviors.

ASSESSMENT OF SUICIDAL RISK

The belief in a unifying paradigm has led suicide risk assessors to search for the supposed one and only set of conditions that is assumed to be linked to the unity. It follows, from such a belief, that there exists a set of measurable conditions which reflect the existence of the mediational process. Research, it is thought, will discover the set of conditions linked to suicide. Once these conditions are discovered and their presence noted in a particular person, the assessor would then be able to predict a suicidal outcome for that individual. However, if the unity is a fragment of conceptual imagination, then the above described program is futile.

The papers in this volume have highlighted many of the failures and some of the successes of the assessment of suicidal risk. The readers have been assailed by the descriptions of the methodological problems encountered by the research evaluators. Foremost among them is that we do not know enough about suicide and that we cannot even adequately define it (i.e., the rubric has been stretched too far). This vagueness of definition has led to accusations of "sloppy design and methodology." However, such consequences are inevitable when there is confusion about the nature of the object of study. Accordingly, the most promising techniques for assessment of suicidal risk are those which de-emphasize specificity of definition and concentrate on evaluating the presence or absence of symptomatic behaviors. Progress in the assessment of suicidal risk can only be made when the concept of suicide as a mediational process is abandoned. The concept of suicide as a mediational unity has forced us to think of suicide as a disorder rather than a symptom. The symptom needs treatment, but efforts directed at building ego-strength and mitigating the effects of various suicidogenic agents (poverty, poor parental upbringing, drug-dependency, etc.) may well be the "true" key to suicide prevention.

NAME INDEX

SUBJECT INDEX

A

Aggression, 96, 99, 197
  and the TAT, 103-107
  and suicide, 107-109
Aggressive content scale, 101
Attempted suicide
  definition of, 8-9
  factors associated with, 180
  populations, 19
  predictive factors, 165, 166, 169, 172, 174
  rates, 180
  research with, 180
  sex differences, 19
  social indicators, 180

B

Beck signs, 194
Behavior-specific predictions, 225
Bender-Gestalt Test, 140-143
  evaluation of, 147
  predictive utility, 143
  research with, 140-142

C

Catalogic, 156
Classifications of suicide, 7-10, 90
Cognition in suicide, 150-151, 156, 160-161
Computer analysis, 43, 191
Consensus Rorschach, 196
Contaminated logic, 156
Critical incidents technique, 131, 199

D

Data banks, 4
Definition of suicide, 229 (*see also* Classifications of suicide)
Depression, 107, 118, 189, 190, 202
Dichotomous thinking, 150, 151, 152, 157, 160
Dimensional analysis, 4

Discriminate function analysis, 4, 46-47, 50, 51, 183

E

Edwards, Personal Preference Scale, 145, 146, 147
Ethology, 107, 108

F

Factor analysis, 4, 202
Failures of prediction
  methodological problems, 18, 186
  nongeneralizability of predictive indicators, 187
Fallacious logic, 150, 151, 156
Field dependency, 157, 158, 159
Follow-up technique, 178
Frustration-aggression hypothesis, 107-108

G

Gatekeepers, 3

H

Hertz signs (*see* Rorschach Test)
High risk criteria, 183
High risk factors, 182
Hildreth Feeling and Attitude Scale, 143-144
  evaluation, 147
  predictive utility, 144
  research, 143-144
Hostility (*see* Aggression)

I

Intention
  definitions of, 23
  evaluation of, 96
  lethality of, 109
  measurement of, 20, 21, 22
  measurement problems, 21
  range, 19-20